blue
rider
press

Chuck Klosterman
X

Also by Chuck Klosterman

BLUE RIDER PRESS
NEW YORK

Chuck Klosterman

X

A Highly Specific, Defiantly Incomplete History of the Early 21st Century

blue
rider
press

An imprint of Penguin Random House LLC
375 Hudson Street
New York, New York 10014

ISBN 9780399184154

Printed in the United States of America
1   3   5   7   9   10   8   6   4   2

Book design by Amanda Dewey

Contents

The book you are about to read is a collection of stories I've published in various media outlets over the past ten years. I like these stories and wouldn't republish them if I didn't. But I certainly hope you like them more than I do. The process of compiling old articles is not difficult, but it also isn't pleasant. It's just not enjoyable to reread things you've written in the not-so-distant past (I think this is true for most writers, discounting those real crazy motherfuckers who believe the world would be radically different if they weren't involved). Every positive memory is coated with the ooze of regret: You want to delete every semicolon and alter every joke. Moments that once seemed revelatory now seem banal. You're forcibly reminded how rapidly society evolves, and it's disheartening to revisit an arbitrary event from five years ago that suddenly feels like a factoid from 1958. It's the worst kind of time machine.

Yet I must admit something else here, even though it will make me seem like a megalomaniac: I love reading the index to any book I publish. It's always my favorite part. Exploring the index from a book you created is like having someone split your head open with an axe so that you can peruse the contents of your brain. It's the alphabetizing of your consciousness. Sometimes I will pick up one of my old books and sing a random section of the index to the tune of Billy

Joel's "We Didn't Start the Fire," purely for pleasure. (Actually, I'm lying. I don't "sometimes" do this. I did this once, just now, simply to see if it would work, solely for the purposes of writing this introduction. There was no pleasure involved and I'll never do it again. I don't even like making this joke. But the experiment *was* successful, so feel free to try this at your leisure. In fact, try it a hundred times, even if you don't really remember the original song. I'm sure all the people in your life will love it.)

I only note this indexical preoccupation as a warning to you, the consumer: This book is deceptive. It is not as panoramic as it appears. Taken at face value, its index suggests an anthology about many divergent topics (wizards, chemical weapons, Donald Trump, Thai sandwiches, et al.). And—technically—that diversity is real. Those references do exist. There are stories in this collection about literature and zombies and postmodern television and the essentialism of Charlie Brown and the capricious nature of our illusionary universe. One could even argue that the only reason any interesting story is "interesting" is because it's not actually about whatever it superficially appears to suggest, and that the only significant purpose of text is to provide a superstructure for subtext (which always matters more). All of that is true. But here's the deal—*I wrote these stories.* I know what these stories are about. And almost all of them are about one of two things: music or sports. Consumed in aggregate, this omnibus equates to a short book about music, a short book about sports, and a short book about everything else that could possibly exist.

It is not a portrait of what the world is, or of what the world could be.

It is a portrait of my interior life: I watch games, I listen to music, and I daydream about the rest of reality.

When I started as a reporter in the early nineties, there was an incontrovertible firewall between music culture and sports culture, spawned (I suspect) from dark memories various members of the music community still carried from high school. There was this ingrained Reagan-era belief that "jocks" and "meatheads" terrorized "punks" and "goths" and "miscellaneous longhairs," and that the type of alienated teenager who liked art had a condescending view of the type of teenager who liked football. Now, I'm sure some of that social derision was authentic. I'm sure that negative experience did happen to somebody, and it was certainly baked into every teen movie of the era. But nothing like that ever happened to me. I was obsessed with music and I was obsessed with sports, and the synthesis never seemed uncomfortable. I suppose it's possible my hometown was just too small to have stereotypical cliques. It's also possible I was so emotionally engaged with both concepts that I couldn't feel anything else. Maybe the estrangement went over my head. Maybe I was just too dumb to care. Still, I knew this conflict existed for other people, even if I didn't relate to it or understand why. I knew that people who wrote about music rarely wrote about sports, unless they weren't especially serious about either. It seemed like you had to choose one or the other. I went to college in 1990 and started my career as a sportswriter. One of the first beats assigned to me was collegiate wrestling, a subject I knew nothing about. I didn't even fully understand the scoring system, so I just described every match like a correspondent for *National Geographic*. Every single story included the phrase "catlike quickness." My only memory of covering wrestling is comparing humans to animals.

In 1994, craving the facade of legitimacy (and maybe the potential access to drugs), I switched over to culture journalism. I wanted to generate theories about why the guys in Anthrax wore shorts, and this was the only way. Once I made the switch, I didn't write another sports story for five years. I'm not sure any traditional newspaper editor would have let me—the fact that I was interested in Radiohead somehow annihilated the possibility that I could be equally informed about Scottie Pippen.

But this imaginary war eventually ended, at least for me. At some point, I stopped caring about this nonproblematic problem. I just started writing about sports and music at the same time, occasionally in the same article. I haphazardly jammed them together, even when they barely fit. And to my mild surprise, everyone else decided this was okay. As it turns out, the divide between music and sports had dissolved during the nineties, so slowly and incrementally that no one even noticed.[1] Pearl Jam named their first album after NBA point guard Mookie Blaylock's jersey number. Power pitcher Randy Johnson became an arena rock photographer. Members of Pavement and Sleater-Kinney joined fantasy leagues with members of Quasi and Built to Spill. Master P played in the CBA. Public Enemy's liner notes made reference to Pooh Richardson. Drew Bledsoe jumped off the stage at an Everclear concert and injured a female spectator. All the coked-up Britpop dudes refused to shut up about Manchester United. Or was it Man City? I've already forgotten. But by the time the twenty-first century started, the notion of being a rock critic *and* a sportswriter was no longer awkward (or even contentious), which nicely coincided with the period of my life when I tried to earn a living by doing so. Which is what this book is, more or less. The surgery was a success and the patient is resting comfortably. I'm not fully accredited by either side of the professional equation

---

1. This evolution was almost entirely due to the mainstream acceptance of hip-hop. Prior to 1990, any relationship between music and sports was seen as a noteworthy aberration (Tony Mandarich talking about Guns N' Roses in *Sports Illustrated*, Rod Stewart kicking soccer balls into the audience at concerts, John McEnroe playing electric guitar and marrying Patty Smyth, etc.). But with a group like N.W.A, an association with sports became almost expected, in the same way everyone immediately viewed Allen Iverson as an extension of rap culture long before he recorded a rap album. There is, certainly, a troubling racial component to this shift in perception. But at least the end result was positive.

(sportswriters think I'm too pretentious and music writers don't think I'm pretentious enough), but I'm able to write about whatever I want, as long as it actually happened. Which, from my limited perspective, is a dream I could not anticipate.

Please enjoy this collection of nonfiction dreams.

Like Sands Through

the Hourglass, So Are

the Days of Our Lives

"Three-Man Weave" is the best story I've ever published, or at least my personal favorite. My emotional investment was high. It took a long time to complete and the research was unorthodox. The presentation is straightforward and traditional. It ran on the very first day the website Grantland came into existence, so it felt significant (simply due to how maniacally obsessed the rest of the Internet was with the idea of Bill Simmons launching a website). I also think the socioeconomic underpinnings of the narrative are slightly more meaningful than the sociocultural underpinnings of the various celebrity-driven pieces I've written, even though those stories inevitably get more attention.

My personal relationship with Grantland was complicated. I still have conflicted emotions over what Grantland was, how it operated, and how it ended, even though my direct involvement with the publication had become virtually nonexistent by the time ESPN shuttered the site in 2015. But the fact that I was able to write this story in 2011 is enough to make me retrospectively pleased with the entire enterprise. Grantland was the only place I've ever worked where you could say, "I want to write about something kooky that happened twenty-three years ago that nobody cares about except me," and the response from everyone working there would be, "Well, of course." Concepts like time and space were not relevant issues. There was a real commitment to not being like the rest of the Internet. But the Internet was where it lived, so that goal was impossible.

Three-Man Weave

I t was 1988. It was a very good year, assuming your name was George Bush or Melanie Griffith. *Miami Vice* was on television, Guns N' Roses and George Michael were on the radio, and gas cost 91 cents a gallon. But none of those things matter to the story I'm about to describe. The story I am about to describe happened in the geographic equivalent of a vacuum. A flat, frozen, fatalistic vacuum.

The abstract details seem boring on purpose: A pair of low-profile junior college basketball teams played a forgotten game on a neutral floor in southeast North Dakota. The favored team was a school best known for its two-year forestry program. The underdog was a minuscule all–Native American college whose campus is located outside the Bismarck, N.D., airport. You've (probably) never heard of either school, and—in all likelihood—you will (probably) never hear of either one again. And if you remember this game at all, you (probably) played in it.

Games described as *forgotten* typically earn that classification because they deserve to disappear; it's a modifier historians employ to marginalize or dismiss a given event, often for dramatic effect. But this game is "forgotten" in a non-negotiable context. There's almost no record of its existence. Fewer than five hundred people saw it happen. It was not televised and there's no videotape. It wasn't broadcast on the radio. No official box score was compiled (statistics were kept, but most have been lost over time). Only a couple of small-circulation newspapers made mention of what transpired, and—because it happened before the Internet—googling the game's particulars is like searching for a glossy photograph of Genghis Khan. The contest has disappeared from the world's consciousness, buried by time and devoid of nostalgia. This (of course) is not abnormal. Junior college basketball games from 1988 are not historic landmarks. We are conditioned to forget who won or lost the opening round of the North Dakota state JUCO tournament because those are moments society does not need to remember. They don't even qualify as trivia.

But something crazy happened in this particular game.

In this particular game, a team won with only three players on the floor. And this was not a "metaphorical" victory or a "moral" victory: They literally won the game, 84–81, finishing the final sixty-six seconds by playing three-on-five. To refer to this as a David and Goliath battle devalues the impact of that cliché; it was more like a blind, one-armed David fighting Goliath without a rock. Yet there was no trick to this win, and there was no deception—they won by playing precisely how you'd expect. The crazy part is that it worked.

The only reason I know about this game is because I saw it happen, totally by chance: I was a tenth-grader, and my older brother and I drove to this JUCO tournament because we had passing interest in the second game of that night's doubleheader (it was also a Sunday evening and we didn't have cable, so there was nothing else to do). The tournament's opening game was between the United Tribes Technical College and North Dakota State University at Bottineau—the Thunderbirds vs. the Lumberjacks. In the years that have passed, I've sometimes wondered if the game I thought I saw actually happened. I've wondered if maybe I'd imagined the circumstances or unconsciously exaggerated the details. Whenever I found myself talking about the game to other people, the scenario I heard myself describing struck me as increasingly implausible. Like Wilt Chamberlain's untelevised, scarcely witnessed 100-point game in Hershey, Pa., it seems like a story someone made up for mythological impact. But this happened. And the game that occurred in reality is even weirder than the game I'd reconstructed in my mind.

"IF YOU WRITE a story about this," Barry Webster tells me, "you need to explain how much I ripped it up that season." I'm speaking to Mr. Webster over the telephone. He lives in Macy, Neb., the same reservation town where he grew up. He's standing in his kitchen, having just taken his Labrador and his dachshund for a walk around the town, which probably did not take very long (the population of Macy is 1,200). When his son meanders into the room, Webster hands him the phone, just to prove that a guy from ESPN is on the other line. Barry can't believe someone is asking him about a game that happened more than two decades ago, but that doesn't mean he's not ready to talk: Our extemporaneous interview lasts over an hour.

"I really did rip it up that year," he repeats. "I think I averaged twenty-seven points a game, with a high of forty-six. I really remember that . . . As a Native, you always start with a strike against you. People always thought they were gonna kick our ass when we showed up in the gym, and that made me want to blow them away. I know I must sound cocky, but that's not how it was. I just knew the world was against me."

I don't need to remind Webster that he was the leader of the '88 Thunderbirds. He knows he was the star. A five-foot-ten lead guard with dynamic quickness (he claims to have run a 4.3 40 as a high school quarterback), Webster received casual attention from a few Division I programs, but he knows he never had a real chance of going there. "According to my high school coach, I was getting looked at by Colorado," Webster says. "But I was a jack around. I didn't take academics seriously. The junior college route was really my only option."

Webster's trajectory is not unusual—in fact, it's the reason 1980s junior college basketball intermittently bordered on the spectacular. Since major colleges were finally growing cognizant of academic standards and potential scholastic violations, there tended to be two types of kids who played hoops at the JUCO level: undersized high school gunners and D-1 prospects who didn't like to read. The master of this universe was San Jacinto's Walter Berry, the southpaw superfreak who dominated the 1984 NJCAA tourney before transferring to St. John's and winning the John Wooden Award. JUCOs were the collegiate equivalent of the ABA, saturated with shoot-first superpowers. Webster wasn't even the best junior college player *in North Dakota* that year; that was Dan Schilz of UND–Lake Region, a 2-guard who led the nation in scoring with 35.3 points a game (still the ninth-highest single-season tally in JUCO history, one slot ahead of Latrell Sprewell).

It was into this world that Webster stumbled, almost by accident. He majored in auto mechanics.

"I'd never been to North Dakota," Webster recalls. "I didn't even know the United Tribes existed."

Not many people do. At the time, enrollment at United Tribes Technical College was somewhere between two hundred and three hundred students.[1] The school was founded in 1969 by the five tribes of North Dakota, but its brick campus buildings were built at the turn of the twentieth century, intended as a military base. During World War II, the base was used as an alien internment camp. Attending school at UT is the polar opposite of *idyllic*. But that's how

---

1. Today, that number is closer to 1,700.

college life was (and still is) for so many Native American students—it's just that nobody pays attention. No American minority is less represented in the national consciousness.[2] This was a collegiate program where the basketball team could not afford to print the name of its school on the front of their jerseys.

"We didn't even have warm-up clothes," says former United Tribes coach Ken Hall. "And Bottineau had those tear-away sweatpants! Half their team was dunking during pregame, and I didn't have one guy over six foot. But as anyone who ever played for me will tell you, everybody on our roster was in the best shape of his life. We could run all day."

This is how five Indians—and then four, and then three—defeated a team that should have crushed them by 30: They ran and they ran and they ran. And then they stopped.

"THEY HAD FIVE KIDS they called the Iron Five."

These are the words of Buster Gilliss, the current athletic director at Bismarck Junior College and the head coach of NDSU-Bottineau in 1988. In his high school and collegiate coaching career, Gilliss won 508 games. When I reach him by phone, he's not especially excited to talk about a loss that (a) the world doesn't remember, but (b) he can't forget. But he talks anyway.

"They had those five kids they called the Iron Five, and they played the whole game. They were a little older than most junior

---

2. Need proof? Recall the military mission that killed Osama bin Laden: What code name did U.S. Navy SEALs assign to bin Laden, the most hated man in the world? "Geronimo." They referred to bin Laden as "Geronimo," for no reason whatsoever. They could have picked anything, but that is what they selected. Now, I realize referring to an enemy target as "Geronimo" is not exactly a crime against humanity—yet how many members of the mass media complained about this? How many even noticed? The conversational bias against Native Americans is so ingrained that nobody even recognizes when they're insulted.

college kids—I feel like a few of them were in their mid-twenties. But these were good players. I think they shot something like seventy-eight percent from the field that night."

The actual percentage was 61, but his general perception is accurate: The Thunderbirds were on fire, especially during the first half. Coming into the game, NDSU-Bottineau had a record of 17-8 and had beaten United Tribes twice during the regular season; nobody seems to recall what UT's record was, but it was definitely below .500 (Webster thinks they might have won ten games that year, but Hall suspects it was more like seven or eight). The Tribe opened the season with a full twelve-man roster, but people kept quitting or getting hurt or losing their eligibility. By tournament time, they were down to five. It was peculiar to watch them take the court before tip-off— they didn't have enough bodies for a layup line. They just casually shot around for twenty minutes.

"It was always so goofy to play those guys," says Keith Braunberger, the Lumberjacks point guard in 1987–88. Today, Braunberger owns a Honda dealership in Minot. "I don't want to dis them, but—at the time—they were kind of a joke. They would just run and shoot. That was the whole offense. I remember they had one guy who would pull up and shoot from half court if you didn't pick him up immediately."

The five Thunderbirds would have dominated any six-foot-and-under league—they were all guards and wings, and everyone had range. But they were completely overmatched by NDSU-Bottineau. Gillis was in his second year as head coach and had developed a recruiting pipeline into Illinois and Maryland. The Lumberjacks roster included hyperbolic talent like Jerome Gaines[3] (a six-five helicopter)

---

3. Gaines had the flu in the game vs. United Tribes and finished with just 13 points.

and Keith "The Total Package" Offutt[4] (a six-six rebounding machine). Offutt had nicknamed himself.

"You had to know Keith to understand," explains Darrell Oswald, the Jacks' six-six swingman. "He'd had a terrible upbringing and some emotional problems. He gave himself that name. Probably the best athlete I've ever been around. Had a forty-two-inch vertical."

The Bottineau roster represented the template for North Dakota JUCO basketball throughout the 1980s: a handful of hyperathletic (read: black) players who were destined to play elsewhere, and a core group of local (read: white) players who were small-town legends. Braunberger was from Max, N.D., a community of 334. Oswald hailed from Wing, N.D., a town with fewer than two hundred people (there were nine kids in Oswald's graduating class—and that included Anika, an exchange student from Sweden). The Jacks' leading scorer was shooting guard Dan Taylor from New Rockford, N.D. (pop. 1,400), a player everyone called "Opie" due to his resemblance to a young Ron Howard. On paper, there's no way the United Tribes should have been able to compete with this team. They probably shouldn't have been in the same tournament.

But they did. And they were.

"You'd think a game like that would have made national headlines, because the idea of playing three-on-five is so odd," says Taylor, now a banker in his old hometown. "But no one even noticed."

Even by North Dakota standards, Bottineau[5] is a pretty small town to have its own college; according to the 2011 census, there are only 2,211 residents in the metro area. That's part of the reason so

<hr />

4. Offutt declined to be interviewed for this story.

5. NDSU-Bottineau was founded in 1906, originally as a forestry school. It became a satellite campus for North Dakota State in 1968, but switched its affiliation to Minot State in 1996. It's now known as Dakota College of Bottineau. Despite a population of only 672,500, there are twenty colleges in North Dakota (that's one for every 33,625 residents). It's probably the easiest state in the union to get a college education in.

little is known of this game: The Lumberjacks had a good team and real talent, but the weirdness of their season-ending defeat was like a comedic rumor that died in the translation. It wasn't that embarrassing, simply because there weren't enough people to mock it.

"By the time our bus got back to Bottineau, we'd supposedly played the whole second half against three Indians, which of course is not what happened," says Gilliss. "But you know, to be honest, there were probably ten people in the whole town who cared that we got beat."

FEBRUARY 21, 1988, was an extremely North Dakota–like day in southeast North Dakota: It had been 45 degrees during the afternoon, but the temperature had plummeted to 7 when the sun disappeared. There was a trace of snow, but nothing cataclysmic; the United Tribes van arrived in Wahpeton, N.D., without any problem. The official site of the game was the North Dakota State College of Science campus, the host school for that season's NDJCAA tournament (with the tournament winner advancing to the regional). With a seating capacity of 4,100 and a pristine red-and-black tartan floor, NDSCS's facility was as good as that of any junior college in the country. It was also empty as a mule barn. As the Tribes and Bottineau got loose, the squeak of sneakers and the cacophony of dribbling dwarfed any murmuring from the stands. There might have been two thousand people in the gym by the time NDSCS took on Bismarck State at 8:30 p.m., but the 6:30 opener didn't even feel like a high school game. It was more like a swim meet without water.

This was Ken Hall's first JUCO tournament, as this was his first year as the United Tribes coach. At the time, he was twenty-eight. Hall is arguably the most recognizable Native American athlete in North Dakota history, but not because of this game or anything else that happened at UT—regionally, he's best known as a high school icon, first as a player in Newtown, N.D. (where he twice took the team to state in the '70s), and later as the head coach in Parshall, N.D. (ending his twenty-two-year career with a Class B title in 2007). But 1987–88 had been a frustrating season for Hall. He couldn't keep anyone on the roster. With only five guys on the team, it became impossible to hold normal practices; when I asked Hall how they scrimmaged, he said (only half joking), "Shadows." But after a while, they got used to it. And over time, he figured out how to win with a nonrotating five-man rotation.

"We had a very strict game plan," says Hall. "This was '88, so the shot clock was still forty-five seconds. We set up a shot clock during practice and got used to running it down to ten seconds on every possession. We'd spread the floor, and then Barry [Webster] would try to take his guy one-on-one. Bottineau played man-to-man the whole game. Barry would collapse the defense and kick it out to the perimeter. And if they didn't collapse, Barry just went to the hole. We controlled the whole game, start to finish. It was really Barry who controlled it. He was a coach's dream."

Webster finished the night with 33 points. He remembers scoring 35, but that's still pretty accurate for a twenty-three-year-old memory.[6] Webster fouled out with four minutes remaining (he'd picked up his third foul before halftime), which initially felt like a deathblow. "Truthfully, I threw in the towel when I fouled out," he says. "I was dejected. I thought the season was over. But then I looked over at the other

---

6. Tim Purdon's memory is remarkably accurate, too. Currently the U.S. attorney for the state of North Dakota (appointed by Barack Obama in February 2010), Purdon was a freshman at NDSCS in 1988. He happened to have a work-study job with the athletic department and operated the scoreboard that night: "This is so crazy. I've been talking about this game for twenty-three years," Purdon says. "The one guy I really remember is Barry Webster. I will never forget that name. He was incredible. And he wasn't just a great shooter—he would routinely get into the paint and get to the rim against these much taller guys. He'd drive the lane and make physical contact with the Bottineau kids, but he'd still manage to get his shot off. He was a little like Allen Iverson."

coach, and he was just so confused. How do you play defense against four people? Who prepares for that situation? I could see them panicking. So we still ran our basic set. We just didn't have a fifth option."

"THERE WASN'T A LOT of teamwork," concedes Oswald. "There might have been a little panic. When it was five-on-four, we should have just pounded the ball inside. But defense wasn't our forte, and we were behind by four points. We still wanted to run. We pushed the panic button and tried to get it all back in two possessions."

This, it seems, is what paradoxically slew the Lumberjacks: their own tempo. They refused to make the Tribes play half-court defense, which fueled Hall's strategy. The Jacks were designed to outscore people; when I finally located Mr. Oswald,[7] he assumed I wanted to ask him about an altogether different game—a 1989 track meet vs. Northland College where the two squads combined for 308 points.[8] Taylor echoed that sentiment. "Most of our games were more like 120 to 118," he says. "I made 115 three-pointers as a freshman.[9] That was just how we played."

When Webster fouled out at the four-minute mark, the Thunderbirds were still ahead by 4. The remaining Birds—Miles Fighter, Vernon Woodhall, Roger Yellow Card, and Harold Pay Pay—were now tasked with breaking the Jacks' press without their best ball handler

---

7. I found his phone number on a website—he's currently president of the Wing Horse Club.

8. The final was NDSU-Bottineau 160, Northland 148. Roger McGillis had 44 points for the Lumberjacks.

9. One of the more amusing details within the reporting of this story was the level of accuracy most of these players had about their own statistics. Though they often misremembered other major details (for example, Taylor remembered the Tribes' best player as "Kurt Keplin from Belcourt," who was not involved in the game in any context), they all had astounding recall for their own contributions. At one point, Webster casually mentioned that he also scored 38 against NDSU-Bottineau in one of their regular-season losses, just in case I was curious.

(and with no one to physically replace him). The lead melted. Fighter picked up his fifth foul with 1:06 on the clock,[10] allowing Bottineau to tie the game at 81. With a two-man advantage, it seemed unfathomable that the Tribes could hold on. But then they got a break: The Lumberjacks' Mark Peltier was called for charging, giving the rock back to UT. Hall called time-out, and the Thunderbirds had to inbound the ball at midcourt.

This is when it happened.

Now, imagine you're Ken Hall or Buster Gilliss. What do you do in this dead-ball situation? Hall had limited options; all he could really do was stack up two of his remaining three players and hope they set screens for each other. But Bottineau made a tragic—yet perhaps understandable—mistake: They covered the man throwing the ball in, and they *surrounded* the other two Thunderbirds. It was like a little human prison—they face-guarded the front Bird, they played directly behind the back Bird, and they sandwiched the stack from both sides. Since one Thunderbird had to throw the ball in, it was a four-on-two situation. The Jacks assumed United Tribes would skew conservative and simply try to sneak the ball inbounds. Instead, Pay Pay spontaneously broke to the basket. Woodhall[11] lobbed the ball over Pay Pay's shoulder, which he converted into a breakaway layup. United Tribes were now up 2 with less than a minute to go, and it suddenly seemed obvious that they were going to win. There were still 40 seconds on the clock, but it was over. The Jacks had broken.

The crowd lost its collective mind. It felt like we were watching the Olympics.

"We had a psychological advantage, and that increased as the game went on," says Hall, slightly understating the situation. "We

---

10. Fighter fouled out with 11 points. Along with Webster's 33 (which included five three-pointers), Pay Pay had 18, Woodhall had 12, and Yellow Card had 10.

11. It's possible Yellow Card was actually the trigger man—no one seems to know for sure.

literally had nothing to lose. We were the sixth seed in a six-team tournament."

THE PRECISE CONCLUSION of this game is something of a mess. It's a little like a murder trial where every eyewitness slightly contradicts every other testimony. What we do know is this: The Lumberjacks hustled the ball up court but lost possession without taking a shot. They immediately fouled Pay Pay, who went 1 of 2 from the line. With the Jacks now down 3, Roger McGillis launched multiple treys in an attempt to tie; Offutt kept snaring the offensive rebounds, but Bottineau was never able to convert. Offutt laid in a meaningless bunny as the buzzer sounded, but the officials waved it off. 84–81. It was over.

"We didn't know how to act," says Webster. "We didn't know how you celebrate something like that. We were all jumping around and celebrating, and I got hit right in the nuts. I actually slumped onto the ground. It was almost like someone said, 'Great job,' but then twisted my balls. But that's still a good memory. We all went back to the hotel and called our parents, and then I went to sleep. I was pretty exhausted . . . I probably cried, honestly. I wish my dad could have seen that game, but he was too sickly. He had diabetes real bad. But if I did cry, I didn't cry in front of anyone else."

This being a single-elimination tournament, the United Tribes had to play again on Monday, this time facing UND–Lake Region and the aforementioned Schilz. Amazingly, they somehow won again, 63–61 (Webster had 28). But they didn't advance to the regional. In Tuesday's championship, they lost to NDSCS, 77–65. They were tired. They deserved to be tired: Most of the Iron Five had logged 120 minutes of floor time over the span of three days.

A handful of players from this game ultimately finished their hoop careers at four-year colleges. Webster did not—he hurt his knee and ended up applying to the University of Nebraska, where he got a teaching degree and met his future wife. However, he continues to be heavily involved with the sport: He runs the Native Elite basketball camp in Nebraska, a networking program that tries to connect Native American high school players with college programs searching for talent. It's not easy. There continues to be a curious gap between the American Indian community and the larger world of basketball. Despite the intense basketball tradition within many reservation cultures, there's never been a high-profile Native American player at the pro (or even the collegiate) level. They're almost never recruited.

"The stigma is that Native kids aren't mentally tough," Webster says. "There is this belief that if you recruit a Native kid, he'll get homesick and quit school." I mention that another long-standing prejudice—that Native kids tend to be heavy drinkers—might be just as detrimental (the fact that United Tribes' nickname was the same as a cheap brand of wine was an insular joke when I was growing up). Webster concedes that this is true, but he didn't want to mention it—it's the kind of bias he doesn't even like to demystify (since a denial only reinforces the original perception). Certain ideas will never disappear.

As I end my conversation with Webster, I thank him for talking and reiterate how this game—this random, unremembered JUCO shootout from 1988—will inevitably remain the greatest sporting event I'll ever witness. Nothing has ever come close, before or since.

I could tell he was flattered. But he was not surprised.

"I do remember talking to Ken Hall that night," he tells me, "and I said, 'Somebody should really write about this game.' I did say that. Pretty funny that it's happening now."

[Additional reporting by Jeff Kolpack, Eric Peterson, Don Engen, and Bill Klosterman Jr.]

EPILOGUE: You know what's even weirder than this story? The fact that it more or less happened again, to the same two schools, twenty-eight years later. On February 24, 2016, Bottineau faced the United Tribes in the NJCAA Region 13 tournament. This time, United Tribes was forced to play the final 56.5 seconds with only *two* players on the court, ultimately losing 158–154 in double overtime (the Tribe dressed only five players and lost three to fouls). I don't know what to make of this. It's not like this is some kind of normal occurrence in North Dakota junior college basketball. It would be like if Oakland faced San Francisco in the next World Series and there was another earthquake. But I suppose that's possible, too.

The following essay ran in *The New York Times* in late 2010. It's about zombies (but just barely).

The reason *The New York Times* wanted an essay about zombies was due to the popularity of the AMC television show *The Walking Dead*. When they asked me if I was interested in writing something, I told them, "Sure. I'll do that. I think I understand the Zombie Lifestyle. But I don't watch *The Walking Dead*. I stopped watching after the premiere." Somehow, this convinced them I was *more* qualified to write the essay, as my personal perception of zombies would not be excessively shaped by this one specific program. I was seen as better suited to write about the zombie phenomenon because I had intellectual distance from the most popular extension of the phenomenon I was writing about.

Of course, if I had told my editor at the *Times*, "I love *The Walking Dead*. It's my favorite TV show," I assume her response would have been, "Great! You're clearly prefect for this assignment."

Once people decide they want you to do something, they don't really care what your qualifications are. However you describe yourself becomes proof that you're the ideal candidate. This is true in journalism, and in life.

My Zombie, Myself

Zombies are a value stock. They are wordless and oozing and brain-dead, but they're an expanding market with no glass ceiling. Zombies are a target-rich environment, literally and figuratively. The more you fill them with bullets, the more interesting they become. Roughly 5.3 million people watched the first episode of *The Walking Dead* on AMC, a stunning 83 percent more than the 2.9 million who watched the season four premiere of *Mad Men*. This means there are at least 2.4 million cable-ready Americans who would prefer watching Christina Hendricks if she were an animated corpse.

Statistically and aesthetically, that dissonance seems perverse. But it probably shouldn't. Mainstream interest in zombies has steadily risen over the past forty years. Zombies are a commodity that has advanced slowly and without major evolution, much like the staggering creatures George Romero popularized in the 1968 film *Night of the Living Dead*. What makes that measured amplification curious is the inherent limitations of the zombie itself: You can't add much depth to a creature who can't talk, doesn't think, and whose only motive is the consumption of flesh. You can't humanize a zombie, except to make it less zombie-esque. There are slow zombies, and there are fast zombies—that's pretty much the total spectrum of zombie diversity. It's not like zombies are changing to fit the world's condition. It's more that the condition of the world increasingly resembles a zombie offensive. There's something about zombies that's becoming more and more intriguing to the average person. And I think I know what that something is.

Zombies are just so goddamn easy to kill.

When we think critically about monsters, we tend to classify them as personifications of what we fear. Frankenstein's monster illustrated our trepidation about untethered science; Godzilla was spawned from the fear of the atomic age; werewolves feed into an instinctual panic over predation and man's detachment from nature. Vampires and zombies share an imbedded anxiety about disease. It's easy to project a symbolic relationship between zombies and rabies (or zombies and the pitfalls of consumerism), just as it's easy to project a symbolic relationship between vampirism and AIDS (or vampirism and the loss of purity). From a creative standpoint, these fear projections are narrative linchpins. They turn creatures into ideas, and that's the point.

But what if the audience infers an entirely different metaphor?

What if contemporary people are less interested in seeing depictions of their unconscious fears and more attracted to allegories of how their day-to-day existence feels? That would explain why so many people watched that first episode of *The Walking Dead*—they knew they'd be able to relate to it. It immediately feels familiar, because a lot of modern life is exactly like slaughtering zombies.

IF THERE'S ONE THING we all understand about zombie killing, it's that the act is uncomplicated: You blast one in the brain from point-blank range (preferably with a shotgun). That's Step 1. Step 2 is doing the same thing to the next zombie that takes its place. Step 3 is identical to Step 2, and Step 4 isn't any different from Step 3. Repeat this process until (a) you run out of shells, or (b) you run out of zombies. That's really the only viable strategy.

Every zombie war is a war of attrition. It's always a numbers game, and it's more repetitive than complex. In other words, zombie killing is philosophically similar to reading and deleting four hundred work emails on a Monday morning, or filling out paperwork that only generates more paperwork, or following Twitter gossip out of obligation, or performing tedious tasks in which the only true risk is being consumed by the avalanche. The principal downside to any zombie attack is that the zombies will never stop coming; the principal downside to life is that you will never truly be finished with whatever it is you do.

The Internet reminds us of this every day.

Here's a passage from a youngish writer named Alice Gregory, taken from a recent essay on Gary Shteyngart's dystopic novel *Super Sad True Love Story* in the literary journal *n+1*: "It's hard not to think 'death drive' every time I go on the Internet," she writes. "Opening Safari is an actively destructive decision. I am asking that consciousness be taken away from me." Ms. Gregory's self-directed fear is thematically similar to how the zombie brain is described by Max Brooks, author of the fictional oral history *World War Z* and its accompanying self-help manual, *The Zombie Survival Guide*: "Imagine a computer programmed to execute one function. This function cannot be paused, modified, or erased. No new data can be stored. No new commands can be installed. This computer will perform that one function, over and over, until its power source eventually shuts down."

This is our collective fear projection: that we will be consumed.

Zombies are like the Internet and the media and every conversation we don't want to have. It all comes at us endlessly (and thoughtlessly), and—if we surrender—we will be overtaken and absorbed. Yet this war is manageable, if not necessarily winnable. As long as we keep deleting whatever's directly in front of us, we survive. We live to eliminate the zombies of tomorrow. We are able to remain human, at least for the time being. Our enemy is relentless and colossal, but also uncreative and stupid.

Battling zombies is like battling anything else . . . or, I suppose, everything else.

BECAUSE OF THE *TWILIGHT* SERIES, it's easy to manufacture an argument in which zombies are merely replacing vampires as the monster of the moment, a designation that is supposed to matter for metaphorical, non-monstrous reasons. But that kind of thinking is deceptive. The recent five-year spike in vampire interest is *only* about the multiplatform success of *Twilight*, a brand that isn't about vampirism anyway. It's mostly about nostalgia for teenage chastity, the attractiveness of its film cast, and the fact that contemporary fiction consumers tend to prefer long serialized novels that can be read rapidly. But this has still created a domino effect. The 2008 Swedish vampire film *Let the Right One In* was fantastic, but it probably wouldn't have been remade in the United States if *Twilight* had never existed. *The Gates* was an overt attempt by ABC to tap into the housebound, preteen *Twilight* audience; HBO's *True Blood* is a camp reaction to Robert Pattinson's flat earnestness.

The difference with zombies, of course, is that it's possible to like a specific vampire temporarily, which isn't really an option with the undead.

Characters like Mr. Pattinson's Edward Cullen in *Twilight* and Anne Rice's Lestat de Lioncourt (and even boring old Count Dracula) can be multidimensional and erotic. It's possible to learn who they are and who they once were. Vampire love can be singular. Conversely, zombie love is exclusively communal. If you dig zombies, you dig the zombie concept. It's never personal. You're interested in what zombies signify, you like the way they move, and you understand what's required to stop them. And it's a reassuring attraction, because those aspects don't shift. They've become shared archetypal knowledge.

A few days before Halloween, I was in upstate New York with three other people, and we somehow ended up at the Barn of Terror, outside a town called Lake Katrine. Entering the barn was mildly disturbing, although probably not as scary as going into an actual abandoned barn that didn't charge twenty dollars and doesn't own its domain name. Regardless, the best part was when we exited the terror barn and were promptly herded onto a school bus, which took us to a cornfield about a quarter of a mile away. The field was filled with amateur actors, some playing military personnel and others portraying what were referred to as "the infected." We were told to run through the moonlit corn maze, if we wanted to live. As we ran, armed soldiers yelled contradictory instructions while hissing zombies emerged from the corny darkness. It was designed to be fun, and it was. But just before we immersed ourselves in the corn, one of my companions sardonically critiqued the reality of our predicament.

"I know this is supposed to be scary," he said. "But I'm pretty confident about my ability to deal with a zombie apocalypse. I feel strangely informed about what to do in this kind of scenario."

I could not disagree. At this point, who isn't? We all know how this goes: If you awake from a coma and don't immediately see a member of the hospital staff, assume a zombie takeover has transpired during your incapacitation. Don't travel at night and keep your drapes closed. Don't let zombies spit on you. If you knock a zombie down, direct a second bullet into its brain stem. But above all, do not assume that the war is over, because it never is. The zombies you kill today will merely be replaced by the zombies of tomorrow. But you can do this, my friend. It's disenchanting, but it's not difficult. Keep your finger on the trigger. Continue the termination. Don't stop believing. Don't stop deleting. Return your voice mails and nod your agreements. This is the zombies' world, and we just live here.

But we can live better.

If you intend to make a living as a culture writer, here's a question you must ask yourself: Can I see politics within nonpolitical scenarios? If the answer is "yes," you must ask a second question: Am I willing to *impose* politics upon nonpolitical scenarios? If that answer is likewise "yes," you need to ask a third question: Does the creative upside to this practice outweigh the social detriment?

The autumn 2011 piece you're about to read anatomizes the complexity of nostalgia. Obviously, most normal people don't see nostalgia as particularly complex; it merely describes a pleasurable, bittersweet, cerebral sensation. But within culture writing, nostalgia is a fucking minotaur. As a culture writer, you must decide how you feel about nostalgia *as a concept*, because it usually suggests something deep and insidious. If you're a nostalgic person, it means you're mentally projecting a belief that life was better in the past, regardless of the evidence. You are trafficking in sentimentality and arguing that progress has been (on balance) bad for society. If you dislike nostalgia, it means you believe that same projection is an interpretative lie and that the world is constantly improving, even if it feels significantly worse. When Donald Trump says "Make America Great Again," he is subtextually supporting the concept of false nostalgia. When Kim Kardashian is venerated as a dynamic genius reflecting the mediated brilliance of The Way We Live Now, her disciples are subtextually assaulting genuine nostalgia.

Now, is this *really* true? Is any of this *really* happening? No one knows and no one cares. But this is how the game is played, because the game is insane.

That's Not How It Happened

Some problems never disappear. Sometimes that's because there's no solution to whatever that problem is. But just as often, it's because the problem isn't problematic. The alleged crisis is just an inexact, impossible-to-resolve phenomenon about which two reasonable people can reasonably disagree. Our current "nostalgia problem" fits into this class: Every so often (like right now), people interested in culture become fixated on a soft debate over the merits or dangers of nostalgia—as it applies to all art, but particularly to popular music. The dispute resurfaces every time a new generation attains a social position that's both dominant and insecure. I suppose if this ever stopped, we'd be nostalgic for the time when it still periodically mattered.

The highest-profile current example is the book *Retromania: Pop Culture's Addiction to Its Own Past*, written by the British writer Simon Reynolds. Promoting his book on *Slate*, Reynolds casually mentioned two oral histories he views as loosely connected to the phenomenon (the grunge overview *Everybody Loves Our Town* and the '80s-heavy *I Want My MTV*). Those passing mentions prompted writers from both books to politely reject the idea that their works were somehow reliant on the experience of nostalgia (since nostalgia has a mostly negative literary connotation). But this isn't the only example: *New York* magazine music writer Nitsuh Abebe wrote about this subject apolitically for *Pitchfork*, effectively noting what I just reiterated—for whatever reason, this (semi-real) "nostalgia problem" appears to be something writers are collectively worried about at this (semi-random) moment. The net result is a bunch of people defending and bemoaning the impact of nostalgia in unpredictable ways. A few of these arguments intrigue me, but just barely. I'm much more interested in *why* people feel nostalgia, particularly when that feeling derives from something that doesn't actually intersect with any personal experience they ever had. I don't care if nostalgia is good or bad, because I don't believe either of those words really applies.

But still—before a problem can be discarded as fake, we must identify what that fake problem is. This dispute has three principal elements. None of them are new. The central reason smart people (and certainly most critics) disparage nostalgia is utilitarian: It's an uncritical form of artistic appreciation. If you unconditionally love something from your past, it might just mean you love that period of your own life. In other words, you're not *really* hearing "You Oughta Know." What you're hearing is a song that reminds you of a time when you were happy, and you've conflated that positive memory with any music vaguely connected to the recollection. You can't separate the merit of a song from the time you originally experienced it. [The counter to this argument would be that this seamless integration is arguably the most transcendent thing any piece of art can achieve.] A secondary criticism boils down to self-serving insecurity: When we appreciate things from our past, we're latently arguing that those things are still important—and if those things are important, we can likewise pretend *our own life* is important, because those are the things that comprise our past. [The counterargument would be that personal history *does* matter, and that the size of one's reality is the size of one's memory.] A third criticism is that emotively dwelling on the past is lazy and lifeless. [The counter to this would be that even those who hate nostalgia inevitably concede it feels good, and feeling good is probably the point.] There are other arguments that can be made here, but these are the main three. If you're "pro" or "anti" nostalgia, a core version of your thesis inevitably falls somewhere within this paragraph. And in all three cases, both sides of the debate are tethered to that magical bridge between the experience of art and the experience of being alive. It's based on the premise that we are nostalgic for things that transport us back to an earlier draft of ourselves, and that this process of mental time travel is either wonderful or pathetic.

But what if this is merely how we choose to explain it? What if nostalgia has less to do with our own lives than we assume?

What if the feeling we like to call "nostalgia" is simply the by-product of *accidental repetition?*

STARE AT A PHOTOGRAPH of someone you dated long, long ago. The emotional reaction you'll have (unless you're bizarre or depressed or kind of terrible) is positive. Even if this person broke your heart, you will effortlessly remember all the feelings you had that allowed your heart to be broken. This is genuine nostalgia: You are looking at something that actively reminds you of your past (and which exists exclusively for that purpose), and you're reimagining the conditions and circumstances surrounding that image. But you're probably not judging the *quality* of the photo. You're probably not thinking, "You know, it's impossible for me to tell if the composition and framing of this picture are professional, because I remember too much about the day it was taken." You probably aren't concerned with unconsciously overrating the photographic prowess of whoever snapped the image. The picture is just a delivery device for the memory. This is why thinking about old music (or old TV shows, or old films, or old books) is more complicated and unclear: It's not just that we like the feeling that comes along with the old song. We like the old song itself. The song *itself* sounds good, even if we never spend a second thinking about our personal relationship to when we originally heard it (and even if it wasn't a personal favorite at the time of its release). We place this sonic experience into the category of "nostalgic appreciation," because that seems to make the most sense.

Except it doesn't.

It doesn't make sense to assume any art we remember from the past is going to automatically improve when we experience it again, solely because it has a relationship to whatever our life used to be like. We may not even remember that particular period with any clarity or importance. Those things might be connected, but they might also be unrelated. Certainly, some songs do remind us of specific people and specific places (and if someone were to directly ask you, "What songs make you nostalgic?" these are the tracks you'd immediately list). But most other old songs only replicate that sensation. The song connects you with nothing tangible, yet still seems warm and positive and extra-meaningful. It's nostalgia without memory. And what this usually means is that you listened to that particular song *a lot*, during a stage in your life when you listened to a smaller number of songs with a much higher frequency. It might have nothing to do with whatever was happening alongside that listening experience; it might just be that you accidentally invested the amount of time necessary to appreciate the song to its fullest possible potentiality. What seems like "nostalgia" might be a form of low-grade expertise that amplifies the value of the listening event.

Here's what I mean: For a big chunk of my adolescent life, I had only six cassettes. One of these was Ozzy Osbourne's *Bark at the Moon*, which (as an adult) I consider to be the third- or fourth-best Ozzy solo album. But it's definitely the Ozzy album I've listened to the most, solely because I only had five other tapes. It's possible I've listened to *Bark at the Moon* more than all the other Ozzy solo albums combined.

The first song on side two of *Bark at the Moon* is titled "Centre of Eternity." It's a bit ponderous and a little too Ozzy-by-the-numbers. It means nothing to me personally and doesn't make me long for the days of yore; until I started writing this essay, I hadn't listened to it in at least ten years. But as soon as I replayed it, it sounded great. Moreover, it was a weirdly *complete* listening experience—not only did I like the song as a whole, but I also noticed and remembered all the individual parts (the overwrought organ intro, how Jake E. Lee's guitar was tuned, when the drums come in, the goofy sci-fi lyrics, etc.). There may be a finite amount one can "get" from this particular song, but—whatever that amount is—I got it all. And this is not because of any relationship I've created between "Centre of Eternity" and my life from the middle 1980s, most of which I don't remember. It's because the middle '80s were a time when I might lie on my bed and listen to a random Ozzy song 365 times over the course of twelve months. It's not an emotional experience. It's a mechanical experience. I'm not altering the value of "Centre of Eternity" by making it signify something specific to me, or my past. I've simply listened to it enough to have multiple auditory experiences simultaneously (and without even trying). The track sounds better than logic dictates because I (once) put in enough time to "get" everything it possibly offers. So maybe it's not that we're overrating our memories. Maybe it's that we're underrating the import of prolonged exposure. Maybe things don't become meaningful unless we're willing to repeat our interaction with whatever that "thing" truly is.

And this, I think, is what makes our current "nostalgia problem" more multifaceted than the one we had ten years ago. This process I just described? This idea of accidentally creating a false (but powerful) sense of nostalgia through inadvertent-yet-dogged repetition? That's ending, and it's not coming back.

IN THE YEAR 2011, I don't know why anyone would listen to any song every day for a year. Even if it was your favorite song of all time, it would be impossible to justify. It would be like going to the New York Public Library every morning and only reading *Jonathan Livingston Seagull*. Music is now (essentially) free, so no one who loves music is limited by an inability to afford cassettes. Radio is less important than it used to be (which means songs can't be easily inflicted on audiences), MTV only shows videos when no one is watching, and streaming services are game changers. Equally important is the way modern pop music is recorded and produced: It's deliberately designed for digital immediacy. Listen to the first ninety seconds of Rihanna's new album *Loud*—if you don't love it right away, you're not going to love it a month from now. There's also been a shift in how long a critic (professional or otherwise) can be expected to hear a product before judging its value. This is especially true for albums that are supposed to be important—most meaningful responses to Radiohead's *The King of Limbs* and Kanye and Jay-Z's *Watch the Throne* happened within twenty-four hours of their embargoed release. When someone in 2011 complains that a specific song is being "played to death," it usually just means it's been licensed to too many commercials and movie trailers and feels more like a commodity.

Now, no one can irrefutably declare that this evolution is bad, good, or merely different; it seems like it will (probably) be negative for artists, positive for casual consumers, and neutral for serious music fans. But it's absolutely going to change what we classify (rightly or wrongly) as "nostalgia." If you hate nostalgia, this is good news. "Excellent," you probably think. "Now I won't have to listen to people trying to convince me that Pearl Jam's *Riot Act* is secretly awesome, based on the argument that they used to listen to Pearl Jam's *Ten* in high school." From a practical standpoint, there's no historical loss to the genocide of self-made nostalgia. The Internet will warehouse what people's minds do not. (And since the Internet is a curator-based medium, it's a naturally backward-looking medium.) People won't need to "remember" Pearl Jam in order for Pearl Jam to survive forever. In a hundred years, we will still have a more complete, more accurate portrait of Eddie Vedder than of Mozart or John Philip Sousa or Chuck Berry, even if no one in America is still aware that a song titled "Jeremy" once existed. It's uncomfortable to admit this, but technology has made the ability to remember things irrelevant. Intellectually, having a deep memory used to be a real competitive advantage. Now it's like having the ability to multiply four-digit numbers in your head—impressive, but not essential.

Yet people will still *want* to remember stuff.

People enjoy remembering things, and particularly things that happened in their youth. Remembering creates meaning. There are really only two stages in any existence—what we're doing *now*, and what we were doing *then*. That's why random songs played repeatedly take on a weight that outsizes their ostensive worth: We can unconsciously hear the time and energy we invested, all those years ago. But no one really does that anymore. No one endlessly plays the same song out of necessity. So when this process stops happening—when there are no more weirdos listening to "Centre of Eternity" every day for a year, without even particularly liking it—what will replace that experience?

I suspect it will be replaced by the actions of strangers.

Connectivity will replace repetition. Instead of generating false nostalgia by having the same experience over and over, we will aggregate false nostalgia from those fleeting moments when everyone seemed to be doing the same thing at once. It won't be a kid playing the same song 1,000 times in a row. It will be that kid remembering when he and 999 other people all played the same song once (and immediately discussed it on Twitter, or on whatever replaces Twitter). It will be a short, shared experience that seems vast enough to be justifiably memorable. And I don't know what that will feel like, and I don't know if it will be better or worse. But I'm sure it will make some people miss the way things used to be.

When the following essay was published in December 2011, Tim Tebow was (by far) the best-known, most polarizing athlete in America. By the time this book is released, many people will not even remember who he was or what he did, unless they really care about God or Florida or minor league baseball. That entire evolution happened in less than five years. It's starting to feel like Tebow's lasting cultural imprint will be small, unless he runs for Congress (which, I must concede, feels inevitable).

So—just in case—here is who this guy was: He was the best college quarterback of the modern era (one Heisman Trophy, two national titles). He was a bad NFL quarterback, even though he won more games than he lost. He's an openly religious person who's heavily involved with philanthropy. He built a children's hospital in the Philippines. As a college senior at Florida, when asked at a press conference if he was a virgin, he laughed and said, "Yes I am." He starred (alongside his mother) in an anti-abortion commercial that ran during the Super Bowl. He is the only football player in history who became famous for genuflecting in public (Colin Kaepernick doesn't count—he got famous for kneeling, which isn't the same). Half the people who watched him play loved him a little too much. The other half hated him too much.

Some people exist only for the benefit of strangers.

The Light Who Has Lighted the World

I f you've lost interest in thinking about Tim Tebow, don't read the rest of this article. It will only make you mad. But then again, that might be what you want.

I'VE JUST WATCHED the Denver Broncos defeat the Minnesota Vikings 35–32. Tebow was awful in the first half, passing for only 13 yards. He was relatively decent in the second half, finishing 10 of 15 for the game and completing three passes of more than 20 yards, a minor achievement he hadn't accomplished all year. The Broncos won by intercepting a pass in the final minute and kicking an easy field goal, so it would be misleading and reactionary and inaccurate to say that Tebow won them the game. But Tebow won them the game.

When the score was deadlocked at 32 and the Broncos were kicking off with 1:33 remaining, Fox idiotically broke away from the tie in Minnesota to show us the opening kickoff of the Giants–Packers game. Since I couldn't see what was transpiring in Minnesota, I just had to sit in my chair and wonder what would happen next. Did I believe Denver would win? I shouldn't have. Minnesota was getting the ball with multiple time-outs. They'd been the better team for most of the afternoon. Viking QB Chris Ponder had outplayed Tebow and the best athlete on the field was Viking receiver Percy Harvin. The worst-case scenario for the Vikings should have been heading into overtime with a home-field advantage.

Yet I believed Denver would win.

My reasoning?

I had no reasoning. And I did not like how that felt, even though I'm trying to convince myself it felt good.

IMAGINE YOU'RE A DETECTIVE, assigned to investigate a murder in an isolated community of a thousand people. There's no motive for this crime and no one saw it happen. By the time you arrive, the body has already been cremated. There are no clues. There is no forensic evidence. You can't find anything that sheds any light whatsoever on who committed this murder. But because there are only a thousand people in town, you have the opportunity to interview everyone who lives there. And that process generates a bizarre consensus: Almost eight hundred of the thousand citizens believe the murderer is a local man named Timothy.

Over and over again, you hear different versions of the same sentiment: "Timothy did it." No one saw him do it, and no one can provide a framework for how he might have been successful. But 784 people are certain it was Timothy. A few interviewees provide sophisticated, nuanced theories as to why they're so convinced of his guilt. Others simply say, "I can just tell it was him." Most testimonies fall somewhere in between those extremes, but no one has any tangible proof. You knock on Timothy's door and ask if you can talk to him about the crime. He agrees. He does not seem nervous or distraught.

You ask what he was doing the evening of the murder. He says, "I was reading a book and watching a movie." He shows you the book. You check the TV listings from the night of the murder, and the film he referenced had aired on television. You say, "Many people in this town think you are responsible for the killing." Timothy says, "I have no idea why they would think that." You ask if he knew the man who died. "Yes," he replies, "I know everyone in town." You ask if he disliked the victim. "I didn't like him or dislike him," he says. "I knew him. That was the extent of our relationship."

After six months of investigating, you return to your home office. Your supervisor asks what you unearthed. "Nothing," you say. "I have no evidence of anything. I did not find a single clue." The supervisor is flummoxed. He asks, "Well, do you have any leads?" You say, "Sort of. For reasons I cannot comprehend, 784 of the citizens believe the killer is a man named Timothy. But that's all they have— their *belief* that Timothy is guilty."

"That seems meaningful," says your supervisor. "In the face of no evidence, the fact that 78.4 percent of the town strongly believes something seems like our best prospect. We can't arrest him, but we can't ignore that level of accord. It's beyond a coincidence. Let's keep the case open. We should continue investigating this Timothy fellow, even if our only reason for suspicion is the suspicion of other people."

Do you agree with your supervisor's argument?

A SURVEY by the Pew Forum on Religion & Public Life suggests that 78.4 percent of Americans identify themselves as Christians.

I'M NOT INTERESTED in forwarding a pro-Tebow or anti-Tebow argument. I have my own feelings, but I don't think they're relevant.

What I'm interested in is why he's so fascinating to other people. I've spent the last two months traveling around the country, and Tebow was the only person I was asked about in every single city. I even had one debate over whether the degree to which Tebow is socially polarizing has been overrated by the media, a debate whose very existence seems to provide its own answer. I feel *compelled* to write about him, even while recognizing that too much has been written already.

The nature of sports lends itself to the polarization of celebrity athletes. But this case is unlike any other I can remember. In 1996, when Denver Nuggets guard Mahmoud Abdul-Rauf refused to face the flag during the national anthem, it was easy to understand why certain people were outraged and why others saw that outrage as hypocritical. It was *predictably* polarizing. But this "Tebow Thing" is different. On one pole, you have people who hate him because he's too much of an in-your-face good person, which makes very little sense; at the other pole, you have people who love him because he succeeds at his job while being uniquely unskilled at its traditional requirements, which seems almost as weird. Equally bizarre is the way both groups perceive themselves as the oppressed minority who are fighting against dominant public opinion, although I suppose that has become the way most Americans think about everything.

Clearly, religion plays a role in this (we live in a Christian nation, Tebow is a Christian warrior, non-Christians see themselves as ostracized, and Christians see themselves as persecuted). But the real reason this "Tebow Thing" feels new is because it's a God issue that transcends God, assuming it's possible for any issue to transcend what's already transcendent. I'm starting to think it has something to do with the natural human discomfort with faith—and not just faith in Christ, but faith in anything that might (eventually) make us look ridiculous.

JUST BECAUSE A BUNCH of people believe something does not make it true. This is obvious, even to a child. People once thought the earth was flat.[1] But here's a more complex scenario: If you were living in Greece during the sixth century, and there was no way to deduce what the true shape of the earth was, and there was no way to validate or contradict the preexisting, relatively universal belief that the world was shaped like a flat disc—wouldn't disagreeing with that theory be less reasonable than refuting it? And if so, wouldn't that mean the only sixth-century people who were ultimately correct about world geography were unreasonable and insane?

Trust the insane!

TEBOW IS A FAITHFUL PERSON. He's full of faith—filled to the top and oozing over the side. It's central to every part of him. When a reporter suggested that he mentions God too frequently (and that this repetition is what annoys his critics), Tebow said, "If you're married, and you really love your wife, is it good enough to only tell your wife that you love her on the day you get married? Or should you tell her every single day when you wake up and have the opportunity? That's how I feel about my relationship with Jesus Christ." This is the smartest retort I've ever heard an athlete give to a theological question. What possible follow-up could the reporter have asked that would not have seemed *anti-wife*?

---

1. Just for the record, though: By the time Christopher Columbus sailed to the New World, almost no educated European still believed the world was flat. That was a misrepresentation that emerged in the seventeenth century.

And this, I think, is what makes Tebow so maddening to those who hate him: He refuses to say anything that would validate the suspicion that he's fake (or naive, or self-righteous, or dumb). My guess is that Ryan Fitzpatrick or Aaron Rodgers would blow him away on the GRE, but Tebow has social intelligence, particularly when he speaks in public. It's not that he usually says the right things. He *only* says the right things, all the time. And that fuels a quasi-tautological reality that makes his supporters euphoric, even if they can't wholly accept its validity. The reality is as follows:

1. Tebow is a good person who loves God.
2. Tebow throws many incompletions and makes curious, unorthodox decisions.
3. The Broncos' defense keeps every game tight. Underrated running back Willis McGahee eats the clock.
4. The Broncos inevitably win in the closing minutes.
5. Tebow humbly thanks God for this achievement (and for all achievements), thereby crediting God for what just happened (and for what happens to everyone on earth).
6. Tebow connects God to life.
7. Tebow is a good person who loves God.

I doubt many Christians believe that God is unfairly helping Tebow win games in the AFC West. I'm sure a few hardcores might, but not many. However, I get the impression that antagonistic secularists assume this assumption infiltrates every aspect of Tebow's celebrity, and that it explains why he's so beloved by strangers they cannot relate to. Their negative belief is that penitent, conservative Americans look at Tebow and see a man being "rewarded" for his faith, which validates the idea that believing in something abstract is more important than understanding something real. And this makes them worried about the future, because they see that thinking everywhere, and it seems like the kind of thinking that runs this country into the ground.

IT'S DIFFICULT TO TAKE an "anti-faith" position. There's no pejorative connotation of the word "faithful." The only time "faith" seems negative is when it's prefaced by the word "blind." But blind faith is the only kind of faith there is. In order for someone's faith to be meaningful, it has to be blind. Anyone can believe a hard fact that everyone already accepts. That's easy. If you can *see* something, you don't need faith. Faith in the seeable is meaningless. But meaningful faith is dangerous. It simplifies things that aren't simple. Throughout the twentieth century, there were only two presidents who won reelection with a bad economy and high unemployment: FDR in 1936 and Reagan in 1984. In both cases, the incumbent presidents were able to argue that their preexisting plans for jump-starting the economy were better than the hypothetical plans of their opponents (Alf Landon and Walter Mondale). Both incumbents made a better case for what they intended to do, and both enjoyed decisive victories. In 2012, Barack Obama will face a similar situation. But what will happen if his ultimate opponent provides no plan for him to refute? What if his opponent merely says this: "Have faith in me. Have faith that I will figure everything out and that I can fix the economy, because I have faith in the American people. Together, we have faith in each other"?

How do you refute the non-argument of meaningful faith?

You (usually) don't. You (usually) lose.

Since Tebow was installed as the Broncos' starter, they are 6-1.

Trust the insane?

THE TOUGHEST QUARTERBACK in the NFL is Ben Roethlisberger. He's not the best, but he's the toughest. He stands in the pocket longer, absorbs more punishment, exhibits a higher threshold for pain, and plays his best in the clutch. Roethlisberger is also, by all credible accounts, either a jerk or a "former jerk." He has a highly checkered past and an unsympathetic persona. According to a survey in *Forbes*, he's the least popular player in the league who hasn't slept on a prison cot. He is tough, and—maybe—he's mean.

It's difficult to separate those qualities. "Toughness" and "meanness" are always intertwined, often coalescing into "grit." When I think about my own life, the toughest people I've known have (often) been bad, bad citizens. Would you rather fight two super-nice guys simultaneously, or one solitary, diabolical reprobate? It's not a difficult question. When I see Roethlisberger unfazed by a busted nose or a broken foot, it computes. He seems like the kind of semi-terrible person who is flat-out *harder* than those around him.

But try to imagine Tebow as a jerk. Let's say his performance on the field was unchanged, but his off-the-field personality was totally different. Let's say he was alleged to have sexually assaulted a few co-eds and electrocuted a few dogs and fired an unlicensed handgun in a nightclub. If all this were true, he would not be polarizing. He would just be unpopular, particularly with the people who currently adore him. Sales of his jerseys would fall through the floor. But what would be the response after he guts out an ugly 17–13 win against the Jets? What would be the perception? The perception would be that his victory was due to his *toughness*. That's how the media would explain it. It wouldn't necessarily be true, but it would immediately make sense to people: We are comfortable with the idea that extra-bad people possess something real that helps them win football games.

There is a long history of this, especially in places like Oakland. But it's less comfortable to think that extra-good people possess such qualities, because that suggests they're being helped by virtuous forces outside of corporeal reality. And that's too much to handle/accept/consider, unless (of course) you already accept that premise unconditionally, in every day of your life.

Right now, whenever Bronco GM John Elway[2] gets asked about Tebow, he effectively says, "We have no choice but to play him. *He wins games.*" It's not really a compliment. It's almost a criticism. But if Tebow did all this with a prison record, Elway would say the same thing in reverse order: "He wins games. *We have no choice but to play him.*" Which is similar, but not the same.

THERE ARE QUANTIFIABLE ASPECTS of Tebow's game that get ignored, mostly because everything else about him is so uncanny. His proficiency as a short-yardage bulldozer on 3rd and 3 compensates for his defects as an intermediate passer on 3rd and 8. The fact that Tebow only runs selectively gives Denver a psychological edge, particularly on two-point-conversion attempts. He's a hard man to tackle, and that's the crux of what football is. All of these qualities are significant in the Broncos' success. But they're not revelatory, and I don't think they have a big impact on why people feel so passionately about this person.

The machinations of his success don't matter as long as they're inexplicable.

The crux here, the issue driving this whole "Tebow Thing," is the

---

2. It's easy to understand why Elway refuses to embrace Tebow. Elway came to the Broncos as the most pro-ready quarterback of his generation, yet people in Denver hammered him for ten years. They were still making fun of his teeth in 1998. He must look at Tebow's fan base and think, "Why do they love him so much? I was more polished than this guy as a senior in high school. This is insane. What am I not seeing?"

matter of faith. It's the ongoing choice between embracing a warm feeling that makes no sense or a cold pragmatism that's probably true. But with Tebow, that illogical warm feeling keeps working out. It pays off. The upside to secular thinking is that—in theory—your skepticism will prove correct. Your rightness might be emotionally unsatisfying, but it confirms a stable understanding of the universe. Sports fans who love statistics fall into this camp. People who reject cognitive dissonance build this camp and find the firewood. But Tebow wrecks all that, because he makes blind faith a viable option. His faith in God, his followers' faith in him—it all defies modernity. And this is why people care so much. He is making people wonder if they should try to believe things they don't actually believe.

The next piece is the foreword to a 2014 Fantagraphics coffee table book anthologizing all the syndicated *Peanuts* cartoons running in various Sunday newspapers from 1956 to 1960 (in the olden days, these colorful inserts were referred to as "The Funnies"). As a consequence, there are a few references to specific *Peanuts* strips on annotated pages of the coffee table book. Don't worry about it. You don't need to see the cartoons in order to understand what I'm writing about.

I was honored to write this foreword. I still can't believe I was asked to do so. But I wish the essay I ultimately typed into my keyboard remotely reflected the essay that still exists inside my skull. Something was lost in the translation; I think I just choked. My relationship to *Peanuts*—and specifically to the character of Charlie Brown—is so overwhelming that I couldn't describe the things I wanted to describe. It was too uncanny. I feel more intimately connected to Charlie Brown than to any musician or any athlete, and I care about *Peanuts* more than any novel or any film. I'm almost embarrassed by the depth of this feeling. I haven't watched *A Charlie Brown Christmas* in at least twenty-five years, solely because I can't emotionally reconcile the final scene: I can't get over the fact that the other kids don't tell Charlie Brown that his decision to pick the tiny, pathetic tree was ultimately the right call. They wish him a Merry Christmas and help him sing "Hark! The Herald Angels," but they never concede he was correct. This will bother me forever. Even writing this paragraph is making me angry.

The rain falls on the just and the unjust. And as Charles M. Schulz once noted, that's a good system, no matter how it makes us feel.

There's Something Peculiar About Lying in a Dark Room. You Can't See Anything.

I can't write objectively about Charlie Brown. It feels like I'm writing about myself.

This, I realize, is no accident.

I know that Charlie Brown is the type of character consciously designed to make people feel like they're looking at an image of themselves. If you can't empathize with Charlie Brown, you likely lack an ability to empathize with any fictional character. Here is a child continually humiliated for desiring nothing more than normalcy—the opportunity to kick a football, the aptitude to fly a kite, the freedom to walk down the sidewalk without having a random acquaintance compare his skull to a block of lumber. He wants glory, but not an excessive amount (one baseball victory would be more than enough). He has the coolest dog in town, but that plays to his disadvantage. He's an eight-year-old who needs a psychiatrist, and he has to pay the bill himself (only five cents, but still). Charlie Brown knows his life is a contradictory struggle, and sometimes his only option is to lie in a dark room, alone with his thoughts. He will never win. *He will never win.* Yet here's the paradox: Charlie Brown is still happy. He still has friends. He still gets excited about all the projects that are destined to fail. Very often, young Americans are simultaneously pessimistic about the world and optimistic about themselves—they assume everyone's future is bleak, except for their own. Charlie is the opposite. He knows he's doomed, but that doesn't stop him from trying anything and everything. He believes existence is amazing, despite his own personal experience. It's the quality that makes him so infinitely likable: He does not see the world as cruel. He believes the world is good, even if everything that's ever happened to him suggests otherwise. All he wants are the things everyone else seems to get without trying. He aspires to be average, which—for him—is an impossible dream.

I suppose nobody feels this way all the time. But everybody feels this way occasionally.

Charles M. Schulz died on February 12, 2000. The final *Peanuts* strip ran the very next day, a coincidence noted by virtually everyone who cared about the man and his work. In the years since his passing, I've noticed a curious trend: For whatever reason, it's become popular to assert that the spiritual center of the *Peanuts* universe is not Charlie Brown. The postmodern answer to that puzzle is Snoopy— dynamic, indefatigable, and hyperimaginative. Perception has drifted toward what the public prefers to celebrate. It's a little like what happened on the TV show *Happy Days*: A sitcom originally focused on milquetoast Richie Cunningham rapidly evolved into a vehicle for the super-coolness of Fonzie. Obviously, this type of paradigm shift is no crime against humanity, and I love Snoopy almost as much as his owner (he's a wonderful dancer and my all-time favorite novelist). But Snoopy is not the emotional vortex of *Peanuts*. That's simply wrong. The linchpin to *Peanuts* will always be Charlie Brown. It can be no one else. And this is because Charlie Brown effortlessly embodies what *Peanuts* truly is: an introduction to adult problems, explained by children.

THE PROBABLE (read: inevitable) death of daily newspapers will have a lot of collateral damage, to varying degrees of impact. I don't know where the gradual disappearance of the Sunday comics falls on this continuum, or even if it belongs at all. I assume something else will come to occupy its role in the culture, and the notion of bemoaning such a loss will be categorized as nostalgia for a period when the media was controlled by dinosaurs who refused to accept that the purpose of every news story was to provide random people the opportunity to publicly comment on how they felt about it. But I will miss the Sunday comics. I miss them already. As a kid, I loved the idea that there was at least one section of the newspaper directly targeted at my brain; as an adult, it was reassuring to read something that was still the exact same product I remembered from the past. It was static in the best possible way. Like most people, I moved through various adolescent phases where different strips temporarily became my obsession: *Garfield* in fifth grade, *The Far Side* throughout high school, *Calvin and Hobbes* as a college boozehound. But I always considered *Peanuts* the most "important" comic strip, and the one that all other strips were measured against. The fact that *Peanuts* was the first strip on the very top of the Sunday comics' front page verified this subjective belief—if comics were rock bands, it seemed obvious that *Peanuts* was the Beatles.

The strips in this particular collection stretch from 1956 to 1960. It was a transitional period for *Peanuts*—the characters no longer have the generic, unsophisticated appearance of the early *Li'l Folks* era, but their fantasies and dialogue rarely skew as surreal as they will become throughout the mid-sixties and beyond. Snoopy "talks," but not in the way we're accustomed (his concerns are more traditionally doglike), and his jowls and his gut look a tad thin. Linus Van Pelt—still noticeably younger than all the other kids in '57—eventually becomes interchangeable with his slightly older peers (and Schulz was clearly enamored with Linus during this period, as he stars in a majority of the offerings, most notably a three-week serial where he worries about performing at the Christmas program). Around 1959, we meet Sally Brown for the first time (still an infant). But the most critical evolution involves the persona of Charlie himself. It is during this three-year stretch that he becomes "the Charlie Browniest." Throughout the mid-fifties, Charlie Brown was still confident. On page 2, we see a boy who believes his snow fort is an architectural masterwork. On page 20, Charlie violently punishes the kite he cannot fly. He's not arrogant, but he is self-assured. He's almost a smart aleck. Yet by the inception of the sixties, that confidence is gone. From 1960 onward, Charlie Brown is the person we all recognize from all those old television specials: the unironic loser with a limitless heart, endlessly hammered for caring too much.

"Nobody likes me," Charlie Brown says as he stares into space. "All it would take to make me happy is to have someone say he likes me." When Lucy overhears this lament, she's immediately incredulous. "Do you mean to tell me that someone has it within his or her power to make you happy merely by doing such a simple thing?" Charlie assures her that—yes—this simple act is all it would take. In fact, it wouldn't even matter if the sentiment wasn't true. He just wants to know how it feels to be liked. But even this is still too much to ask for.

"I can't do it," Lucy replies. And then she walks away. And this, it seems, is the whole joke.

One of the common assumptions about *Peanuts* is that Charlie Brown and Charles M. Schulz were the same person, and that we are able to see the personality of Schulz by studying the personality of Brown. Certain similarities are undeniable (both of their fathers were barbers, both were obsessed with red-haired girls they never really knew, etc.). But I don't think this connection is fully accurate. The reflection is not as straightforward as it seems. I think that the primordial *Li'l Folks* version of Charlie Brown—the little guy from the forties—was Schulz crafting a fictional version of his literal childhood. Early Charlie was, essentially, who Schulz once was. But the model of Charlie Brown we recognize and love so much more—the model reinvented here, at the end of the 1950s—was Schulz crafting a version of how he *felt*, both in his memory and in the present tense. It was the construct of an adult, suffering through problems only an adult can conceive and recognize. It was also a depiction of how he *wanted* to feel: Schulz, the man, was rumored to be a maniacal grudge holder, unwilling to forget any slight or embarrassment ever levied against him. His creative boyhood doppelgänger is the opposite; Charlie Brown could always wipe the slate clean. And that makes an overpowering difference, both for the character and for everyone else.

"IT'S DEPRESSING to realize that you're so insignificant you haven't got a chance ever to become president," Charlie Brown tells Lucy on page 76 (it's the second week of June, 1957). "It wouldn't be so bad if I thought I had some chance." Like so much of the classic *Peanuts* banter, he makes these remarks apropos of nothing—it's just something he's suddenly worried about, for no clear reason. Lucy, of course, obliterates Charlie for voicing this trepidation, mocking him with a tsunami of faint praise, almost as if he had somehow claimed he was destined for political greatness. Is her response amusing? I suppose it's a little amusing. But it's mostly dark (and entirely true). At the age of eight, Charlie Brown is considering a reality that most people don't confront until much later: a realization that the future is limited. It's not that he desperately wants to become Dwight Eisenhower—it's the simple recognition that this couldn't happen even if he did. He's confronting the central myth of childhood, which is that anyone can be anything. Charlie Brown represents the downside of adult consciousness. And what does Lucy represent? Lucy represents the world itself. Lucy responds the way society always responds to any sudden insight of existential despair: *How did you not know this already, Blockhead?*

It doesn't matter how many times this sort of thing has happened before. It will never stop happening, to Charlie Brown or anyone else. Like I said—Charlie Brown knows he's doomed. He absolutely, irrefutably knows it. But a little part of his mind always thinks, "Maybe not this time, though." That glimmer of hope is his Achilles' heel. It's also the quality that makes him so eminently relatable. The joke is not that Charlie Brown is hopeless. The joke is that Charlie Brown *knows* he's hopeless, but he doesn't trust the infallibility of his own insecurity. If he's always wrong about everything, perhaps he's wrong about this, too. When Charlie mentions the impossibility of his own presidential fantasy, there's a vague sense that he wants Lucy to tell him he's mistaken. And at first (of course), Lucy does exactly that. She says "maybe." And then (of course) she does what she always does. She reminds Charlie Brown that he is Charlie Brown. Which is how I suspect Charles M. Schulz felt about himself, up until the very end: "No matter what I do or what I try, I'm always going to be myself."

In this particular anthology, there are four strips where Charlie tries to kick a football. Unless you're a yet-to-be-conceived archaeologist reading this book a thousand years in the future, the outcome of these attempts will not surprise you. Two of these strips (released roughly a year apart) are so similar they almost suggest a lack of imagination. In one, Charlie Brown expresses his belief that people have the ability to change and deserve the opportunity to do so (and then he breaks his back). In the other, Lucy compliments Charlie's faith in human nature (moments after his back has been broken). This is the reassuring, hypereternal, death-and-taxes aspect to *Peanuts*: The children don't grow up and the conflicts don't change. The pigskin's omnipresent unkickability is the Sisyphean symbol for the whole of Charlie's life and the pivotal metaphor behind why he matters so much to so many people. It is the apex of his failures. But failing is not what makes Charlie Brown my fictional friend and personal protagonist. It's his reasoning for placing himself in a position where failure is inevitable: "I must be out of my mind," he says to himself. "But I can't resist kicking footballs."

He can't resist kicking footballs.

Even though he never, ever does. He still can't resist.

Resistance is futile.

White Dudes

Holding Guitars

I landed at Heathrow airport at eight a.m. on August 26, 2014. I think it was a Tuesday. I took a taxi through the spitting rain to a fancy hotel in order to ask Jimmy Page questions about *Led Zeppelin II*. I will never forget that cab ride. I was exhausted, I had a terrible toothache, and I felt wonderful. I think it was the first time I ever felt professionally successful.

Page, of course, hated our conversation, both in theory and in practice. His mind still resides in an era when media exposure only served as a detriment to artistic aspiration. Led Zeppelin did not need the press to succeed. They did not need to explain what they were doing or persuade people to care. They just had to record and tour. The songs were enough. Forty years after the fact, Page still assumes answering questions about his music can only erode its interpretative potentiality. He looked at me like I was a man who was trying to ruin his life.

Part of my job is annoying people I admire. I hate to admit that, but I have to accept it.

In retrospect, I probably should have pushed him on the accusation that "Stairway to Heaven" is a plagiarized reinvention of the instrumental song "Taurus" by the group Spirit. The eventual 2016 court case over this allegation was hilarious. Zeppelin won the trial decisively, even though "Stairway to Heaven" probably *is* loosely based on the opening strains of "Taurus." There are multiple reasons why I believe this, but the main one is Page's testimony about his (alleged) reaction to the first time he (supposedly) heard "Taurus": "I was confused by the comparison," he insisted. "What's this got to do with 'Stairway'?"

Now, if he had said: "You know, even I was a little shocked by how similar these two songs seem, but it's just a coincidence," I might have believed him. But no reasonable person could hear both of these songs and detect no similarity whatever. Structurally and atmospherically, the relationship is just too parallel.

That said, the guy who sued Zeppelin was not the writer of "Taurus" (the deceased Randy Wolfe, a.k.a. "Randy California") or even an ancillary member of Spirit. He was just an opportunist looking for money, so he deserved nothing, even if his argument was valid. And if Spirit accidentally spawned "Stairway to Heaven," that's worth more than money, anyway. That's arguably the apotheosis of their career (and the rest of their career was pretty good!).

Liquid Food

People still watch *The Song Remains the Same*, or at least they look at it for four or five minutes whenever they're scrolling through the late-night TV menu and suddenly hear a theremin. It is, for reasons both good and bad, the quintessential concert film, produced by the kind of super-popular rock band that no longer exists in contemporary popular culture. Led Zeppelin recorded the live footage for *The Song Remains the Same* at Madison Square Garden in 1973, but the camera magazines ran out of film and missed key sections from certain songs. To compensate, the individual band members created interstitial fantasy sequences that were intended to reflect their respective personalities, all of which were varying levels of opaque.

The last time Zeppelin architect Jimmy Page saw *The Song Remains the Same* was June: He was in Japan, and somebody showed him what it looked like on an iPhone. His contemporary views on the movie are more positive than what they were at the time of its release, but still lukewarm and neutral: He classifies the performances as "good," the fantasy sequences as "diverse," and the overall aesthetic as "quaint." He ultimately concludes, "The film is what it is," which is the critical equivalent of saying "I concede that the film exists." But he also realizes that the appreciation of *The Song Remains the Same* has inverted itself. For three decades, the standard take was that the movie was essential for its musical content, as this was the only way Zeppelin could be witnessed by anyone who didn't see the band when they were still active. The tacked-on fantasy bits were always mocked. But now it has become unfathomably easy to see live footage of Led Zeppelin, on both the Internet and DVD. There's no longer any period of Zeppelin's musical career that cannot be accessed instantly. If, however, you want to understand how the various members of the group viewed *themselves* at the apex of their fame, those weird little interstitial corridors are as close as you're going to come. The most straightforwardly psychedelic passage involves Page: As "Dazed and Confused" drones in the background, we see the (then) twenty-nine-year-old guitarist climbing a rock cliff on a moonlit December night, eventually reaching a wizard who's a decrepit, kaleidoscoped version of Page himself. The footage was filmed near the Boleskine House on the shore of Loch Ness, a mansion that had once been the residence of infamous British occultist Aleister Crowley.

I start to ask Page a question about this fantasy sequence. But I don't get to finish.

"I knew you were leading up to that. I knew you were eventually going to ask me what that sequence represents," says Page. Throughout our two-day interview, he often predicts what he thinks I'm about to ask. "You have the hermit, and you have the aspirant. And the aspirant is climbing toward the hermit, who is this beacon of light. The idea is that anyone can acquire truth at any point in his life."

Jimmy Page is seventy years old. He undoubtedly knows the truth, at least about himself and the most important hard rock band that ever walked the earth. He has become the hermit on the hill. But getting the hermit to share those truths is not easy, because hermits are hermetic for a reason: They don't trust the aspirants, and particularly not the aspirants who want to record whatever they have to say.

I **MEET PAGE** at the Gore Hotel, three minutes from Royal Albert Hall and not far from Page's home in Kensington, London. Founded in 1892, the Gore is an old hotel that feels even older than it is (our conversation takes place in a sitting room filled with multiple sets of the *Encyclopædia Britannica*). Page looks fantastic for a man who once subsisted on food that did not require chewing.[1] Somehow, he appeared slightly older fifteen years ago; he might be aging in reverse, the best remaining argument for those who still believe he sold his soul to the devil. Dressed in black with his hair pulled back, Page is a paragon of restrained dignity. He looks like a man who just finished ratifying the Articles of Confederation. And considering how long it's been since Led Zeppelin's dissolution—thirty-four years this December—that's how distant his cultural imprint should feel: It should feel like colonial history, or perhaps even prehistory. But this is not the case. Finding Led Zeppelin on the radio is easier today than it was in 1973. If you stroll around the campus of any state college, the likelihood of finding kids wearing Zeppelin T-shirts mirrors the likelihood of finding kids trying to buy weed. This autumn, British fashion designer Paul Smith announced the creation of five Zeppelin-inspired scarves, independent of the fact that the members of Zeppelin didn't wear scarves with any inordinate regularity. It appears there will never be a time when this band isn't famous, even if the entire genre of rock becomes as marginalized as jazz. That

---

1. Here's Page in a 1977 interview with the magazine *Rock Focus*: "I prefer to eat liquid food, something like a banana daiquiri—sort of the thing they would give to invalids. I'm not into solid foods very much . . . I do have a blender, but nobody's gotten it together yet. The blender thing is great. I mean, I'll never turn down some alcohol, so a banana daiquiri with all the food protein is the answer to the problem. It got me through the last tour, having that every day and nothing else to eat."

cultural tenacity can be directly traced to the majestic power—and the judicious fragility—of the music itself. And most of the credit for that can be directly traced to Page.

Page is either the second- or third-greatest rock guitarist of all time, depending on how seriously you take Eric Clapton. After a mini-career as a sixties session musician (he's an uncredited guitarist on everything from the Who's "I Can't Explain" to Donovan's "Sunshine Superman"), Page invested twenty-five months with the Yardbirds before handpicking the musicians who would become Led Zeppelin. For the next twelve years, he operated as a perpetual riff machine, reinventing his instrument and recontextualizing the blues; his influence is so vast that many guitarists who copy his style don't even recognize who they're unconsciously copying. Equally unrivaled is Page's skill as a producer, although that's complicated by his curious homogeneity—he only produces his own work. He also operates at his own capricious pace: Once renowned for his coke-fueled, superhuman productivity (he recorded all of the 1976 album *Presence* in a mere eighteen days), he's released only five proper studio albums since 1980 (two with the Firm, one with ex–Zep vocalist Robert Plant, another with Plant sound-alike David Coverdale, and the 1988 solo effort *Outrider*). All five would qualify as intriguing disappointments.

Over that same span, Page's central passion has been curatorial, incrementally mining and remastering Zeppelin's catalog in the hope of reflecting his impossibly high audio standard. In truth, that's the only reason Page even agreed to this interview: All the Led Zeppelin albums are being rereleased as individual box sets that include an updated vinyl pressing of the LP, a compact disc, rough studio mixes and outtakes from the respective recording sessions (in both formats), a code for a high-definition download, and a seventy-page photo book. They're not cheap (each box retails for over a hundred dollars), but the sound quality cannot be disputed. And this is the only thing Page really wants to talk about—the *sound* of the music, and how that sound was achieved. He can talk about microphone placement for a very, very long time. Are you interested in having a detailed conversation about how the glue used with magnetic audiotape was altered in the late 1970s, subsequently leading to the disintegration of countless master tapes? If so, find Jimmy Page. He has thoughts on this.

In order to get Page to talk about almost anything, you always need to start by talking about music. Early in our conversation, I mention his use of "reverse echo" on the song "Whole Lotta Love." This is a studio technique where echo is added to a recording and the tape is then flipped over and played in reverse, allowing the listener to hear the note's echo before hearing the note itself . . .

So when you used reverse echo on "Whole Lotta Love," were you—

Reverse echo is actually on the first record, too, on "You Shook Me." You can hear it pulsating underneath the rest of the track. Today, you would just reverse the files. But it was more complicated in those days. You had to physically flip the tape over, and you had to convince the engineer to let you do it, because engineers didn't think that way. I'd actually had an experiment of sorts on this with the Yardbirds. In the Yardbirds we had to release singles, which was a total soul-destroyer for the band. But some of the singles had brass instruments on them, so I was trying to make the brass sound like something interesting. So I would put echo on the brass and then play the tape backward, so that the echo would precede the signal. And I could tell that was a really good idea, so I used that technique across a lot of Led Zeppelin.

But how do you come up with that kind of idea in the first place? Do you start by imagining a sound in your head and then try to figure out how to create it, or do you first come up with the idea of flipping the tape and then just see what happens? I have to assume this is a technique no one had ever tried before.

That's true. No one had ever done this. I just thought of it. I would picture it, and sort of hear it in advance in my head, and then I just tried to see if it would work. And I obviously knew what tape sounded like when you played it backward.

What makes music "heavy"? It's one thing to make music louder, but how do you make music feel heavy? Is it mostly technological or mostly ethereal?

I don't want to say it's just the attitude, but attitude has a lot to do with it. One of the things that was employed on the Zeppelin records was the fact that I was very keen on making the most of John Bonham's drum sound, because he was such a technician in terms of tuning his drums for projection. You don't want a microphone right in front of the drum kit. Sonically, distance makes depth. So employing that ambience was very important, because drums are acoustic instruments. The only time John Bonham ever got to be John Bonham was when he was in Led Zeppelin. You know, he plays on some Paul McCartney solo tracks. He plays on the song "C Moon," for example. But you'd never know it was him, because of the way it was recorded. It's all closed down. He was a very subtle musician. And once he was introduced to the world on that first Zeppelin album, on the very first track, when it's just one single bass drum—drumming was never the same after that. It didn't matter if it was jazz or rock or whatever: If drums were involved, he had changed them.

I was surprised that in the recent documentary on Ginger Baker (Beware of Mr. Baker), Baker takes some shots at Bonham's musical ability. You just never hear other drummers making that criticism. He's usually so untouchable.

That's an interesting film, because of the way the film starts. Doesn't it start with Ginger hitting the director with a cane? I did see the film and I know what you're talking about. I was a bit disappointed by that. His criticism was that Bonham didn't swing. I was like, "Oh, Ginger. That's the *only* thing that's undeniable about Bonham." I thought that was stupid. That was a really silly thing of him to say.

If any other musician obsessed over technological details with this level of exacting specificity, he would likely be classified as a "nerd," as that has become a strange kind of compliment in the Internet age. People *want* to be seen as nerds. But that designation does not apply here. Jimmy Page does not seem remotely nerdy. He is, in fact, oddly intimidating, despite his age and physical frame. He rarely raises his voice, yet often seems on the cusp of yelling. And while he's polite and charming when making casual conversation, his posture instantly changes the moment a tape recorder is brought into the equation: He becomes adversarial, and sometimes condescending. He does not compromise.

On the flight over here, I was reading this compilation of interviews conducted with you over the span of several years by Brad Tolinski and—

Yeah, somebody showed me that book. I used to like Brad, until he published that book. It's just articles from a magazine. My God.

Did you feel ripped off?

Let me put it this way: I don't do things like that.

Well, regardless, here is one quote I found especially interesting: You once said, "I can't speak for the others, but for me drugs were an integral part of the whole thing, right from the beginning, right to the end." This makes me wonder—are there specific tracks that would not exist if not for your experiments with drugs?

I'm not commenting on that. Let's not talk about any of that.

So you don't want to comment on anything about Zeppelin's relationship with drugs?

I couldn't comment on that, just like I wouldn't comment on the relationship between Zeppelin's audience and drugs. But of course you wouldn't ask me that. You wouldn't ask me what the climate was like at the time. The climate in the 1970s was different than it is now. Now it's a drinking culture. It wasn't so much like that then.

Did you ever need to go to rehab?

No.

But you supposedly had a serious heroin problem at one time, so how did you quit?

How do you know I had a heroin problem? You don't know what I had or what I didn't have. All I will say is this: My responsibilities to the music did not change. I didn't drop out or quit working. I was there, just as much as anyone else was.

So does it bother you that the conventional wisdom is that your alleged heroin addiction impacted your ability to produce In Through the Out Door? *The way that story is always presented is that John Paul Jones and Robert Plant took over the completion of that album, because you were heavily involved with drugs.*

If anyone wants to say that, the first thing you have to ask them is, "Were you there at the time?" The second thing to take on board is the fact that I am the producer of *In Through the Out Door*. That's what I did. It's right there in black-and-white. If there were controversy over this, if John Paul Jones or Robert Plant had done what you're implying, wouldn't they have wanted to be listed as the producers of the album? So let's just forget all that.

Okay, I get what you're saying. But there are just certain things about your life that remain unclear, and—

I'll tell you what: When I'm good and ready, I will write an autobiography.

Didn't you once claim you would only write an autobiography if it wasn't published until after you were dead?

Well, that's the way to do it, isn't it? Because everyone is going to die, so you gotta make sure that you don't. When I'm good and ready, I will talk about what I want to talk about. I was just telling this to someone else who wanted to talk about Led Zeppelin and the mud shark. You haven't asked me about the mud shark—yet—but I will tell you this: Most people would be far more interested in the length of a Led Zeppelin track than they would be in the length of a mud shark.

What do you mean?

You see, you don't even get it. The length of a song matters more than the length of a fish.

Here's something else I've always wondered: Why did you choose not to produce albums by other bands?

I wanted to keep everything in-house with Zeppelin. I didn't want to hedge my bets by doing other things.

*Sure, but what about **after** Zeppelin? Particularly in the 1980s, it seems like you would have been a natural choice for so many of those metal acts trying to model themselves after your work. I mean, why not produce a Rush album or something?*

That's a good question. There was certainly a period where that could have happened. Maybe the bands thought I was un-approachable. I don't think I was ever asked. Not that I know of, at least.

I know John Paul Jones produced some albums and—

Oh, I don't know what he did.

He made a Butthole Surfers album in 1993.

Well, good.

This kind of prickly exchange was not uncommon, and it's illustrative of two points. The first is that Zeppelin was the last colossal band who saw no meaningful relationship between their own musical invention and how it was interpreted by the media. It did not matter that they rarely gave interviews and never released radio singles; Zeppelin's massive success was totally disconnected from how they were covered or what they said in public. As a result, Page sees interviews as devoid of purpose. And that indifference prompts the second point, which is that almost every salacious detail we know about Led Zeppelin comes from outside sources. The band members themselves almost never discuss any of the assumed debauchery that defined their reputation. That aforementioned "Mud Shark Incident"? The entire concept of the band pleasuring a female groupie with a shark they caught while fishing out of the window of a Seattle hotel? You will find that story in the unauthorized biography *Hammer of the Gods*, written by a man who spent only two weeks with the group and explained to him by a deceased road manager the band disowned while he was still alive. Now, this is not to say the event didn't happen, just as it's undeniable that Page was intensely involved with drugs. But these are not things he talks about. These are simply things he chooses not to deny. And that makes the extraction of reality profoundly complex.

Take, for example, Page's current relationship with Plant. Robert Plant continually expresses ennui toward his tenure in Led Zeppelin, seemingly uninterested in potential reunions and entirely focused on making new, less-heavy music that moves him further and further away from the yowl he unleashed on "Immigrant Song." Page is the opposite. Page is fixated on celebrating the legacy of Zeppelin and affirming their musical primacy. Very often, this dissonance is framed to suggest that Plant remains vital while Page is mired in the past; of course, it would be just as reasonable to argue that Page understands who he is while Plant is still wondering. My suspicion is that Page thinks about this conflict a lot. But I can't say for certain, because his official statements are purposefully prosaic.

This question requires speculation, but I suspect your speculation would be more accurate than most other people's: Why is Robert Plant so adamant about his disinterest in Zeppelin?

(*pause*) Sometimes I raise my eyebrows at the things he says. But that's all I can say about it. I don't make a point to read what he says about Zeppelin. I really don't. But people will read me things he has said, and I will usually say, "Are you sure you're quoting him correctly?" It's always a little surprising. But I can't answer for him. I have a respect for the work of everyone in the band, and I can't be dismissive of the work we did together. I sort of know what he's doing. I can see what he's doing. But I don't fully understand it.

Is it personally offensive?

No. It doesn't matter. There is no point in getting down to that level. I'm not going to send him messages through the press.

THE FOLLOWING DAY, I meet with Page at a photo studio in Camden Town. We sit at a spartan table in a space designed for portraiture, which means everything is blindingly, seamlessly white: the walls, the floor, the lighting. It feels like I'm conducting an interrogation on the set of *2001: A Space Odyssey.*

If I asked you, "What was the best period of your life?" would the answer be the same as if I asked, "What was the best period of your career?"

That's an interesting question, isn't it? I would have to say the most profound parts of my life involve the birth of my children. But in a professional capacity, it was really two things. The first was getting the first gold disc with Zeppelin. I remember the day that came in, and I knew what that meant, especially in America. The other was playing at the Olympics in Beijing. I knew that was going to beam out over the whole planet, and I loved working with [vocalist] Leona Lewis, who I think is astonishing. And it was a full version of "Whole Lotta Love." Not an edited version!

Does audience response impact how you perceive your own work?

I don't want to sound arrogant about this, but—when those Zeppelin records were being put together and the song selections were being made—we all knew it was good. We were very confident about what we were presenting. So that was what was important to me. People have their own interpretation of the songs. Take a song like "When the Levee Breaks." The lyrics are clear. The story is clear. But people still have a different interpretation of how it touches them, which is what you want to achieve. You want there to be modular impressions. You don't want a blanket impression of what a song means.

Musically, you're so confident. Are there aspects of your musical life that you're insecure about?

Yes. But you're not going to find out about them. (*laughs*)

When you'd hear other artists make music that seemed like obvious attempts at replicating what you were doing—those early Billy Squier albums, Kingdom Come, even a song like "Barracuda" by Heart—what did you think? Were you flattered or annoyed?

I actually thought it was alright. They were playing in the spirit of Led Zeppelin. I mean, I've had so many songs that sound like "Kashmir" come to my attention, but you always know what it is. People were inspired by Zeppelin, so that's part of Zeppelin's legacy. Those Zeppelin albums are such essential texts for any new musician, regardless of what instrument they play.

Do you remember hearing the first Beastie Boys album, which opens with the drums from "When the Levee Breaks"?

I thought it was a bit cheeky, but I wasn't going to lose any sleep over it.

*In the 1970s, the word everyone used to describe you was
"reclusive." Well, you're obviously no longer reclusive. So the
word they use now is "unknowable."*

You know who knows me? My clothes. My clothes know me
very well.

*Would you generally prefer other people not to know about
your life? And I don't mean as a celebrity. I mean just as a
normal person.*

I don't know what other people need to know, really. I don't see
the necessity of that, and I'm not going to start now.

*But when you were young, were you not interested in the life
of someone like Robert Johnson? Were you not interested in
the life of Elvis Presley? Didn't what you knew about them as
people partially inform how you consumed their music?*

Robert Johnson is an interesting one. I'm sure we'd all have wanted
to be around when he was playing, if we could teleport ourselves
to that time . . . What's important about Elvis was that he changed
absolutely everything for youth and that he came in right under
the radar. But that's all I need to know about his life. I guess
I'm interested in how those recordings were done with Sam
Phillips, and about Phillips's vision of having this white guy sing
black music. But the music is what turned me on. Chuck Berry,
for example: It was what he was singing about in his lyrics. The
stories he was telling. He was singing about hamburgers sizzling
night and day. We didn't have hamburgers in England. We didn't

even know what they were. You know? It was a picture being painted.

But I think most people who love Elvis are also interested in how his life was connected to his music. Who he was impacted what he did as an artist. Which is why a person who loves Zeppelin might wonder the same things about you. He might wonder, "What kind of man buys Aleister Crowley's mansion?"

A man with good taste.

There's a Led Zeppelin book by Mick Wall—

I haven't read it.

I'm not surprised. But there's an implication in the book that you almost joined the Rolling Stones on three separate occasions. Is that possibly true?

If it's in a book, it probably isn't true. This is something I supposedly said?

The implication is that you were considered as a replacement when Brian Jones died, again after Mick Taylor left, and as a possible fill-in when Keith Richards was arrested in Toronto in 1977. Is any of that accurate?

(*long pause*) No. I mean, I've played with the Stones. I play a little on *Dirty Work*. The reality is that it would have just meant I was going in with the Stones when someone else wasn't there.

But I know what you're getting at. Put it this way: Not that I know of.

Have you ever met Bob Dylan?

Not really. I think I bumped into him once at a hotel in New Orleans, but we didn't have a chance to have a musical conversation. I wish I could have. I was aware of his music before he ever came to England. There's an interview with me from 1965, when I was still a session musician, where I'm asked who my favorite composer is, and my answer is Bob Dylan.

Are you a nostalgic person?

Yeah. I can be quite nostalgic. Although not to the point of melancholia.

Do you miss the 1970s? Do you miss your day-to-day life from, say, 1973?

I miss how life was for everybody in the '60s and '70s. Music had just exploded. The Beatles had revitalized everything and the record companies were taken by surprise. There was positive freedom in society in general. That was a really good period for everybody. I don't hanker after it, but I see it for what it was. I was improving as a guitarist.

The degree to which you see everything through music is amazing. Considering how insane your life was in 1973, I'm surprised that one of your key memories is that you made technical improvements as a guitar player. Is there any separation between who you are as a musician and who you are as a person?

When my parents made a move from an area near the London airport to [the Surrey suburb of] Epsom in 1952, there was a guitar in the house. It was just there, like a sculpture. No one knew how it got there. It was just in the house. So there was this immediate connection between this guitar and what I was listening to on the radio. It was almost like an OCD thing. I was obsessed with it. But I don't know how that guitar got there, and I don't know where it went. I have no idea where it is now. My mother is still alive, and she doesn't know where it went. But that guitar was like an intervention. I have to look at this in a philosophical way, or maybe in a romantic way. Either way, for me, it's reality.

Was part of your motive for making that Coverdale/Page album an attempt to annoy Robert Plant?

(*smiles*) That's pathetic. I'm not going to answer that. I'll give you one more question.[2]

Okay, how about this: Was your interest in the occult authentic, or were you just interested in that stuff as a historical novelty? Did you ever actually attempt magic?

---

2. On paper, it probably seems like Page was offended by this question. He actually found it rather amusing. Sitting across from him, that was obvious. But this is often a problem with the Q&A format: Though you get a more accurate portrait of *exactly* how the subject responded to a specific question, you can't always tell when one or both parties are being sarcastic.

Well, we can finish the interview with me saying I won't answer that question, either.

We shake hands and chat a bit more, mostly about Elvis. As we get up to leave, I casually mention the room's aesthetic similarity to *2001: A Space Odyssey*. Page starts talking about his love of Stanley Kubrick. With open admiration, he notes that the soundtrack to *A Clockwork Orange* was likely produced before the advent of the polyphonic synthesizer, and that this was an amazing accomplishment. As I exit the building, I find myself fixated on how curious that comment is—that of all the things to take away from *A Clockwork Orange*, Page remains most interested in the arcane technology used to make its score. Yet this explains as much as everything else he told me: There is music, and there is everything else. And if other people can't understand that, he feels no need to explain.

From the standpoint of pure, unadulterated *talent* at his chosen craft—technical execution, natural proclivity, and formal inventiveness—Eddie Van Halen exists at a level slightly beyond everyone else I've ever interviewed. Jimmy Page matters more historically, because his riffs are more timeless and his songs are more sophisticated. But EVH has total command of his instrument. He's a genius in every sense of the word, literally and nonhyperbolically.

He was also slightly paranoid and does not seem like a particularly happy person.

We met in the summer of 2015. Even as we spoke, I was skeptical of certain things he said and of the veracity of his memories. But I don't think Eddie Van Halen cares if strangers see him as paranoid or unhappy or mendacious. My impression is that the only things he truly cares about are (a) his immediate family, and (b) if other high-level musicians respect his ability as a guitarist. His worldview is small. It's roughly the size of his studio.

Eddie Van Halen is the rare example of a celebrity I was excited to meet for completely nonprofessional reasons. When I was in first grade, my older brother would drive me to school and play the first Van Halen album on the 8-track. I probably heard "Eruption" fifty times before I turned seven. I had no idea what we were listening to or who the band was or what a guitar was supposed to sound like. Five years later, I saw "Jump" on *Friday Night Videos*. It was everything I'd ever wanted from art. As I proceeded through high school, I methodically acquired all the old Van Halen albums, including that 1978 debut (which, at the time, felt like buying a fossil). I was shocked to discover I already knew every lyric and every solo. I had involuntarily memorized the whole record. It turns out I loved Van Halen before I even knew what rock music was.

C'mon Dave,
Gimme a Break

Eddie Van Halen doesn't listen to music.

This is not a fake-out or a misdirection, nor is it a seemingly straightforward statement that actually means its opposite. Eddie Van Halen does not listen to music. "I don't listen to anything," he tells me from a greenish couch inside 5150, the expansive home recording studio built on his seven-acre residence in Studio City, Calif. I'd just asked if he ever revisits old Van Halen albums, but his disinterest in those records is merely the tip of a very weird iceberg: Unlike every other musician I've ever met, he does not listen to any music he isn't actively making. He maintains that the last album he purchased was Peter Gabriel's *So*, when it came out in 1986. He's not familiar with the work of Radiohead, Metallica, or Guns N' Roses. He appears to know only one song Randy Rhoads played on, and it's "Crazy Train." He scarcely listened to Pantera, even though he spoke at the funeral of the group's guitarist and placed the axe from *Van Halen II* in the man's casket. He doesn't listen to the radio in his car, much to the annoyance of his wife ("I prefer the sound of the motor," he says). He sheepishly admits he never even listened to most of the bands that opened for Van Halen and worries, "Does that make me an asshole?" Sometimes he listens to Yo-Yo Ma, because he loves the sound of the cello. But even that is rare.

"It's an odd thing, but I've been this way my whole life," he continues. "I couldn't make a contemporary record if I wanted to, because I don't know what contemporary music sounds like."

As a high school student, he was obsessed with Eric Clapton and interested in Black Sabbath and Deep Purple. That's pretty much the extent of his investment as a consumer.[1] He can intuitively learn almost any song he hears twice and works on his own music every day—the 5150 archive is filled to the rafters with unreleased recordings—but he simply isn't intrigued by the music of other people (the last "new" guitarist he liked was jazz artist Allan Holdsworth, who's older than he is). And if that seems strange, here's something stranger: A few minutes after explaining this, I casually mention Taylor Swift as an example of modern songwriting; before I finish my thought, Van Halen rhetorically speculates on the role Max Martin might play within her songwriting process. So how is it possible to not listen to music for three decades, yet still know the reputation of a faceless Swedish songwriter who specializes in high-gloss pop?

"I have a lot of Google alerts set up," says Van Halen. "I think I read something where somebody said, 'If Max Martin played guitar like Eddie Van Halen, he'd be dangerous.' I know he's like the modern Desmond Child. He makes all the hits. But that's all I know about him."

It's a contradiction—but not the first one, or the last.

---

1. Part of what makes this so insane is the massive number of songs Van Halen has covered live, particularly when they were playing rock clubs and house parties before getting signed by Warner Bros. in 1977. It would appear that Eddie Van Halen can flawlessly replicate several hundred songs he does not necessarily like. His older brother would just hand him a record and say, "Learn these songs," and he would learn them overnight.

EMERGING FROM THE BACKYARD PARTY SCENE of mid-seventies Pasadena, Van Halen radically modernized the trajectory of American metal by simultaneously making it less heavy, more melodic, less gothic, and more inclusive. The band's first six albums sold 56 million copies, punctuated by the mammoth #1 single "Jump" in 1984. But that volcanic success melted into a never-ending carousel of high-profile reinvention: Vocalist David Lee Roth went solo, prompting the group to relaunch its identity with Sammy Hagar. Over the next ten years, this more refined, less bombastic version of Van Halen sold another 27 million records—but that lineup was similarly doomed, leading to Hagar's acrimonious departure and an ultra-brief, ill-fated reconciliation with Roth at the 1996 MTV Video Music Awards. That debacle spiraled into an awkward three-year union with ex–Extreme frontman Gary Cherone, the only singer Van Halen officially terminated.

"It was a strange thing with Cherone," Eddie explains. "He joined Van Halen, and he was living in my guest house. We were getting ready to go on tour, and all of a sudden I see this John Travolta outfit—these big lapels and a crazy jacket. He's like, 'This is my stage outfit.' That's when I realized it wasn't going to work. And when we tried to make a second record with him, he wouldn't take any direction. But I don't dislike Gary at all."

Hagar rejoined in 2003 (mostly for touring purposes) but exited again after two years, this time followed by bassist Michael Anthony (eventually replaced in Van Halen by Eddie's son, Wolfgang). Rumors that Roth would return once more progressively bubbled to the surface; in 2007, it finally happened. Which leaves us where we are today, at least for the moment. The current lineup released *A*

Different Kind of Truth in 2012, trailed by a 2015 live album cut in Japan. Interestingly, *A Different Kind of Truth* included a handful of old songs abandoned from the band's earliest demos from the seventies, selected by Wolfgang and lyrically updated by Roth.

Eddie Van Halen looks back on these transactions the way a Vietnam vet recalls Cambodia—certain details are vivid while others blend together, but he has no nostalgia for any of it. The most hyperkinetic guitarist of the past forty years has become, for lack of a better term, exceedingly normcore. "I'm a T-shirt and jeans guy," he says while compulsively vaping. He no longer smokes cigarettes, having surgically lost a third of his tongue to a cancer that eventually drifted into his esophagus. Still, he's not certain if the cigarettes were totally to blame.

"I used metal picks—they're brass and copper—which I always held in my mouth, in the exact place where I got the tongue cancer," he says. "Plus, I basically live in a recording studio that's filled with electromagnetic energy. So that's one theory. I mean, I was smoking and doing a lot of drugs and a lot of everything. But at the same time, my lungs are totally clear. This is just my own theory, but the doctors say it's possible."

The surgery has slightly impacted his speech, in the same way his 1999 hip replacement slightly impacted his mobility. But he works out several times a week and appears remarkably spry. As proof, Mr. Van Halen is about to embark on a thirty-eight-date North American tour. He will be joined by his drummer brother (who he loves), his bassist son (who he loves), and vocalist Roth (with whom he has no relationship whatsoever).

"He does not want to be my friend," Van Halen says, seemingly bemused. "How can I put this: Roth's perception of himself is different from who he is in reality. We're not in our twenties anymore.

We're in our sixties. *Act like you're sixty.* I stopped coloring my hair, because I know I'm not going to be young again."

Eddie would love to make another Van Halen album, but that plan has obstructions. "It's hard, because there are four people in this band, and three of us like rock 'n' roll. And one of us likes dance music," he says. "And that used to kind of work, but now Dave doesn't want to come to the table." That said, Eddie still seems more magnanimous to Roth than he does toward Hagar and Anthony. The guitarist swears he has no hatred for anyone, but his grudges run deep (he's still pissed that longtime producer Ted Templeman forced him to waste an original minimoog composition for the single "Dancing in the Streets" in 1982: "The whole reason I built this studio was to shove it up Templeman's ass").

The fundamental nature of his genius confounds logic: He is an autodidact who can play any instrument he gets his paws on (he owns an oboe, for instance), but he's also the rare rock artist who studied music at college (both he and his brother Alex attended Pasadena Community College in the early seventies). He's a classically trained pianist, but he can't read music. And he insists that—had he taken proper guitar lessons—he would have never developed the innovative techniques that are now regularly taught by proper guitar instructors. His entire career has been built on astonishment and influence. The first question every rival guitarist asked upon hearing the '78 instrumental song "Eruption" was, "How is he making those sounds?" The second tended to be, "And how can I copy it?" As a consequence, the 1980s were saturated with EVH clones, all of whom tried to prove that they, too, could hammer on the neck of their guitar with maximum dexterity. But it never really worked for anyone else.

"That was a different trip," Van Halen recalls. "It was like, 'What the hell did I start here?' Because [that technique] had been a part of my playing for so long, and then everybody else started doing it. I did not take it as flattery. But it ultimately didn't matter, because I still play that way and none of those other people stayed with it." He further notes that all the Big Hair replicants ignored a subtle aspect of his methodology—he always held the neck of the instrument with both hands while he hammered (as opposed to just popping the strings with the fingers of an open hand). Now, why that detail makes a difference is hard to deduce. But that's just one of myriad mysteries within Van Halen's populist catalog. There are many who can instantly recall the first time they heard songs like "Panama" and "Unchained" and "D.O.A."—but Eddie Van Halen is not among them.

"I have no memory of coming up with any of those riffs," he says. "Even the stuff I wrote for the last record, I don't remember. It just comes to me. I never sit down and decide to write a song. I've never done that."

This sentiment becomes more explicable when you hear the explanation for how Eddie used to work. For most of his career, he wrote on tour. After every show, the other three members of the band would hit the town and carouse ("My brother was the biggest horndog of them all," he says). But not Eddie. Eddie would remain alone in his hotel room, where he'd spend the entire night drinking vodka, snorting cocaine, and noodling into a tape recorder.

"I didn't drink to party," he says now, sober since 2008. "Alcohol and cocaine were private things to me. I would use them for work. The blow keeps you awake and the alcohol lowers your inhibitions. I'm sure there were musical things I would not have attempted were I not in that mental state. You just play by yourself with a tape running, and after about an hour, your mind goes to a place where you're not thinking about anything."

Here again, the contradiction is stark: While directing the

ultimate California party band, Eddie Van Halen took little pleasure from partying. Drugs and booze were merely intertwined with a relatively hermetic lifestyle. In fact, most rumors about Van Halen's drinking adopt an unusually dark tone, most notably a passage from Sammy Hagar's autobiography *Red* that portrays Eddie as a violent, booze-addled vampire, living inside a garbage house resembling the mansion from *Grey Gardens*.

"I was an alcoholic, and I needed alcohol to function." For years, he awoke every morning with dry heaves. "I started drinking and smoking when I was twelve. I got drunk before I'd show up to high school. My ninth-grade science teacher, he could smell the alcohol, and he told me, 'Don't drink anything you can't see through.' And I was like, 'So, vodka?' And he said yeah. Which was great, because that was my drink . . . I'm not blaming my father at all, but he was an alcoholic, too. So in our household, it was normal. But it never affected his work, although I guess it didn't affect my work, either. Around 2004, I suppose I became a very angry drunk. But [the stuff in Hagar's book] was definitely embellished. That's him painting a picture of something that never happened."

Not surprisingly, Hagar stands behind his book's depiction. "There is what Eddie says and there is the truth," he says. "I'm happy to see that he's healthy, sober, and playing music again."

PART OF WHAT MAKES Van Halen's persona difficult to interpret is his tendency to swing between unyielding perfectionism and mild apathy. When making the early VH albums, he would often sneak back into the studio at four in the morning to fix mistakes only he could hear. Yet he can also be confoundingly laissez-faire about significant career accomplishments. For example, it's widely known that he received no compensation for playing the solo on Michael

Jackson's "Beat It." What's less known is that he (probably) deserves a chunk of the track's songwriting credit, too. But he doesn't care about this at all. It's almost like he doesn't comprehend the magnitude of the song, the fame of the person who sang it, or the singularity of his contribution.

"I think it's funny the way people talk about that," he says. "It was twenty minutes of my life. I didn't want anything for doing that . . . I literally thought to myself, 'Who is possibly gonna know if I play on this kid's record?' So I went to the studio and listened to the song twice, and I didn't like the section they wanted me to solo over. They wanted me to solo over the breakdown. I asked [*Thriller* producer] Quincy Jones to edit the chords underneath the solo. Then I could play the solo in the key of E, but it was the chords underneath that made the solo interesting. So I guess I did re-arrange it."

He expresses similar detachment from his own sense of auditory reality. For years, it's been rumored that Van Halen has synesthesia. It's wholly possible that this is true. But it's impossible to say for certain, because he doesn't seem to know what synesthesia is—inadvertently spawning a long-standing error about the sound of his guitar:

Do you have synesthesia?

I think I read something about this. What is that, exactly?

It's the ability to see sound, which is supposedly why you call your guitar tone the "brown sound"—you supposedly see the color brown when you hear that specific tone.

That's funny, because people took that whole "brown sound" thing totally out of context. I was never talking about my guitar tone. I was talking about Alex's snare drum. I've always thought Alex's snare drum sounds like he's beating on a log. It's very organic. So it wasn't *my* brown sound. It was Alex's.

Then how did this confusion happen?

It happened years ago. People would ask me about his drumming, and the only way I could explain it was that it had a very brown sound. I'm glad you brought this up, actually, so people can finally understand what I was talking about.

But even so, you must realize that this was a weird way to describe a sound. You thought his drums sounded like a log, so you describe the color of the log itself? Why didn't you say it was a wooden sound, or a log sound?

I don't know. It's an organic sound. Brown is an organic color.

This makes me suspect you do have synesthesia. Does sound always have a color to you?

Alex's snare drum does, definitely. Otherwise I wouldn't have called it brown.

Right now, the only new music Eddie seems excited about is a forthcoming solo project from Wolfgang, who's also crafting the set list for the upcoming tour (they're including a handful of songs they've never played live—"Dirty Movies," "Drop Dead Legs, "Top Jimmy"). To classify Eddie as the consummate family man might be a tad overstated, but he takes familial ties seriously: Alex is his un-impeachable best friend, a relationship forged by their childhood immigration from Amsterdam in 1962 (when they arrived in the U.S., the brothers could speak only four English words—"yes," "no," "motorcycle," and "accident"). He still has a good relationship with Wolfgang's mother, actress Valerie Bertinelli (when Eddie married stuntwoman/publicist Janie Liszewski in 2009, Bertinelli was one of the hundred guests in attendance). Eddie dislikes Van Halen's '82 cover version of "Big Bad Bill," but he's overjoyed his musician father was able to play clarinet on it. And he's adamant that his son is a better bass player than the exiled Michael Anthony, almost to the point of overkill.

"Every note Mike ever played, I had to show him how to play," Van Halen claims. "Before we'd go on tour, he'd come over with a video camera and I'd have to show him how to play all the parts." He doesn't even credit Anthony for his harmonic backing vocals, which fans classify as an integral part of the group's signature. "Mike's voice is like a piccolo trumpet. But he's not a singer. He just has a range from hell," he says. "Mike was just born with a very high voice. I have more soul as a singer than he does. And you know, people always talk about Mike's voice on Van Halen songs, but that's a blend of Mike's voice *and* my voice. It's just not him." (Anthony's rebuttal to these accusations is diplomatic: "I am proud to say that my bass playing and vocals helped create our sound. I've always chosen to take the high road and stay out of the never-ending mudslinging, because I believe that it ultimately ends up hurting the Van Halen fans.")

The reasons Van Halen split with Anthony in 2006 are predictably complex—it involves Anthony's relationship with Hagar, his lack of contribution to the songwriting process, and the fact that he did not phone when Eddie contracted cancer (or when Eddie and Alex's mother died). But that conflict feeds into a larger question that's even more complicated: Why does Eddie Van Halen so often work with people he doesn't seem to like? It does not appear that he needs the money or enjoys the fame. He concedes that he barely knows the words to most Van Halen tracks, which means he doesn't care about the lyrics to songs he doesn't recall inventing. He could spend the rest of his days making music by himself, in his own isolated studio, and no one would question the decision. So why, at the age of sixty, does he continue to tour with a singer who drives him insane?

Because he feels obligated to do so.

"I think it's now built into people's DNA, that it just won't be Van Halen if it's not Roth's voice," he says. "This conversation brings me back to being in Pasadena Community College with Alex, where all these strict jazz guys would call us musical prostitutes, because we would be gigging at rock clubs every night and then stumbling into class the next day. They said we were musical prostitutes. But there is an element of music that is for the people. You make music for people. Otherwise, just play in your closet. And how do you reach the most people? By giving them the band that they know. To do it any other way would be selfish."

Van Halen is hitting the road. And they're hitting the road *for you*.

Noel Gallagher is the funniest person I've interviewed and among the nine or ten funniest people I've encountered in any context whatsoever. The words on the page cannot reflect the effortlessness of his humor; the only other celebrity who comes close is David Lee Roth. And as with Roth, Gallagher's virtuosity at comedic conversation detracts from his reputation as an artist: Because he doesn't take himself seriously, the audience feels no obligation to take the work seriously, either. He makes everything seem too easy. By the time we spoke in 2011, people wanted to hear him lecture more than they wanted to hear him play, which is a little disheartening. Although to be fair, I sometimes get the sense Gallagher enjoys talking more than playing, too. Or perhaps he sees those activities exactly the same, but talking doesn't force him to haul a twelve-pound guitar around his neck.

Though there are a handful of groups I like more than Oasis, I find that I'm extraordinarily willing to *defend* Oasis, anytime someone says anything negative about their legacy. This seems to be a central connective fluid among their fan base. "I was definitely on their side," British music writer Roy Wilkinson admitted in 2016, roughly nineteen years after giving *Be Here Now* a hyperpositive review he can no longer justify. "There weren't many bands who were demonstrably from a council estate background. The way they became part of the establishment was pleasantly absurd. I remember thinking in my heart of hearts there was something not quite right about what I was saying, but such was the phenomenal momentum, you did want it to keep going—for them and the wider world."

I know what he means. I still feel that way now.

Where Were You While We Were Getting High?

Noel Gallagher's first official solo record won't be released in America until November, but there's already a party for it in August. It's described as a "listening party," so that's what I expect it to be: six or seven people sitting in an otherwise quiet room, listening to an album titled *Noel Gallagher's High Flying Birds*. For those who care about the music of Oasis, anticipation for this record is greater than for anything Oasis has done in the past ten years. This is not only because Noel was the principal songwriter for the band, although that's certainly part of it; equally significant is the fact that the finest moments in Oasis's two-decade trajectory have generally occurred when Noel was singing: "Don't Look Back in Anger," the chorus on "Acquiesce," their live cover of Neil Young's "Hey Hey My My (Into the Black)," the rarity "D'yer Wanna Be a Spaceman," and a 1996 episode of *MTV Unplugged* (where Noel sang the whole set while his brother drank beer in the balcony). Oasis completists are interested in Liam Gallagher's new project, Beady Eye, the way Smiths fans were interested in Electronic, but Noel's material is what matters. The potential is real. Considering the circumstances of the Oasis split, it seems possible that Noel might make a fascinating album purely out of spite.

The so-called listening party is not what I anticipate. It's not six or seven people, but sixty or seventy. It's held in the penthouse of the Mondrian luxury hotel and sponsored by (or is perhaps just uncommonly supportive of) UV vodka. The walls are white, the couches are white, the light is white. Everything is white (except the audience, which is maybe 4 percent Asian). There are at least two guys who look and talk like Adam Scott's character from *Step Brothers*. At 7:35 p.m., Mercury Records president David Massey picks up a microphone and explains how most people in the 1990s incorrectly assumed Oasis would "just flame out in a drug haze." This is an odd compliment, particularly since that's precisely what many casual fans concede must have happened. After his speech, we get to hear six tracks off *High Flying Birds*. No one even pretends to listen. The partygoers talk the whole time and stand in line for free vodka. I'm told that Noel is allegedly coming to this party later, but I don't stay long enough to find out. As I ride the elevator down from the twenty-sixth floor, I find myself hoping he never shows up at all, because I suspect he'd really hate it.

THE NEXT DAY, I'm scheduled to meet Gallagher at a similar hotel in a different sector of Manhattan. He is forty-three minutes late for our forty-five-minute interview, so I sit and listen to a pair of publicists discussing a third hotel that's 2,462 miles away. It's the Friday before New York will be hit by Hurricane Irene, presenting the Gallagher camp with a strange problem: Noel is now flying to Los Angeles a day early, but he can't get into his room because the King of Tonga (George Tupou V) has supposedly booked an entire floor of the Sunset Tower Hotel. The King of Tonga rocks harder than anyone you know. I have a brief conversation with one of the publicists about a lawsuit Liam recently filed (and then dropped) against Noel: During a July 6 press conference, Noel claimed Liam had missed a 2009 festival date because of a hangover. Liam saw this as an attack on his professionalism and legally charged Noel with slander, which is a little like Kanye West charging Rickey Henderson with overconfidence. Noel publicly apologized and the problem seemed to evaporate, although Liam continues to insist otherwise.[1] It will likely drag on indefinitely. Ever since Oasis was propelled into existence, Noel and Liam have behaved like boyish versions of Andy Capp who despise each other equally—but this recent schism feels different. It's less fun, somehow. There will undoubtedly be a day in the distant future when Oasis reunites, because just about every group eventually does. But it probably won't be because these guys suddenly stopped disliking each other.

When I finally meet Gallagher (he'd been having a long lunch with his wife), he seems tired. He looks healthy but grouchy. My suspicion is that he's probably spent his morning talking to other people like me, most of whom have either asked him leading questions about Liam or tried to goad him into insulting other bands at random (as this is something he does not mind doing). He slouches on a couch while we navigate ten minutes of small talk. We chat about the weather and about why he finally married his girlfriend after dating for eleven years. For no clear reason, he's wearing a garish class ring from a high school in Louisiana, purchased in a Japanese pawnshop twenty-one years ago. He briefly imagines the backstory of the ring: "I reckon the previous owner was a G.I. who was stationed in Tokyo and pawned this ring for prostitutes." I momentarily get the sense that this is never going to become a real interview. But I start to ask a few questions and Gallagher starts answering them.

---

1. Liam's take on the affair, as reported by the BBC: "I didn't want this to happen. It's not nice suing your family, but like I said, he was telling porkies for the sake of his mates and journalists to get a wise crack on me." (Porkies fired!)

And everything he says is hilarious. I don't even know if this can be properly reflected in a profile, because it's not so much what he says as it is the way he says it—Gallagher just has a naturally comedic, endlessly profane delivery that seems unbound by the parameters of normal conversation. He doesn't even have to try. It just happens. I suppose this might all be premeditated, but that's not how it seems. Gallagher's dialogue is like his music: The straightforward virtuosity is a by-product of its apparent effortlessness.

"I've never understood musicians who don't enjoy doing promotional interviews," he says. "I just can't believe it. I always think, 'Your life must have been so brilliant before you were in a band.' Because my life was shit, and this is great. Even after all these years, at forty-four years of age, whenever the label asks if I want to go to New York to do promos, I always say yes immediately. And the label is always like, 'Are you sure? It's going to require a lot of interviews.' And I'm like—I don't give a fuck. You're gonna fucking fly me first class to New York and put me in this amazing hotel? And my wife can go fucking shopping four hours a day? I fucking love doing press conferences. I don't want to suggest it's all a joke, but come on—the president holds fucking press conferences. Why am I here? Why not enjoy it? I've never felt like I had anything important to say. I can tell a few jokes and we can talk irreverently about fame and success and sport and bullshit and all the crazy people you meet. But I have nothing to say."

This is not accurate.

WHEN YOU LIKE A BAND, you want to hear about the good times. When you love a band, you want to hear about the bad times.

I want to hear about *Be Here Now*.

"At the time, I was taking a lot of fucking drugs, so I didn't give a fuck," Gallagher says. "We were taking all the cocaine we could possibly find. But it wasn't like a seedy situation. We were at work. We weren't passed out on the floor with a bottle of Jack Daniel's. We were partying while we were working. And when that record was finished, I took it back to my house and listened to it when there wasn't a party happening and I wasn't out of my mind on cocaine. And my reaction was: *'This is fucking long.'* I didn't realize how long it was. It's a long fucking record. And then I looked at the artwork, and it had all the song titles with all the times for each track, and none of them seemed to be under six minutes. So then I was like, 'Fucking hell. What's going on there?' But you know, those were just the songs I wrote, and we recorded them to the best of our abilities. When we had recorded *(What's the Story) Morning Glory?*, nobody from the label bothered us, and we hatched the Golden Egg. So the label was like, 'Don't bother those guys. They're geniuses. Just let them do what they want.' The producer was really just the recording engineer. There was nobody around to say, 'These songs are too long.' It was a good wake-up call, to be honest. I really wonder what would have happened if *Be Here Now* had sold like *Morning Glory*. What would we have done the next time? Just imagine if that album had sold thirty million copies. I probably would have grown a mustache and started wearing a fucking cape."

Because of how the music industry has evolved (read: collapsed), there will never be a situation like 1997's *Be Here Now* again. There are no more situations where a rock album that's impossible to hear in advance is collectively anticipated by the monoculture. But that's how it was before the release of *Be Here Now*. At the time, Oasis was in an unassailable position: They were of simultaneous interest to the critical community, the tabloid press, and the populace at large. They were the first post-grunge band of the nineties to be massive in every context. But the seventy-one-minute *Be Here Now* failed, even though it supposedly sold eight million copies in six months. The earliest reviews were mostly positive, but the actual reception was disappointing (and the sales proved top-heavy). It's sometimes viewed as the record that killed Britpop. And people turned on Oasis when this happened. The bloated, bass-empty, blow-stretched songs validated critics who'd claimed their early work was overrated, and the absence of a ubiquitous single (such as 1995's "Wonderwall") eroded their catbird position in the culture. From a public opinion standpoint, they never recovered.

"At the end of the cycle of *Morning Glory*, I was hailed as the greatest songwriter since Lennon and McCartney," Gallagher recalls. "Now, I know that I'm not, and I knew I wasn't then. But the perception of everybody since that period has been, 'What the fuck happened to this guy? Wasn't he supposed to be the next fucking Beatles?' I never said that I was the greatest thing since Lennon and McCartney . . . Well, actually, I'm lying. I probably did say that once or twice in interviews. But regardless, look at it this way: Let's say my career had gone backward. Let say this new solo album had been my debut, and it was my last two records that sold twenty million copies instead of the first two records. Had this been the case, all the other albums leading up to those last two would be considered a fucking journey. They would be perceived as albums that represent the road to greatness. But just because it started off great doesn't make those other albums any less of a journey. I'll use an American football analogy since we're in America: Let's say you're behind with two minutes to go and you come back to tie the game. It almost feels like you've won. Right? But let's say you've been ahead the whole game and you allow the opponent to tie things up in the final two minutes. Then it feels like you've lost. But the fact of the matter is it's still a fucking tie. The only difference is perception. And the fact of that matter is that Oasis sold fifty-five million records. If people think we were never good after the nineties, that's irrelevant."

The premise of Oasis's career happening in reverse is an interesting thought experiment and not altogether incorrect (had this inverted sequence actually transpired, it's easy to imagine the kind of person who'd argue that "Supersonic" sucks and that the real Oasis music can only be found on the likes of *Heathen Chemistry*). But it ignores a key element of artistic endeavor: motivation. The album that followed *Be Here Now* was the lowest artistic point in the group's career—and that was due to everything that preceded it.

"We should have never made *Standing on the Shoulder of Giants*," Gallagher says of the 2000 release, an album whose worst moments sometimes sound like an attempt at satirizing *Rubber Soul*. "I'd come to the end. At the time, I had no reason or desire to make music. I had no drive. We'd sold all these fucking records and there just seemed to be no point. Liam, to his credit, was the one who was like, 'We're going to make a record, we're going into the studio next month, and you better have some fucking songs written.' We should have gone to wherever it is the Rolling Stones disappear to, wherever the fuck that is. Rent a boat and sail around the Bahamas or whatever. But I went ahead and did it, even though I had no inspiration and couldn't find inspiration anywhere. I just wrote songs for the sake of making an album. We needed a reason to go on a tour. But at the time, I wasn't thinking like that. We all thought the song 'Go Let It Out' was good. I was off [street] drugs, but to get off those I had to go on prescription drugs, which is fucking worse because they come from a doctor. It's just uppers and downers that replace the cocaine and booze. But after that, Gem [Archer][2] and

---

2. Formerly the guitarist of Heavy Stereo, now a member of Beady Eye. In an interview with *Mojo*, Gallagher mentioned that Archer is one member of Oasis he openly misses.

Andy [Bell][3] joined the band, and we started to split up the songwriting duties because they wanted to write songs, too. I'd slowed down as a writer and didn't feel like I could keep writing twenty songs every two years."

GALLAGHER MAKES a lot of reference to *perception* (both his own and other people's), so I try to reframe our conversation: I tell him that I want to run through various points of his life and have him try to recall how other people viewed him and how he viewed himself. He is totally willing to do this, but we never get past 1991.

"I was living in the center of Manchester, so I was always in clubs and at shows and kind of living on the periphery of the music business," he says. "The people at the center of the music scene would have seen me as an outsider. The people who were further outside than me, though, would have thought I was some kind of insider. But I just believed I was at where I would always be. It never occurred to me to be in a band or write songs, even though I played guitar. I'd always thought I might be in the music business, because I loved collecting records and reading about records and all of that. But just being in a road crew, I thought, 'This is fucking great.' I was making seven hundred dollars a week to plug in some other guy's guitar. I loved it. I never felt like I needed to be onstage. I liked

---

3. Formerly the guitarist in Ride, now also in Beady Eye. One detail that's somewhat unexplained is the reason why the remaining members of Oasis have sided with Liam in this dispute, at least professionally. For elderly citizens who may recall the acrimonious breakup of Uncle Tupelo, this awkwardly positions Liam as Jeff Tweedy to Noel's Jay Farrar. Speaking to the *Japan Times*, Bell accused Noel of being more manipulative and media-conscious than he appears on the surface: "I know him, so I'm not disappointed [about what he said about Liam's hangover]. That's what he's like. I know how he spins the press. He's used the press for years. Interviews and press are secondary for us, that's his life."

being behind the fucking amplifiers. I had no ambitions. I got to travel the world—drugs, women. Nobody knew who I was after I left town. I didn't have to be anywhere or do anything. But then Liam said, 'You should join my band, because you know how to write songs.' So I went down there on a few Sundays to jam, and it was the first time I'd ever heard other people play my songs. It was amazing to have that happen. And there was another pivotal moment about two years in, before we'd done anything or anyone knew us: I wrote the song 'Columbia.' And the next song I wrote immediately after that was 'Up in the Sky.' And then right after that, I wrote 'Live Forever.' All of this happened in a row, very easily. And I just thought, 'These songs are fucking great.' Especially 'Live Forever.' I remember thinking, 'I know enough about music to know that this is a good song.' So I took it to the band and we played it, and I instantly knew that I had written a bona fide classic song, even though nobody knew who the fuck we were. So that's when I started to take things quite seriously."

It's hard to tell exactly what "quite seriously" means in this context, since Gallagher is so consciously adamant about not taking himself seriously. Is his work on *High Flying Birds* more "serious" than his work with Oasis? That depends on what you thought of him before. It's very much in line with the music he's always made—the first single ("The Death of You and Me") has the most satisfying hook he's composed in many years, and the track "If I Had a Gun" would fit comfortably on any Oasis album after *Definitely Maybe*. All the lyrics are oblique and there are only two guitar solos on the entire album. Gallagher also has a companion LP coming out in 2012 that he made with the British electronic duo the Amorphous Androgynous, better known in some circles as the Future Sound of London. It still doesn't have a title, but it's an elongated seventies psychedelic record Gallagher compares to *Dark Side of the Moon*.[4] How well these albums will perform is uncertain, mostly because gauging the true success of modern records has become increasingly impossible. It's not the same as fame, which Gallagher understands completely. He is not the type of artist who longs for success while hating the baggage of celebrity. In fact, he feels the opposite. He sees success as a much more complicated predicament.

"Fame is something that is bestowed upon you because of success. Success is something you have to chase," he explains. "And once you've had success, you have to keep having it in order not to be a failure. In business, you can have one massive success that earns fifty million dollars overnight, and that's it. You're successful. End of story. But in the music business, you have to keep on doing it. You have to constantly chase success. The fame you just *get*. I enjoy being famous, because I don't have to do anything. I can just turn up at nice restaurants and people are like, 'Oh, it's Noel fucking Gallagher. Brilliant. Sit down.' But success can ruin people, because you have to chase it, and that can drive you insane. You can get obsessed with the idea of a formula, and you start wondering, 'Why did I sell twenty fucking million albums in less than two years during the nineties, but now I can't sell twenty million albums over the span of ten years?' And it's not like I sit around thinking about that, but it's always there. And when you start really chasing success, you start to make mistakes, and that's when things spin out of fucking control."

As he says this, I suspect that he's talking about the real reason he can no longer work with his brother. Here again, the issue is not reality, but perception. The two brothers were able to maintain a working relationship for roughly twenty years, through periods of feast

---

4. This album was never released. In 2015, Gary Cobain of the Amorphous Androgynous expressed deep annoyance over this, claiming it was killed because Gallagher was "too afraid to be weird."

and phases of famine. Yet the perception during that whole time never changed: Noel was always the talented one and Liam was simply the charismatic singer. When they were younger, that perception was tolerable. But now that Liam is thirty-nine—and now that it's so clear that this assessment will always be the defining image of what Oasis was—he simply could not accept the conditions of the contract.

"I think that's what it was," Gallagher says. "He'd never admit that, though. In the beginning, when I was writing all the songs and he was partying until the break of dawn, he didn't give a shit. D'you know what I mean? He was fine with it. But when he started to write songs . . . You know, this is really more of a question for Liam than it is for me, although you'd never get a straight answer from him. In my experience, you never see an older brother jealous of a younger brother.[5] Maybe he did get cast in the role of the performing fucking monkey by the press, and maybe I got cast as the man behind the curtain. Maybe he wanted to be the Wizard of Oz instead of the monkey. Maybe if I'd been a little more tolerant of his behavior things would be different. But at some point he had to take responsibility for the fucking words he was saying. I have a circle of friends, and he kept saying things that were upsetting to these people. And for years I ignored it, because I thought the band was more important. But at some point, I just decided I'd had enough of this. And when things got violent, I left. There is no point in being in a fucking violent rock band. That's nonsense.[6] We've always had a different

5. There is, of course, an even older Gallagher brother named Paul who maintains a good relationship with both Noel and Liam. I asked Noel how Paul views the situation in Oasis: "Oh, he's a crazy character. He's a DJ, so he's not really the voice of reason."
6. To be fair, it should be noted that while recording *(What's the Story) Morning Glory?* in 1994, Noel allegedly hit Liam over the head with a cricket bat.

view of the band: I thought the most important part were the songs, and he thought the most important part was the chaos."

As one might expect, Noel also tries to downplay the degree of antipathy the two brothers share, since this type of breakup is more multidimensional than a typical, nonfamilial implosion. Certain issues between them might still stem from when they shared a bedroom as truculent teenagers. Sometimes, Noel seems amused by their fighting (I can tell he's still kind of proud that one of their 1995 arguments was recorded in the studio and released as a bootleg single in the UK). But sometimes he seems angry in a manner that's impossible to fake. There was a period when people assumed the animosity in Oasis might have been a marketing ploy, and perhaps—for a time—it was. But it's not anymore. Their dislike for each other is at least as genuine as their music.

"We never hung out together outside of the band, ever," he says. "Now, of course, at some point I'm going to have to sit in a fucking room with Liam again. Hopefully time will heal some of these wounds. But if you're asking me if it's going to be this Christmas— not a fucking chance."

AS OUR INTERVIEW DRAWS to a close, I notice that Gallagher is sniffling and coughing, so I ask if he's getting sick. At first he says yes, but then he gets up for a cup of coffee and says, "To tell you the fucking truth, I'm kind of hungover." It turns out he did show up at the album release party the night before, just before it ended. And it turns out he hated it a little less than I suspected.

"In England, we don't go for that kind of stuff," he says. "You just put the record out and people buy it or they don't. Over here, things are a little more corporate. You have to go to parties like that. I find it always helps to get drunk beforehand—not too drunk, but just a little. D'you know what I mean? You have to shake a lot of hands. I have no idea who those people were. My wife was like, 'How can you stand doing this?' But it wasn't that bad, except that now I'm hungover."

This, it seems, is the real explanation as to why Noel is different from Liam (and always will be). Liam denies his hangovers and sues people for joking about them; Noel confesses his hangovers and will shake hands with anyone. And when you've been in a band that's been drunk for twenty years, that difference tells you everything you need to know.

There's a quote late in my interaction with Stephen Malkmus that I still find intriguing, though I didn't fully recognize its intricacy at the time it was said. "If we had signed to Gold Mountain management, or if we had signed with Geffen, maybe *Crooked Rain, Crooked Rain* sells 750,000 copies instead of 250,000 copies," he explained. "But it was really just the difference between being Pavement or being Weezer."

This statement interests me for three reasons. The first is that I can't tell if Malkmus is arguing that (a) Pavement and Weezer were fundamentally similar or (b) they were fundamentally different (and this type of decision illustrates why). The second is that it suggests (probably correctly) that there were five hundred thousand kids in the nineties who would buy (or not buy) an album simply due to how it was framed and promoted. But here's the main thing I keep wondering about: Assuming Pavement would have been allowed to write and record *Crooked Rain* for Geffen in the same way they wrote and recorded it for Matador, wouldn't tripling the size of the audience have been desirable? Or would those extra five hundred thousand consumers have only served as a detriment? Did they represent the type of person he actively did not want to like his music?

Malkmus was not born a multimillionaire, but he was never poor (or even lower middle class). That gave him an advantage guys like Eddie Van Halen and Noel Gallagher never had—he could be cool *on purpose*. Which is probably why he was so good at it.

I'm Assuming
It's Going to Be Fun

I suppose you don't like sports, do you?"

This is what Stephen Malkmus—the enigmatic architect of Pavement—asks me as he sits in a Thai sandwich restaurant, waiting for his bacon and bread. He's casually pawing at a Portland alternative newspaper that features Trail Blazer center Greg Oden on the cover; it's the day before Thanksgiving,[1] so Oden's patella is still unexploded. Malkmus seems slightly (but unspecifically) annoyed—his wife's parents are in town for the holidays, he's just spent the last ninety minutes at a school party for his five-year-old daughter, and now he has to waste two hours with some bozo who probably doesn't know why Greg Oden is interesting. He keeps his head down as he speaks. At this moment, Stephen Malkmus looks so much like Stephen Malkmus that it feels like sarcasm. In fact, he looks like someone playing Stephen Malkmus in an ill-conceived Cameron Crowe movie: He's unshaven, he's wearing Pony high-tops that no longer exist on the open market, the bottoms of his blue jeans are caked

---

1. The year was 2009.

with mud, and his baseball cap promotes the Silver Jews. His T-shirt features the logo of the Joggers, a Portland-based rock act whose greatest claim to fame is being mentioned in a *GQ* story about Stephen Malkmus eating at a Thai sandwich shop. The restaurant is loud, so I initially mishear his question. He asks it again.

"I said, I suppose you don't like sports?"

I tell him that I do like sports. I tell him that—honestly—I'm probably more qualified to talk with him about sports than I am to talk with him about Pavement. Immediately, everything changes. He looks up quickly. He's no longer irritated, except when I suggest that Greg Oden might be no better than Erick Dampier. For the next forty-five minutes we discuss our respective fantasy teams, pretty much nonstop. I cannot exaggerate the degree to which Malkmus enjoys fantasy sports; he almost seems to like it more than music. His fantasy football team was devastated by the loss of Ronnie Brown to injury, but he's stayed in the playoff hunt by getting Viking WR Sidney Rice as a free agent ("You could just immediately tell he was going to be Favre's guy"). He serves as commissioner for (what has to be) the finest indie rock fantasy basketball league in America—other owners include Built to Spill frontman Doug Martsch and ex–Matador Records executive Gerard Cosloy. ("But Gerard doesn't take it very seriously," Malkmus says with mild disdain. "He barely even changes his lineup.") The most productive player on his NBA team is underpublicized Indiana Pacer forward Danny Granger, but he's more satisfied about stealing the Nets' Chris Douglas-Roberts off the waiver wire. Malkmus does not watch the NHL, yet he still participates in a fantasy hockey league. He's that kind of guy. I don't even try to talk with him about rotisserie baseball.

After almost an hour has passed, I realize we need to start talking about music. We leave the restaurant and jump in his Audi. He rolls a cigarette with a brand of tobacco from Holland called Samson. I notice that Malkmus does not wear a seat belt, nor does he tell me to wear mine. I am immediately more comfortable.

THE ORIGINAL PLAN was to meet at Malkmus's Pacific Northwest home around one p.m. and talk about the upcoming Pavement re-union shows, four of which sold out in New York a full twelve months in advance. The plan does not work. Malkmus meets me at the front door, shakes my hand, and says this: "Okay, here's the new plan. I'm sure you can roll with the new plan. My daughter has this Thanks-giving feast at her school, right? And I'm going to go there for an hour. Do you like coffee? Actually, that doesn't matter. I will meet you at a coffeehouse in an hour." He points up the street and gives me walking directions to the coffeehouse, and that is where I go. I get the sense that Malkmus is very used to telling people what to do; he's polite, but he speaks in clear, declarative sentences. When he shows up at the coffeehouse 100 minutes later, the first thing he tells me is that—despite the aforementioned school feast—he needs to get food. "It was potluck," he says. "I don't eat potluck." We drive five minutes to the Thai place; he buys a nine-dollar bacon-oriented sandwich and we talk about sports. I try to persuade him to take me back to his house. I want to see what his house looks like. "It's kind of crazy over there right now," he says. "Maybe not today." Of course, today is the only day I'll ever be with him, but that's life. We go to a park instead. I try to talk about music on the drive over, but Malkmus wants to talk about books. He just returned from a festival in Copenhagen that featured both musicians and authors, and he talks about who he saw—Nick Kent ("My wife really loved his Stones books when she was in college"), Denis Johnson ("He's got a lot to be proud of"), a slightly drunk Jay McInerney ("He looks exactly like his author photo"). Malkmus is more gossipy than one might expect—he's never cruel, but he likes to talk about how a given artist's perception is both detached from and irrevocably tied to how their art is consumed. He likes to talk about authors the way Pavement fans like to talk about Pavement.

There's an inherent problem with writing about Pavement, and the problem is this: People tend to know nothing or everything about them. There are very few "casual" Pavement fans. To most of the music populace, they were a band with a funny name, one minor MTV hit (1994's "Cut Your Hair"), and a lot of abstract credibility among people who get mad at the radio. They view Pavement as a minor act. But to the kind of hyperintellectual, underemployed people who did not find it strange to buy concert tickets a year in advance, Pavement is the apotheosis of indie aesthetics, the "finest rock band of the '90s" (according to former *Village Voice* critic Robert Christgau) whose first full-length record is better than the original Velvet Underground album (according to the now-defunct music magazine *Blender*). They are remembered as the musical center of the Clinton-era lo-fi universe, a designation that's spiritually true but technically wrong.[2] Over the span of five albums and nine EPs, Pavement became decade-defining music, widely regarded as dazzling and essential and game changing (at least among those who cared). Malkmus is aware of this. As such, I return to our vehicular discussion about Jay McInerney: Since just about everyone now concedes that McInerney's self-perception as a writer was adversely impacted

---

2. "Lo-fi" is an abbreviation of the term "low fidelity," and *fidelity* means how faithful something sounds when compared to its original source. In truth, albums from bands like the Electric Light Orchestra or Def Leppard have a much lower fidelity than anything Pavement produced, as those recordings have no relationship to what a living, breathing band could sound like live. A better term for Pavement would actually be "mid-fi," because their material falls somewhere between amateur authenticity and imaginative construction. But—as always—technical reality rarely matters when discussing pop music. Whenever a normal person says they prefer lo-fi music, it means they prefer bands like Pavement: imperfect sound forever.

by the avalanche of negative criticism he received in the years following *Bright Lights, Big City*, I ask Malkmus if he's had the opposite experience. Does being endlessly told you're a genius make you feel like one? Did having so many people insist that *Slanted and Enchanted* was brilliant change the way he now thinks about those songs?

"Of course it does, in a way. But no matter how much positive feedback you get, it's never enough," Malkmus says. "I'm not a particularly needy person, but it always seems like every review could be better. With a record like *Slanted and Enchanted*—that was so much a timing thing, along with the fact that its flaws are a big part of what makes it good. It's not like some Radiohead record where the whole thing is good, and you wonder how those guys made the album because the individual parts are all so good. Our records aren't good in that way. Our records are more attitude and style, sort of in a punk way. We're good in the same way the Strokes are good, even though we're not like the Strokes. I think *Slanted and Enchanted* probably *is* the best record we made, only because it's less self-conscious and has an unrepeatable energy about it."

Three years later, Pavement teetered on the brink of classic rock with 1994's *Crooked Rain, Crooked Rain*, but that didn't last—the following project (*Wowee Zowee*) drove them back into experimental semi-obscurity. Since their dissolution in 1999, Malkmus has recorded four solo albums with a backing band called the Jicks. He plans to record a fifth Jicks album in 2010. Much of this solo material is competitive with anything he made with Pavement. However, it's clear Malkmus does not believe that. Not completely. His assessment of the music-making process has evolved. He doesn't seem to mind that he's forty-four years old, but he's conscious of what aging means to any creative person.

"I barely think about music anymore," he says, although *somebody* must have come up with all the songs on those Jicks albums. "I have other interests now. ADD things, like fantasy sports. Things I can think about while thinking about something else, as opposed to songwriting, where you have to focus really hard on what you're doing. That's not the only reason people make inferior music when they're older, but that's probably a factor. Your ambition and confidence change. It's not right to say any music I make now is not going to be as good as music I made when I was younger, but it's probably not going to be as intense. I'm not going to yell as loud—figuratively or literally. I used to drunkenly yell on a record. I wouldn't do that again . . . I played some Pavement songs when I was in Holland, and I played 'Range Life,' and when I got to the part at the end [which criticizes Smashing Pumpkins and Stone Temple Pilots], I just didn't feel like singing those words. It seems so dated now. At the time, it was an attempt to be topical, kind of like an ironic rap song and a way to make fun of the whole indie 'We're cool, you're not cool' thing. But I probably wouldn't do that now."

I LIKE PAVEMENT. I suppose I really like Pavement. But I don't *love* Pavement, or at least not in the way every smart rock critic I've ever met seems to love them. Very often, I don't understand the band's intentions. So I tried an experiment. I asked various people who identified themselves as Pavement fanatics one fundamental question: "What is Pavement's music about?" I then posed these answers to Malkmus and asked if he agreed or disagreed with each analysis.

THEORY ONE: Pavement is the musical equivalent of a little boy trapped in a library with all his favorite books and records, and that little boy decides to spend the rest of his life writing music about this interior world.

That's nice. That sort of makes our music seem like a curatorial exercise, and that's kind of true. But we have a relationship to the outside world that had an impact too. That theory sort of discounts the physicality of the music.

THEORY TWO: *Pavement is a synthesis of everything that was compelling about '80s indie rock, but performed at a higher level. The lyrics are nonessential and Malkmus is overrated as a lyricist—but he's underrated as a vocalist and a guitar player.*

That could be true. That speaks to how I feel about it. I like that. But I would add this: Even though we don't have classic, Bob Dylan lyrics, I think my lyrics have a tone that holds up better and is less cringeworthy than most other lyric writing. I don't think any of my lyrics are literal. The way somebody's voice sounds is much more important than how meaningful the words are. I just look for lyrics I can say with conviction.

THEORY THREE: *Pavement is about class dynamics. Malkmus is well educated and was raised in the affluent community of Stockton, California, and he could have pursued any life he wanted—yet he consciously chose to pursue an art form that typically represents the disenfranchised underclass. As a result, Pavement's music is about reconciling that class dichotomy.*

That's not true. The fact of the matter is, when we went to New York and the band was getting some attention for the first time, the scene we were in was really . . . well, at the time, I called it preppie scum rock. That scene was populated by *really* rich people—Ivy League millionaire kids who were in punk bands and noise bands. But we always had jobs. When you get down to it, I was middle class. I was upper middle class. My dad's an insurance broker. But there are no airs in central California. I had some relatives who became kind of wealthy through California real estate, but they built their house to look like Tara from *Gone with the Wind*. They had Clydesdales! It wasn't classist. It wasn't classy. It was more like . . . *new*. I mean, I like Clydesdales, you can have Clydesdales if you want. But people in Westchester County aren't breeding Clydesdales, you know? The actual source material for our music had more to do with going to college at the University of Virginia. That was when I got into Can and the Clean and the Velvet Underground. Before that, I just liked dumb teenage punk—Bad Religion, that sort of stuff. I thought Social Distortion was high art.

AFTER AN HOUR at the park, Malkmus needs to go home. We start walking back to his car, and I try to ask the principal questions I need to address: Why is Pavement reuniting now? Why are they reuniting *at all*? I mention that this could actually hurt the band's legacy, since there's a certain romantic cachet in going away and never coming back. "Oh yeah, I know," he says. I also mention, on the upside, that these massive sellout concerts will allow Pavement to earn some of the money they never made when they were musically peaking. He says, "That's a consideration." I keep waiting for him to unleash some fake enthusiasm, because that's what musicians always do whenever they're promoting something in a magazine. And he tries. But he just can't make himself do it.

"I think people really want to do it. I . . . I want to do it. I want to do it. I mean, I don't want to be the person who only *kind of* wants to

do it." Malkmus laughs. He knows he is not being particularly convincing. "Our booking agent had a lot to do with it. He's been pushing for it for a while. If we're going to do it, everyone says this is a
good time. And we want to do it. We're doing the interviews. We're
going to be on the cover of *SPIN*. I don't know why. It's a big hassle
to take all the pictures and stuff, but we're going to do it. I guess I
will be able to eventually show that magazine to my kids, but is that
really why I do things? I suppose what I like about this whole reunion
is the openness. Will it be fun for us? Will people in the audience
have fun? Who knows? It's not like I'm gagging to get out there and
play those songs, but I am curious to see what it will be like, and I'm
curious to see the other guys and watch them play onstage again. I'm
assuming it's going to be fun."

I ask if he has much of a relationship with the other members of
Pavement. He says he does, but it's tendril. The only member he consistently communicates with is multi-instrumentalist Bob Nastanovich, but that's mostly because they're in some of the same fantasy
leagues. "Stephen is a pretty difficult guy to access," Nastanovich
explains via telephone, calling over lunch break from his job at the
Hawthorne racetrack[3] in Illinois. "If you're not in the same town
with him, you don't really hear from him. I've found that the easiest
way to get in touch with him, even if it's about a Pavement-related
issue, is to propose a trade in one of our fantasy leagues and attach
my question in an email memo." Nastanovich is pretty open about
the things he does not know about Pavement. "I have no idea why
we're doing this now. I only talked to Stephen for about five or ten
minutes about this reunion, and the only things he clarified were that

---

3. Nastanovich has a fascinating occupation: He does computer charting and analysis for the horse
racing industry, compiling data on both animals and jockeys. He's like the Elias Sports Bureau for
Thoroughbreds. If you pick up a racing form at any track, Nastanovich undoubtedly contributed
some of its information. "Not everyone in Pavement needs a job," he says. "But I do."

I would need to be comfortable quitting my job, that I'd have to practice, and that I had to promise not to blow the money I made on horses."

In the midst of any band-related conversation, Malkmus always makes a point to mention that Pavement is a democracy. But Pavement is a democracy the way the Replacements were a democracy, or the way Creedence Clearwater Revival was a democracy, or the way Zimbabwe is a democracy. The rest of the group has wanted to reunite for years, and nobody has ever fully explained why they broke up in the first place. I phone guitarist Scott Kannberg and ask him about this. He tells me how much he misses playing their old songs. Kannberg (who performed in Pavement under the moniker Spiral Stairs) cryptically says they broke up because "Malkmus got tired of it" and feared the band would become a cliché. Whenever he talks about Malkmus, it feels like he's describing someone distant— someone he thinks about, yet barely knows. He never refers to him by his first name.

"Maybe Pavement is just not as important to him as it is to me," Kannberg says toward the end of our conversation. "That's probably all it is. But I've come to accept that."

As soon as the Pavement reunion concludes, Kannberg says, he's moving to Australia. I ask if he would make another Pavement album, if—for whatever reason—Malkmus decided he wanted to do so. "Absolutely," he said. "But I'd still move to Australia."

KANNBERG'S DETACHED DIFFIDENCE is easy to understand: Malkmus is a hard person to read. We talk a little about his wife, sculptor Jessica Jackson Hutchins, whose work will appear in the prestigious Whitney Biennial; he tells me their wedding song was "What Love Can Be" by Kingdom Come. I believe him, but I'm not sure if this indicates weird sincerity or next-level mockery. Sometimes he's amazingly straightforward, like when I ask if he thinks Pavement could have been bigger if that had been what they wanted. This was always the core criticism of the Pavement posture—some may remember an especially insightful episode of *Beavis & Butt-head* wherein Beavis watches the "Rattled by the Rush" video and reprimands the band for being "too lazy to rock."

"If we had signed to Gold Mountain management, or if we had signed with Geffen, maybe *Crooked Rain, Crooked Rain* sells 750,000 copies instead of 250,000 copies. But it was really just the difference between being Pavement or being Weezer," he says. "I never had a great deal of confidence in my ability to write hits. I don't think I could have done it, honestly. There's a formula to that, and I'm not a good chorus writer. I'm better at the verses. Sometimes I don't even *get* to the chorus."

This feels like honesty, but it might just be conversational misdirection—Malkmus often comes across as cagey because he doesn't like constructing obvious answers to pointed questions. He often starts his responses by saying, "I've never thought about that before," even when his ensuing reply clearly indicates that he has. It's impossible to totally understand how he feels about Pavement, or about this reunion in general. I think the closest he comes is when he talks about the experience of fatherhood, even though that was not his intention.

"You just do it," he says. "There's not much time for self-absorption about what it means. It's great, because it's primal and sort of feels like the reason you're on earth. It's a deep part of life. But on the other hand, it's not that deep. It just happens. It's biology. And I assumed being a parent would be pretty hard, because I'm a pretty selfish person. It's hard for me to sacrifice anything or to take care of other people's needs. Our society is meant to work—or, say, capitalism is supposed to work—when everyone takes a little bit of what they want and gives something else back. But with a kid, it's not like that. There is no give-and-take. In theory, I suppose the idea is that you *want* to give yourself completely to your child, and then you'll get something back from that experience." He waits a beat and stares at nothing in particular, almost as if he's preparing to say something that will blow me away forever. Instead, I get this: "But that does not seem true when you want to sleep more." Which, I suppose, is about as honest as it gets.

And I Said to Myself,
"This Is the Business
We've Chosen!"

[Here's something I wrote in 2008, in Europe, when I was pretend depressed.]

Last weekend I was in a hashish bar in Amsterdam. It was post-dusk, pre-night. The music was terrible (fake reggae, late-period Eric Clapton, Sublime deep cuts). I was sitting next to a British stranger with a shaved head and a speech impediment. Our conversation required subtitles, so I imagined them in my mind. He told me he had lost three family members within the past year: his mother, who was sixty-six; his uncle, who was fifty-six; and his sister, who was forty-six. He said he'd just turned thirty-six. He asked if I saw a pattern developing. "Yes," I said. "But only numerically."

I asked what he did for a living. He said he was a housepainter. He asked me the same question about myself. "I manufacture opinions," I said.

"Really?" he asked. "How do you know if you're any good at that?"

"By the number of people who agree or disagree," I said in response. "If a large number of strangers seem to think one of my opinions is especially true or wildly wrong, there is somehow a perception that I am succeeding at this vocation."

"That's interesting," said the bald British man who could barely speak. "I guess house painting is a totally different thing."

I Need to Be Alive
(in Order to Watch TV)

My life is split into two halves. They're not equal halves, but sometimes they feel that way. The first half is spent trying to figure out how reality works, if time is real, and what it means to be alive; the other half is spent scheduling my life around sporting events I am compelled to watch, even though I usually don't care who wins and won't remember anything significant about the game in two weeks' time. It makes no sense: All winter long, I'm constantly trying to catch random mid-major basketball games between second-tier teams going nowhere, all while realizing I can't even remember who played in the Final Four just three years ago. It's a (very minor) paradox. But another (less minor) paradox is why the achievement of my second goal is so consistently unsatisfying, even though technology has made it remarkably simple.

This is where the two halves of my life intersect.

If that statement makes no sense, let me rephrase it as a straightforward question: Why is watching a prerecorded sporting event less pleasurable than watching the same game live?

This phenomenon is inescapable (I'm sure some might disagree, but not any sports fan I've ever met). It's going to be the principal issue TV audiences have with coverage of the upcoming summer Olympics, since live events in London will almost never match up with the prime-time window when NBC will want to show them. For most North Americans with normal jobs, the 2012 Olympics will not be experienced as living history; they will be experienced as recent history. And that will create an ethereal loss.

It doesn't matter how much I sequester myself or how thrilling the event is—if I know the game has finished, it's difficult to sustain authentic interest in what I've recorded. I inevitably fast-forward to the last two or three minutes, even when I have no vested interest in the outcome. Since I'm watching the game purely for entertainment, it shouldn't be any different from the real thing. It should, in fact, be better, just as it's more enjoyable to watch self-recorded episodes of *Parks and Recreation* or *The McLaughlin Group* or *Storage Wars* or any other traditional show that lives inside my DVR. In theory, I should be able to enjoy every single game I want to see, on my own schedule— all I need to do is avoid the Internet for a few hours and not glance at the ESPN ticker on public TV screens. But it never works: I get home, I start watching the recent past, and I find myself rushing toward the present.

So why is this?

I believe there are five reasons this happens. I've broken them down into two categories—the rational explanations (which play a minor role) and the irrational explanations (which matter way more).

The Rational

1. The removal of commercials erodes drama: If I record a sporting event, there's no way I'm sitting through the commercials. That would be like volunteering for a DUI. One of the central pleasures of self-recorded TV is eliminating our forced exposure to advertising. Yet this is probably an error, at least when consuming sports. It's during those moments when *nothing* is happening that the drama of a game becomes most palpable. This is why static sports like baseball and golf generally feel more gut-wrenching than fluid sports like soccer and hockey. By purposefully skipping all the game breaks, I'm inadvertently skipping the gaps that manufacture tension. I should probably just sit through every commercial and let the tension build. But I'll never do that, because that would make me an idiot.

2. By watching a game after the fact, I am consciously distancing myself from the actual experience: Do you remember the controversy following Ricky Gervais's hosting of the Golden Globe Awards? In all likelihood, it's the *only* thing you remember about the Golden Globes, if you remember them at all: Gervais made a handful of funny, mean-spirited jokes about *The Tourist* and Charlie Sheen and Scientologists, and it changed the trajectory of his entire career. But here's the twist—the reaction to those jokes varied wildly, depending on how and when you saw them. If you watched those clips on the Internet a day later, they didn't seem remotely problematic (if anything, they came across as a bit too obvious). But people watching the show live on TV were more polarized, and people who attended the event in person were actively disturbed (even if they weren't necessarily targeted or offended).

This, I suppose, is a non-stoned way to describe the (completely unscientific) concept of *levels of reality*. The celebrities and media members in the same room with Gervais were experiencing a "hard reality"—they were sharing the same space in real time, tangibly connected to what was happening. If someone in the room was humiliated, they could feel that humiliation; they could look over at Robert Downey Jr. and watch him pretend not to care. For people watching live on television, it was a "soft reality"—they were sharing time, but they weren't sharing space. TV audiences were surprised by what Gervais was saying, but it still looked and felt like television (the participants seemed less like actual people and more like actors playing themselves). For those of us who watched those same clips twenty-four hours later, there was no ingrained emotive response whatsoever—if you liked (or didn't like) the jokes, it was for personal or aesthetic reasons. The entire affair was now a construction (i.e., the softest reality possible).

The same thing happens with sports. If you watch a game in person, you're forced to connect with it emotionally (even if you don't want to be there). If you watch it live on television, the network airing the game compensates for your physical distance by maximizing the pertinent details—they shoot the game from the best possible vantage point, they show replays from different perspectives, and they hire announcers to contextualize what you're already seeing. But here's what the networks *can't* do: They can't make you forget what time it is. They can't trick you into believing that this game is still happening. They can't make you forget that the outcome of the game has been established, and that what you're now seeing has been scripted by the rotation of the earth. You know this, and you can't unknow it.

As a result, a 7:05 p.m. Yankees–Red Sox game viewed at midnight becomes the equivalent of watching the 2011 Golden Globes in the year 2015—a distant event where nothing is at stake (even if you want it to be).

3. Digital recording gives me too much control: This seems backward, but it's closer to common sense. The most reassuring thing about television is that it's a passive experience—it's one-way entertainment. You sit motionless and watch what's happening, and it's acceptable to totally surrender your agency. The show is being shown, the decision to air it was made by some stranger in Hollywood, and you just happen to be seeing it. Even if you were dead, it would still be there. But if you're watching a game that has already occurred (and that you decided to record), you're constantly forced to decide whether or not it's worth the investment of your time. You suddenly have *too much* agency. You know you could just walk over to your computer and learn everything important in seconds (i.e., who won, what were the highlights, what is the takeaway), so the play-by-play action needs to be more entertaining than *every other life option* you have at that given moment. As soon as one team takes command, it feels wasteful to wait and see if the trailing opponent makes a comeback. When I watch a bad football game live, I tend to unconsciously place the blame on the players and coaches; this reaction is misguided and childish, but it's a natural reaction. But if I watch a bad football game three hours after it has finished, I can only blame myself.

The Irrational

1. "Perhaps my personal involvement with this game will impact the outcome." This, certainly, is a crazy thing for anyone to believe. But whenever I discuss this topic with other people, they inevitably allude to the notion of being *involved* with what they're seeing. There is a massive sector of the populace who think they are partially responsible for what occurs in the games they're watching on television; they believe their psychic energy plays a role in what happens to other people in other cities. These consumers tend to fall into one or more of the following categories:

a. People who get mad at strangers for not standing up and cheering at live events.
b. People who swear at inanimate objects.

c. People who refer to teams composed of people they've never met as "We."

d. People who think God has a vested interest in certain teams succeeding.

e. People who applaud at the conclusion of movies, just in case the director happens to be sitting in the theater.

f. People who worry about Susan Miller.[1]

g. People who refuse to accept that even "live" TV events are on a seven-second delay.

h. People who set their watch five minutes ahead in order to fool themselves into being on time.

Now, is this compulsion bad? I suppose it isn't. It's egocentric and baseless, but it increases the degree to which people enjoy sporting events (and since sports are ultimately entertainment, this is good for everyone involved). Yet this perverse, illogical dream is killed by the prerecorded event: If you think your mind and heart play a role in the game you're watching, a DVR'd game is like trying to hug a dead body. Your hopes and desires immediately become irrelevant. Which, of course, they *always* were . . . but now you can't even pretend.

2. "If this game has already ended and I don't know anything about what happened, it was probably just a game." This sentence is so obvious that it's almost nonsensical, but I suspect it's the point that matters most. It's the central premise behind the entire concept of "liveness," which is what this problem really comes down to.

Just over five years ago, Kobe Bryant scored 81 points against the Toronto Raptors. That game wasn't on TV (it might have been on NBA TV, but I didn't have that network at the time). I had no chance to watch it *or* record it. Yet someone sent me a text that evening

---

1. A subset of this category would be "People who know who Susan Miller is."

around midnight, informing me that Kobe had 53 points at the end of three quarters. If Bryant had eventually scored 101 points, I suspect I would have received eighteen texts, three phone calls, and a fax.[2] Seven years ago, the Pistons and the Pacers were involved in a brawl that spilled into the stands, ultimately resulting in 146 game suspensions (86 for Ron Artest alone). When that fight happened, I was in a tiny bar in Brooklyn with no TV, listening to "Buffalo Stance" at a semi-intimate birthday party. Twitter did not yet exist, and—even if it had—my 2004 phone didn't have Internet access. Yet I knew everything about this fight long before I got home. Late-arriving party guests told us what had transpired the moment they walked into the bar. It was the first thing they said, even before "Happy birthday." It was like they *needed* to tell us, even if they themselves did not particularly care.

What I've come to accept (and this is both good and bad, but mostly bad) is that—for the rest of my life—I will never not instantaneously know about any marginally insane event. There's just no way to avoid the information. The world is too mediated and interpersonal relationships are too connected. Since most adult relationships are now based around new technologies,[3] it's almost like there's a built-in responsibility to immediately distribute whatever interesting information we acquire. People constantly complain about Facebook, but that doesn't mean it hasn't changed them; they're complaining because it *has* changed them. And they know it. They can feel it. Everyone has become a special-interest newspaper. Everyone wants to break news.

---

2. I do not own a fax machine.

3. This seems like a bombastic statement, but it's almost irrefutable. How many "relationships" do you have in your life? Probably hundreds, and perhaps thousands. But think about how you interact with most of those people: In how many cases does social networking, texting, and email comprise more than 51 percent of your interaction?

If I record tomorrow's Mavs–Heat game and wait until Friday morning to watch it, will I be able to avoid discovering that Miami won in overtime? Probably. I can probably avoid hearing the score or knowing that it was an especially thrilling game. But could I avoid hearing that LeBron James scored 85 points? Could I avoid hearing that Dirk had 51 at halftime? Could I keep from learning that the roof of the American Airlines Center tragically collapsed? What if Miami never missed a single field goal for the entire second half? What if Mark Cuban grabbed the P.A. microphone seconds before tip-off and publicly announced he was gay? What if a bear broke into the stadium and started attacking players on the court, forcing Shawn Marion to tackle the bear and break its neck? Is there any chance I could avoid hearing *that* news before pressing "play" on the DVR remote? No. No way. There's no possible way I could avoid hearing about any of those situations. And—sure—those scenarios are preposterous and implausible. But so was the likelihood of an NBA title game being interrupted by the LAPD slowly chasing a Hall of Fame tailback down the freeway in order to arrest him for double homicide. So was Monica Seles getting stabbed in the middle of a tennis match in Hamburg. So was Dock Ellis throwing a no-hitter on LSD, Reggie Miller scoring eight points in less than nine seconds, and the conclusion of the 1982 Cal–Stanford football game.

It's difficult to project fictional scenarios that are more oblique and unexpected than the craziest moments from reality. We all understand this. And that understanding is at the core of the human attraction to *liveness*. We don't crave live sporting events because we need immediacy; we crave them because they represent those (increasingly rare) circumstances where the entire spectrum of possibility is in play. They're the last scraps of mass society that are totally unfixed.

When you watch an event in real time, anything is possible.

Someone could die. Something that has never before happened could spontaneously happen twice. When there's :03 on the clock, not one person in the world can predict how those seconds will unspool. But if something happens within those three seconds that is authentically astonishing and truly transcendent . . . well, I'm sure I'll find out three minutes after it happens. I'm certain someone would tell me, possibly by accident. You can avoid the news, but you can't avoid The News. Living in a cave isn't enough. We've beaten the caves. The caves have Wi-Fi.

And that, ultimately, is why a prerecorded game can never feel the same as a game that is happening in real time: If I don't know anything about the event I'm about to watch, I can be certain that nothing except a good game is going to transpire. I know I'm merely going to see a slightly different version of something I've seen a thousand times before. And even though I think that's all I want, it doesn't come close to what I unconsciously crave.

—June 2011

I Will Choose Free Will
(Canadian Reader's Note:
This Is Not About Rush)

Though some may disagree (and I'm sure some will, because some always do), there doesn't seem to be much debate over what have been the four best television shows of the past ten years. It feels like an easy puzzle to solve, particularly since it's become increasingly difficult to write about the state of TV (or even the state of popular culture) without tangentially mentioning one of the following four programs— *The Sopranos*, *The Wire*, *Mad Men*, and/or *Breaking Bad*. The four fit together so nicely: two from HBO that are defunct, two from AMC that are still ongoing, and all of which use nonlinear narratives with only minor experimentation. There have been bushels of quality television during the past decade, but these four shows have been the best.[1] Taste is subjective, but the critical consensus surrounding these four dramas is so widespread that it feels like an objective truth; it's become so accepted that this entire paragraph is a relatively mundane argument

---

1. I once wrote in *Esquire* that *Lost* was the best show in the history of network television, but the operative word there is "network." The limitations change everything. Being the best show on network TV is kind of like being the sexiest person at a Dream Theater concert.

to make in public. I'm basically writing, "The greatness of these great shows is defined by their greatness." There's no conflict in stating that good things are good.

Until, of course, you try to suggest that one of these shows is somehow better than the other three. Then it becomes a fucking bloodbath.

Because TV is so simultaneously personal (it exists inside your home) and so utterly universal (it exists inside everyone's home), people care about it with an atypical level of conversational ferocity—they take it more personally than other forms of art, and they immediately feel comfortable speaking from a position of expertise. They develop loyalties to certain characters and feel offended when those loyalties are disparaged. This is what makes arguing about these particular shows so intense and satisfying—even though most serious TV watchers enjoy (or at least appreciate) all four, they habitually feel a greater internal obligation to advocate the superiority of whichever title they love most. As a result, you often hear people making damning, melodramatic criticisms of TV shows they ostensibly like. You hear a lot of sentences that begin, "I love *Mad Men*, but . . ." or "The first two seasons of *The Sopranos* were great, but . . ." And whatever follows that "but" is inevitably crazy and hyperspecific. This is especially true among people who prefer *The Wire*. There's never been a more obstinate fan base than that of *The Wire*. It's a secular cult that refuses to accept any argument that doesn't classify *The Wire* as the greatest artistic endeavor in television history. It's almost like these people secretly believe this show *actually happened*, and that criticizing any detail is like mocking an episode of *Frontline*. This was not a documentary about Baltimore: Wallace is not alive and playing high school football in Texas, Stringer Bell was not reincarnated as a Pennsylvania paper salesman, and you are not qualified to lecture on inner-city education because you own season four on DVD. The citizens on that show were nonexistent composites, and the events you watched did not occur. As a society, we must learn to accept this.

Which is not to say *The Wire* wasn't brilliant, because it was. Of the four shows I've mentioned, *The Wire* absolutely exhibited the finest writing. *Mad Men* has the most fascinating collection of character types. *The Sopranos* was the most fully realized (and, it's important to note, essentially invented this rarefied tier of televised drama). But I've come to the conclusion that *Breaking Bad* is the best of the four, or at least the one I like the most.[2] And I've been trying to figure out why I feel this way. It's shot in the most visually creative style, but that's not enough to set it apart; the acting is probably the best of the four, but not by a lot (and since good acting can sometimes cover deeper problems with direction and storytelling, I tend not to give it much weight). I suspect *Breaking Bad* will be the least remembered of these four shows and the least influential over time. Yet there's one profound difference between this series and the other three, and it has to do with its handling of morality: *Breaking Bad* is the only one built on the uncomfortable premise that there's an irrefutable difference between what's right and what's wrong, and it's the only one where the characters have real control over how they choose to live.

Certainly, all of these series grapple with morality—more than anything else, it's the reason they're better than the shows around them. But the first three examples all create realities where individual agency is detached. *Mad Men* is set in the 1960s, so every action the characters make is not really a reflection on who they are—it's a commentary on the era. Don Draper is a bad husband, but "that's just how it was in those days." Roger Sterling's depravity is a form of retrospective entertainment. People can act however they want without

---

2. Which I realize is not always the same thing.

remorse, because almost all their decisions can be excused (or at least explained) by the circumstances of the period. There is far less at stake.[3] The characters are irresponsible for the sake of plausibility. We don't hold them accountable for what they do.

Now, *The Sopranos* and *The Wire* were set in the present, so the actions of their casts are harder to rationalize away. But both shows had fixed worldviews, so that process is still possible. Every important person on *The Sopranos* was involved with organized crime, and its protagonist was a (likable) transgressive who regularly murdered for money—subsequently, there were never any unresolved questions over Tony Soprano's "goodness." When Tony did something nice, he did it *in spite of the fact* that he's fundamentally bad (otherwise he couldn't exist as the person he was). *The Sopranos* was compelling because we were continually watching innately bad people operate within a world not unlike our own—this, in one sentence, was the crux of the entire series. Meanwhile, *The Wire* was more nuanced: In *The Wire*, everyone is *simultaneously* good and bad. The cops are fighting crime, but they're all specifically or abstractly corrupt; the drug dealers are violent criminals, but they're less hypocritical and hold themselves to a higher ethical standard. There were sporadic exceptions to this rule, but those exceptions only served to accentuate its overall relativist take on human nature: Nobody is totally positive and nobody is totally negative, and our inherently flawed assessment of those qualities hinges on where we come from and what we want to believe. This, of course, is closer to how life actually is (which is why *The Wire* felt so realistic). It's a more sophisticated way to depict the world. However—from a fictional, narrative perspective—it ends

---

3. Semi-related: Of these four shows, *Mad Men* is the only one that doesn't regularly involve violence. This also changes the gravity of the characters' decision-making, because the worst thing that can happen to anyone on *Mad Men* is losing a job or being humiliated. But that, of course, also brings it closer to the lives of most average Americans.

up making the message a little less meaningful. If nothing is totally false, everything is partially true; depending on the perspective and the circumstance, no action is unacceptable. The conditions matter more than the participants. As we drift further and further from its 2008 finale, it increasingly feels like the ultimate takeaway from *The Wire* was more political[4] than philosophical. Which is not exactly a criticism, because that's an accomplishment, too . . . it's just that it turns the plot of *The Wire* into a delivery mechanism for David Simon's polemic worldview (which makes its value dependent on how much the audience is predisposed to agree with him).

This is where *Breaking Bad* diverges from the other three. *Breaking Bad* is not a situation where the characters' morality is static or contradictory or colored by the time frame. Instead, it suggests that morality is continually a personal choice. When the show began, that didn't seem to be the case: It seemed like this was going to be the story of a man (Walter White, portrayed by Bryan Cranston) forced to become a criminal because he was dying of cancer. That's the elevator pitch. But that's completely unrelated to what the show has become. The central question on *Breaking Bad* is this: What makes a man "bad"—his actions, his motives, or his conscious decision to *be* a bad person? Judging from the trajectory of its first three seasons, *Breaking Bad* creator Vince Gilligan believes the answer is option #3. So what we see in *Breaking Bad* is a person who started as one type of human and decides to become something different. And because this is television—because we were introduced to this man in a way that

---

4. If the president tells a reporter your TV show is his favorite, it's de facto political, regardless of the premise or the creator's original intent. Barack Obama loving *The Wire* is a little like Amy Carter adding the Sex Pistols to the White House music library—it shouldn't mean anything, but of course it does. Whenever a president (or even a senator) is asked about what they like to watch on television, they know their answer will be perceived as symbolic of who they are and what they represent. This is why there will never be a modern U.S. president who will not define himself or herself as a sports fan.

made him impossible to dislike, and because we experience TV through whichever character we understand the most—the audience is placed in the curious position of continuing to root for an individual who's no longer good. And this is not a case like J. R. Ewing or Al Swearengen, where a character's over-the-top evilness immediately defines his charm; this is a series where the main character has actively become evil, but we still want him to succeed. At this point, Walter White could do *anything*, and I would continue to support his cause. In fact, his evolution has been so deft that I feel weird describing his persona as "evil," even though I can't justify why it would be incorrect to do so. Gilligan detailed this process in a recent interview with *Newsweek*: "Television is historically good at keeping its characters in a self-imposed stasis so that shows can go on for years or even decades. When I realized this, the logical next step was to think, how can I do a show in which the fundamental drive is toward change?"[5]

In that same *Newsweek* article, the writer suggests Walter White's ongoing metamorphosis is what makes *Breaking Bad* great. But that doesn't go far enough. It's not just that watching White's transformation is interesting; what's interesting is that this transformation involves the fundamental core of who he supposedly is, and that this (wholly constructed) core is an extension of his own free will. The difference between White in the middle of season one and White in the debut of season four is not the product of his era or his upbringing or his social environment. It's a product of his own consciousness. He changed himself. At some point, he *decided* to become bad, and that's what matters.

---

5. Gilligan made an almost identical point in David Segal's recent story on the series for *The New York Times Magazine*: "Television is really good at protecting the franchise. It's good at keeping the Korean War going for 11 seasons, like *M*A*S*H*. It's good at keeping Marshal Dillon policing his little town for 20 years. By their very nature TV shows are open-ended. So I thought, Wouldn't it be interesting to have a show that takes the protagonist and transforms him into the antagonist?"

There's a scene in *Breaking Bad*'s first season where Walter White's hoodrat lab assistant Jesse Pinkman (Aaron Paul) tells Walter he just can't "break bad," and—when you first hear this snippet of dialogue—you assume what Jesse means is that you can't go from being a law-abiding chemistry teacher to an underground meth cooker. It seems like he's telling White that he can't start breaking the law after living a life where laws were always obeyed, and that a criminal lifestyle is not something you can join like a club. His advice seems pragmatic, and it almost feels like an artless way to shoehorn the show's title into the script. But this, it turns out, was not Jesse's point. What he was arguing was that someone can't "decide" to morph from a good person into a bad person, because there's a firewall within our personalities that makes this impossible. He was arguing that Walter's *nature* would stop him from being bad, and that Walter would fail if he tried to make this conversion real. But Jesse was wrong. He was wrong, because goodness and badness are simply complicated choices, no different from anything else.

—*October 2011*

Everybody's Happy When the Wizard Walks By (Or Maybe Not? Maybe They Hate It? Hard to Say, Really)

Here is what I know about Harry Potter: nothing.

I haven't read any of the books, nor have I seen any of the movies. I know the novels were written by a rich middle-aged British woman named J. K. Rowling, but I have no idea what the letters "J" and "K" represent. I don't know the name of the actor who portrays Harry Potter in the films, although I think he has eyeglasses. I don't know the names of any minor characters and I don't know the narrative arc of the plot. I don't know where the stories take place or if they are set in the past or the future. Somebody at a steak house recently told me that Harry Potter doesn't die at the seventh book's conclusion (and that this detail was important), but I wasn't even aware he was sick. Christopher Hitchens wrote something I didn't read about this series in *The New York Times Book Review*, but I'm told it didn't mention Nixon (not even once!). I assume there are dragons and griffons and werewolves and homosexual Frankensteins throughout these novels, but I honestly don't give a shit if my assumption is true or false. In fact, if somebody told me that the final Harry Potter novel was a coded interpretation of the Koran that instructed readers on how to read my thoughts, I could only respond by saying, "Well, maybe so." For whatever the reason, this is one phenomenon that I have missed completely (and mostly, I suppose, on purpose).

Now, do not take this to mean that I dislike these books. I do not. I have a colleague who feels anyone over the age of twenty-one caught reading a Harry Potter novel should be executed without trial,[1] but that strikes me as unreasonable; the fact that they're written for British thirteen-year-olds probably means they're the right speed for 90 percent of American adults. I don't hate these novels at all—in fact, I suspect they're good. Moreover, I find it astounding that the unifying cultural currency for modern teenagers is *five-hundred-page literary works about a wizard*.[2] We are all collectively underestimating how unusual this is. Right now, there is no pop star or film starlet as popular as J. K. Rowling. Over time, these novels (and whatever ideas lie within them) will come to represent the mainstream ethos of our future popular culture. Harry Potter will be the only triviality that most of that coming culture will unilaterally share.

And I have no interest in any of it.

And I wonder how much of a problem this is going to become.

The bookish kids reading Harry Potter novels may not go on to control the world, but they will almost certainly go on to control the media. In fifteen years, they will be publishing books and directing films and writing broad jokes for unfunny situation comedies that will be downloaded directly into our brains. And like all generations of artists, they will traffic in their own nostalgia. They will use their

---

1. This person has since changed his stance to "life in prison." When push comes to shove, all my friends are soft on crime.

2. Or a warlock, or an emo elf, or whatever the fuck he's supposed to be.

shared knowledge and experiences as the foundation for discourse. So I wonder: Because I don't understand Harry Potter, am I doomed to misunderstand everything else?

I HAVE A FEMALE FRIEND who has never seen any of the *Star Wars* movies. If someone on *The Office* makes a joke about a Wookiee, she knows that it's supposed to be funny, but it never makes her laugh. I also know a guy from college who (under pressure) cannot name three Beatles songs unless you allow him to include their cover of "Twist and Shout," and that's only because it was used in *Ferris Bueller's Day Off.* On a practical level, these knowledge chasms do not hinder either of their lives; I'm sure some would argue they're better off *not* caring about such trivial matters. But part of me knows there's an intangible downside to having complete intellectual detachment from whatever most Americans consider to be common knowledge. It's not just that someone who hasn't seen *Star Wars* won't appreciate Kevin Smith films, or that any person who doesn't know about the Beatles won't appreciate the Apples in Stereo. Those connections are obvious (and usually meaningless). What's less clear—and much more important—is the degree to which *all* of culture is imperceptibly defined by whichever of its entities happen to be the most popular at any given time. Which is, I suppose, the fundamental question about why "popular culture" is supposed to matter to anyone.

Within any complex scenario, there are three kinds of information. The three types are as follows:

1. Information that you know you know.
2. Information that you know you *don't* know.
3. Information that you don't know *you don't know.*

I'd like to believe that my relationship with Harry Potter fits into that second category. I'd like to view the information in Rowling's books as something I consciously realize that I don't understand. But this is not the case. The phenomenon around these books is so large that I can't isolate the consequence of my unawareness. My relationship to Harry Potter actually falls into the third category: I cannot even pretend to predict what the social impact of 325 million books will eventually embody. As the years pass, the influence of these teenage wizard stories will be so vast that it will become invisible. In two decades, I will not be alienated or confused by passing references to Harry Potter; very often, I will be unaware that any reference has even been made. I will not know what I am missing. I'll just feel bored, and I won't know why.

HERE IS WHAT I IMAGINE the seven Harry Potter novels are about: I imagine that Harry is an orphan who had a bad relationship with his father (kind of like Tom Cruise in *Top Gun* or *Days of Thunder* or *A Few Good Men* or any of his movies that didn't involve Ireland). He escapes some sort of abstract slavery and decides to become a wizard, so he attends Wizard College and meets a bunch of anachronistic magic-using weirdos and perhaps a love interest that he never has sex with. There is probably a good teacher and a bad teacher at this school and (I'm sure) they eventually fight each other, and then some previously theoretical villain tries to destroy the world and all the wizard kids have to unite in order to protect the universe by boiling black cats in a cauldron and throwing lightning bolts at pterodactyls. Something unremarkable comes to symbolize God (or possibly a pagan version of abstract goodness, or possibly Krishna). Harry learns about life and loss and leadership, and then he doesn't die. The end.

I realize I don't have to guess at these details. I'm sure I could have read the entire four-thousand-page plot summarized in four hundred words on Wikipedia, or I could simply walk into any high school and ask a few questions of the first kid I find who isn't smoking crystal meth. I could just as easily buy and read the books themselves, which—as stated previously—I assume are engaging. But I am not going to do this. It doesn't seem worth it, even though I know it probably is. It's an interior paradox. I mean, is it my *obligation* to "study" these novels, even if I don't want to? Perhaps it is. In many ways, I am paid by *Esquire* to contextualize this sort of phenomenon, and I assume that will still be the case in the future. It's probably to my long-term financial benefit to read Harry Potter books; ignoring them is a little like not investing in my 401(k). Were I a more responsible citizen, I would force myself to consume everything I could about this goddamn teenage wizard, simply for economic self-preservation. Yet I can't make myself do it. I just don't care that I don't understand this.

Which, I realize, is a dangerous position to publicly adopt. I am constructing my own generation gap on purpose. By making this decision in the present, I will be less able to manage the future. My thoughts about entertainment aesthetics will be outdated, and I will not grasp the fundamental lingua franca of 2025. I will be not just old, but old for my age. I will be the pterodactyl, and I will be slain. It is only a matter of time.

—*October 2007*

Speed Kills (Until It Doesn't)

Allow me to spare you the hyperbole: Usain Bolt is fast.

He is, as far as we can tell, the fastest human who's ever lived—in 2009, in Berlin, he ran the 100-meter dash in 9.58 seconds. This translates to an average speed of just over 23 mph, with a top speed closer to 30. His '08 performance in Germany was .1 quicker than the (still astounding) 9.69 he ran at the 2008 Beijing Olympics, the fattest chunk ever taken off a world record at that distance. Considering the unadulterated simplicity of his vocation and the historic magnitude of his dominance, it's hard to argue that Bolt has not been the world's greatest athlete of the past five years. And yet there's an even easier argument to make than that one: Within the next twenty-five years, Bolt's achievements as a sprinter will be annihilated.

This is not *guaranteed*, of course, but it's certainly more plausible than speculative[1]—for the past thirty years, the men's record in the 100-meter dash has been assaulted so continually that many of its former record holders don't even qualify as difficult answers to

---

1. As it turns out, this has not yet happened. Bolt won his third straight 100-meter gold medal at the 2016 Olympics with a time of 9.81, and his victory was decisive—but as I write this today, it does not appear that Bolt (set to retire in 2017) will ever again run as fast as he did in 2009, and neither will any of his current peers. The record will be broken eventually, but it might stand at 9.58 for a while.

difficult trivia questions. This was not always the case: In 1968, Jim Hines broke the 10.00 barrier with a 9.95 at the (high-altitude) 1968 Olympics. That mark stood for fifteen years, until Calvin Smith ran a 9.93 (also at altitude) in Colorado Springs. But since 1983, the record has been shattered more than a dozen times. Ben Johnson's steroid-fueled 9.83 in '87 was the first massive blow, but eight others have chipped away at the record with increasing regularity (Bolt just happened to use a sledgehammer).

The big-picture upshot to all this measured subtraction is simple: Over the past forty years, man has improved his ability to run 100 meters by .37 seconds. That's a rough average of .01 a year, but such math is deceptively understated—though the year-to-year improvement isn't exponential, it also isn't gradual. The rate of change keeps accelerating. As of this June, seventeen men had already run sub-10.0 100-meter dashes, the most ever in the span of a year (with six months still on the calendar). Were he to get in the same physical condition he was in in 2009, most track experts concede that the twenty-five-year-old Bolt has the potential to breach the 9.50 barrier at any moment. And this raises the central question fans of track and field have always wanted to know: Is there a ceiling to how fast a man can run? Will there be a day—maybe in fifty years, or maybe in five hundred—when someone runs the 100-meter dash in 8.99 seconds? In 7.99 seconds?

"In order to answer this question, you have to think like a sprinter. And sprinters believe that—someday—somebody will run the hundred meters and the clock will read 0.00." Ato Boldon tells me this over the telephone. Boldon is currently known as the lead track analyst for NBC and CBS, but he's also a four-time Olympic medalist and the fastest man the island of Trinidad has ever produced (in 1999, he ran the 100 in 9.86). "And when a sprinter thinks like that, he's not trying to trick himself. It's how you have to think. This idea of human limitation is exactly what we're competing against. It's thinking about running an 8.99 that gets you down to 9.58. That's how it works."

OBVIOUSLY, IT'S IMPOSSIBLE to talk about sprinting records and human potentiality without mentioning steroids. It's more than the rhino in the room—it's possibly the true reason why the WR in the 100 didn't move for fifteen years and then started falling like an air conditioner shoved out an open window. But for the sake of this specific discussion, PEDs don't really matter. This isn't a moral (or even competitive) issue. The question is not what speed a man *should* run; the question is how fast a man *could* run, through any means necessary. In fact, steroids tend to be a secondary issue for hardcore track fans, principally for two reasons:

1. Though nobody will talk about it on the record, PEDs have become an integral, irretraceable component of sprinting. It's pretty much like cycling: There's just an unspoken "Everybody does it" concession. There are sanctioned rules, and athletes get penalized if they get caught breaking them. But nobody really worries about this, simply because . . .
2. People who love track want to see guys run fast. That's the whole game. There is nothing else to care about. The sport is not built on personal rivalries or constructed purity or nationalism or tradition; the sport is solely driven by the excitement of people moving at speeds never before experienced. In this one instance, the ends truly do justify the means. And unlike other sports, there's no rhetoric or concern about steroids warping statistics, because the only stat that matters is who's fastest *right now*. Once a record has been broken, it

instantly becomes meaningless. Not even track historians use comparative times as a way to establish greatness. Easy example: Which of these men was the greatest sprinter— Jesse Owens (who won the 1936 Olympics with a time of 10.3), Carl Lewis (whose career best in the 100 was 9.86), or Leroy Burrell (who ran a 9.85)? Track and field is about running fast *today*. It's a bottom-line endeavor.

This is not to say that steroids don't make debates about human speed complex, because they do. Around the same time Ben Johnson ran his (then unthinkable) 9.83, Florence Griffith Joyner destroyed the women's 100-meter mark with a 10.49, and that record has not been seriously challenged in the twenty-three years since. Was something happening with PEDs in the late 1980s that has since been removed from the sport? Why do men keep getting faster, but women do not? These are questions science cannot seem to answer (or even guess at).[2]

"Bolt's 9.58 is so low that perhaps no one gets close to it for a very long time, just like Flo-Jo's record," says Boldon. "But scientists are always wrong about this stuff. Scientists once believed that if a man ran a four-minute mile, his lungs would explode."

"THE SCIENTIFIC UNDERSTANDING OF SPRINTING is pretty immature," concedes Peter Weyand, and—since Weyand is the de facto American expert on the science of sprinting—that tells you just how

---

2. Worth noting: Because many PEDs generate and amplify a body's level of testosterone, PEDs tend to help female runners far more than their male counterparts (since women naturally produce very little testosterone on their own). This is sometimes cited as the reason Flo-Jo's record is so untouchable—the one thing modern drug testing is especially good at is flagging unnaturally high testosterone levels, which was not the case in 1984.

mysterious this phenomenon is. A physiologist and biomechanist at Southern Methodist University, Weyand specializes in terrestrial locomotion. While at Harvard in the '90s, he directed experiments at Concord Field Station, a facility where researchers regularly placed animals like cheetahs,[3] wolverines, and kangaroos on treadmills to understand the mechanics of movement. Now fifty, Weyand was also a fairly swift runner in his younger days, having run the 100-yard dash in 10.8 as a high school student. "The one thing about sprinting we all understand is that speed comes from how hard the runner's foot hits the ground. Someone like Bolt is hitting the ground with a thousand pounds of force, and we just don't know how he does that. For example, we have a very accurate understanding of how much weight someone can lift—we can take a person's frame and muscle mass and accurately estimate how much weight he'll be able to bench press. But world-class sprinters deliver twice as much force as our estimates indicate, and we don't know why."

With Bolt, there's also a key second component: height. While most world-class sprinters are short, Bolt is six-foot-five and his stride is an insane 2.44 meters long. When Bolt ran 9.58 in Berlin, he needed only 41 strides to traverse those 100 meters; the man who placed second, five-foot-eleven-inch Tyson Gay (who still managed an incredible 9.71), needed 44½ strides. This has led to a popular pet theory about the future of sprinting: Bolt has the proportions and mechanics of a conventional sprinter, but he comes with an inordinately long skeleton. So what would happen if an even taller man were able to move with this kind of fluidity? What if someone with Kevin Garnett's seven-foot frame moved as naturally as Bolt does at six-foot-five? Would this hypothetical super-sprinter be able to travel

---

3. "To be honest, I missed the cheetah experiments," Weyand admits with some regret. "That happened before I got there."

100 meters in only 33 strides? Might sprinting become dominated by sleek, long-stepping giants?

Perhaps. But probably not.

"Being tall is really a disadvantage," says Weyand. "Bolt is just a freak. Generally, the smaller you are, the stronger you are in relation to your weight. Bolt defies the laws of biology in terms of his start. He's good out of the blocks, and he shouldn't be. It's so strange, because Tyson Gay is basically as fast as Bolt once they hit full speed."

The idea that Bolt's height is his not-so-secret weapon makes sense geometrically, but not in practicality—he seems to be the only person who somehow benefits from (what should be) a disadvantage. Francis Obikwelu (the 2004 Olympic silver medalist for Portugal) is almost six-five, and he once ran an impressive 9.86—but he simply can't turn his legs over[4] as quickly as Bolt. His length gets in the way. For whatever the reason, Bolt is flat-out superior at every aspect of high-speed locomotion—stride length, stride power, and the amount of time it takes to reach his top speed. It's almost like he was designed to do this by a track-obsessed God.

IS THERE AN IRREFUTABLE DEAD-END to the 100-meter dash? Is there a speed where a human body would just break down and disintegrate, no different from a machine pushed beyond the capacity of its individual components? Some have been arguing "yes" for years. Reza Noubary, a professor of mathematics, computer science, and statistics at Bloomsburg University in Pennsylvania, has estimated "with 95 percent confidence" that the ultimate time for the 100-meter dash is 9.44. That number seems as good a guess as anything

---

4. This is a term that describes the time it takes to make a stride with your left leg after completing the previous stride with your right (or vice versa). Basically, it just means how fast your legs are moving in succession. It's what "running" is.

else. But if Noubary is correct, it would force us to accept a depressing, unreliable notion—it would essentially mean we're roughly twenty-five years away from the pinnacle of human performance. It would mean that most of us will see the fastest man *who could ever possibly exist* within our own lifetimes. And something about that just seems unlikely. Beyond the (pretty clear) evidence that people are getting bigger, faster, and stronger at the same time, there's also been a massive uptick in cultural motivation: There has never been a time when being the fastest man in the world[5] was worth so much money (particularly in the 100 meters, where the difference in notoriety between who's #1 and #2 is especially vast).

"I wouldn't take 9.0 off the table," says Weyand. "Scientists don't like making these kinds of predictions, and for good reason. A world record is the most extreme fringe of performance, and weird things happen at those fringes. I need to take off my scientist hat to make that statement and just speak as the Average Joe. But my gut feeling

---

5. Contradictory side note: We should not overlook the large contingent of long-distance runners who find the whole question of "the fastest man alive" patently ridiculous, simply because humans are all relatively slow (at least compared to most other mammals). Humans are designed for distance running. Christopher McDougall, author of the best-selling book *Born to Run*, actually thinks this debate is borderline sexist. "My bedrock feeling about sprinting is that we only get excited about it because boys are better than girls. Men set the entertainment agenda, so we pick the events that give us an edge over women. As a species, we're awful sprinters. Really bad. The average amputee dog can hold his own against any high school track star . . . It takes a really prosperous, secure society to perfect frivolous pursuits. In a way, our quest for speed isn't far removed from [the MTV show] *Jackass*. But I'm a grouch." Daniel Lieberman at Harvard (who, coincidentally, was Weyand's anatomy instructor) makes a similar point, albeit for different reasons: "It's useful to keep in mind that we should not be too impressed by Bolt and other speedsters. By mammalian standards, they are comparatively slow. Most decent quadrupeds out there—dogs, horses, zebra, lions—can run about twenty meters per second, twice as fast as Bolt, and they can do so for much longer (up to a few minutes). No Olympic sprinter could ever outrun a lion. We humans gave up the ability to run fast by mammalian standards many millions of years ago when we became bipeds and lost the ability to gallop. Instead, what humans excel at is endurance, especially on a hot day." Of course, if we took all these arguments at face value, the Olympics would be pretty bizarre.

is that it will probably happen in our lifetime, and that feeling is driven by the incentives of modern sports."

Boldon is less confident than Weyand. He says he'd bet against a man running 9.0 in the next forty years, based on the premise that "a pen is harder to refine than a tractor." The race is short and the moving parts are minimal—at some point, you simply run out of details to improve upon. For a more personal perspective, I emailed Tyson Gay (who was nice enough to return my email on the same day he underwent surgery for a torn hip labrum). Gay is the fastest American of all time, having run a 9.69 in the 100 (he's also the first man to break all three magic barriers within the sprints—he's run under 10 seconds in the 100, under 20 seconds in the 200, and under 45 seconds in the 400). I posed him two simple questions: (1) If you ran a perfect race under perfect conditions, what time do you think you'd run? and (2) When you're an old man, how low do you think the world record in the 100 meters will be? His response was rather curious:

> I think with everything perfect I possibly could run 9.4, hahahaha. I know that sounds crazy but just being honest. I think the record will be in the 9.4 to 9.3 [range]. Maybe 9.2 range and that's only if people can grasp and believe that's possible. All about the mind.

What's so interesting about this answer is the dissonance between Gay's self-perception and his perception of the world at large. He believes he could run almost .3 seconds faster than he ever has—yet he also assumes that specific time will almost be the top of the mountain, even fifty years from now. When I read this email to Boldon, he laughed with an immediate sense of recognition. "Typical sprinter narcissism," said Boldon. "*I* could run a 9.4, but *nobody* could run a

9.2." Even sprinters don't understand what they do (or how they do it). In an era when science is able to explain and predict almost everything, it's amazing how little we know about the potential of rudimentary movement. Sprinting has represented half of the "fight or flight" instinct for the totality of human existence, yet we still have no idea about our true limitations . . . which explains why track and field will always matter, even if no one in America seems to care.

—July 2011

Not a Nutzo Girl,
Not Yet a Nutzo Woman
(Miley Cyrus, 2008)

Whenever a teenage entertainer becomes semi-famous, it's usually for vaguely predictable reasons. Often, it's because the performer happens to possess an unorthodox attractiveness that only like-minded kids instantly recognize (case in point: the Olsen twins). Sometimes it's because an artist capitalizes on a marketing scheme other people ignore. (Tiffany's 1987 barnstorming tour of shopping malls is perhaps the best example.) Occasionally it's because an act will combine a modicum of genuine talent with a craven desire to *seem* young, purely for commercial purposes. (This was the case with Hanson, a trio whose debut album was both not terrible and not credible.) There is always an unlimited demand for teenage idolatry; as such, there are proven, long-established techniques for constructing an impermanent cult of personality around whatever ambitious, sexier-than-average fifteen-year-old the mass media happens to select. But all those conventional techniques can only spawn semi-fame. The sensation they produce is limited and transparent, and it's (generally) not symbolic of anything. It's what makes people use modifiers like "disposable."

This, however, is not the case with that rarefied class of teenage entertainers who become authentically, dangerously metaphoric. These are people like Ricky Nelson, Brooke Shields, and Britney Spears: teenage superstars whose existence hinged on sweeping social evolutions they (a) could not have possibly anticipated and (b) played almost no active role in creating. In all three of those cases, the teenagers unknowingly represented something that was changing about the way American young people looked at themselves in relation to the world—they were "accidentally transformative." And they subsequently remain important, even as they become adults, often for reasons unconnected to their artistic purpose. Which brings us to the strange case of Hannah Montana, a sixteen-year-old entertainer who helps adolescents deal with a self-identity problem they created themselves.

If you already know who Hannah Montana is, skip to the next paragraph. If you don't, here are the pertinent details: She is the most famous teenager in America, which makes her the third or fourth most powerful person in the universe. *Hannah Montana* is a highly rated TV show on the Disney Channel that focuses on a (nonfictional, I guess) pop star named "Hannah Montana," who secretly lives an unassuming life as California citizen "Miley Stewart." Both roles are played by Miley Cyrus, a likable, enthusiastic vessel who is (a) actually named Destiny Hope Cyrus and (b) the daughter of country goofosaurus Billy Ray Cyrus (who also portrays her dad on the program). She's a good singer. Besides appearing on TV, Miley Cyrus records and tours as Hannah Montana and succeeds with Madonna-like tenacity. During concerts in 2007, she would be momentarily replaced onstage with a body double who lip-synched her songs while Cyrus changed clothes. The body double was a cloned replicant of Cyrus, built with DNA from the singer's saliva and rapidly aged through the unsanctioned, experimental process of hypermaturilization.[1] She has also toured with the Cheetah Girls.

The narrative core of most *Hannah Montana* episodes is established by the show's expository theme song, "The Best of Both Worlds." The hook is supposed to be a contradiction—instead of working to achieve fame, Miley craves anonymity. When the show was created, I'm sure this reversal of desire was expected to serve as a novel twist on an old theme. It was supposed to operate as fantastical irony. But that is not what happened. Instead, Hannah Montana/Miley Stewart became a concept Web-obsessed teenagers could understand innately: They, too, struggle to reconcile who they are with the quasi-real persona they consciously construct. Hannah Montana is the Internet incarnate.

Like all techno-media advances, the Internet is good for the world in the short term and bad for the world in the long term. But its most meaningful impact is neutral—it provides an opportunity for average people to create public identities that are entirely their own vision. The self-portrait you upload on Facebook is what you always look like. Always. It does not matter if you've honestly enjoyed the movies you list as favorites or read the books you claim to love; by typing those titles, they constitute your aesthetic. Who is going to disagree? You want to be a stoner kite enthusiast? K-I-T-E E-N-T-H-U-S-I-A-S-T 4-2-0. There you go. That's who you are. You can buy the kite and the vaporizer later.

This, I have no doubt, has been wonderful for the self-esteem of countless people who are not designed to thrive in a less pliable, more judgmental, wholly nonvirtual society. There are now two distinct worlds that people can inhabit simultaneously. But that also creates a

---

1. [Citation needed.]

new kind of problem: Because of technology, the gap between the life one inherits and the life one creates has become exponentially vast. The fake world is much, much larger. Every online existence is a noncommercial simulation of celebrity culture: Users develop a character (i.e., the best-case portrait of themselves) and then track the size of its audience (via the number of friends they acquire or page views they receive). Private citizens now face a dilemma previously reserved for the authentically famous: How do they cope with the disparity between how they are seen in the communal sphere and how they live in private?

This is why Hannah Montana works.

Teenagers can relate to her.

Obviously, the idea of young people having secret lives is old. But the idea of having a secret *public* life is new—and it's a different kind of secret. It's more creative than escapist, and it requires the person to self-identify as a public figure. Over time (or at least on occasion), that online creator will desire separation from that celebrity construction and return to the simpler, unimagined existence that was always there. And this, in a nutshell, is the framework for most episodes of *Hannah Montana*. It also explains why that show has become accidentally important—it premiered at a specific point in history when millions of young people arbitrarily decided they were "kind of famous." Most of them would never say that overtly, because no reasonable person ever would. But this is how they feel.

In January, the PBS series *Frontline* aired an episode called "Growing Up Online," which was widely criticized for fear-mongering. One of the segments focused on a New Jersey teenager named Jessica Hunter who turned herself into an online Goth sexpot called Autumn Edows. She explained how she would spend "all day" on the computer, constantly hitting the refresh button to see what new person was validating her existence. "I didn't feel like myself," she explained, "but I liked the fact that I didn't feel like myself. I felt like someone completely different. I felt like I was famous." Within the context of the report, it was suggested that her actions were dangerous, mostly due to the kind of photos the girl was posting. The photos were sexual. But that strikes me as far less troubling than the idea of a fourteen-year-old trying to feel normal while consciously generating a bipolar existence *for an audience she'll never meet.* I mean, is living like a celebrity a good way to live? Judging from the day-to-day happiness of real celebrities, the answer seems pretty obvious. But obvious rules don't apply to Miley Cyrus, and maybe not to her fans, either.

—April 2008

When Giants Walked the Earth (and Argued About China)

The McLaughlin Group has been on television for twenty-six years. I began watching it in 1986. I can't think of any program that has taught me more about human interaction, if not necessarily about politics or journalism. Right now, there are roughly 388 shows on television that feature lunatics yelling at each other, but this is still the only good one. Critics sometimes suggest that the success of *The McLaughlin Group* has led to the erosion of serious discourse in American media, but that's like complaining about AC/DC because of Rhino Bucket. The failures of its clones only serve to illustrate why *The McLaughlin Group* is—almost exactly—what televised arguing should look, sound, and feel like. All the shows plagiarizing the "McGroup" format copy the wrong things—the only quality they duplicate is the volume. What actually makes *The McLaughlin Group* so continually watchable is (a) its inherent understanding of how personal dynamics operate, (b) its supernatural ability to incarnate idealized semiotics, and (c) the force of one specific personality. The show remains brilliant.

These are the reasons why.

I. Adversaries who hate each other must love each other.

I am sitting in the *McLaughlin Group* greenroom at the NBC studio in Washington, D.C., chatting with Pat Buchanan about Eleanor Clift (who has not yet arrived). It is Friday, December 7, 2007. "People assume we aren't friends, but we have a lot in common," Buchanan says. "For example, Eleanor and I share a great affinity for cats." He goes on to tell me that he had a cat named Gipper for eighteen years, and when Gipper died, Eleanor commiserated with Buchanan over the loss.

I was not surprised to discover Buchanan and Clift are friends. I assume anyone who has watched *The McLaughlin Group* over time would come to that same conclusion. The friendship seems palpable. But that palpability is superficially contradictory; outside of their views on the war in Iraq, Clift and Buchanan don't agree on anything. Most of their relationship has been built on attacking the other person's worldview. From a production perspective, this is imperative. It is not fun to watch public arguments between two people who legitimately hate each other, as they will inevitably spend 95 percent of the conversation pretending they're cordial. Real enemies can only disagree once; after that, they will only do battle in absentia or in court.[1] If you want people to go for the jugular every single weekend, they need to enjoy the foe they're assaulting. It's worth noting that the panelists on *The McLaughlin Group* make very little money for appearing on the show; they would not tell me the exact amount, but a producer indicated it was well below $1,000 per appearance and did not include travel expenses.

"Pat is a very generous debater," Clift later told me. "He will often

---

1. Case in point: William F. Buckley and Gore Vidal.

say, 'Eleanor is right on this point,' and I can't believe how good that makes me feel. It makes me feel way better than it should."

II. Simplify, then exaggerate.

The McLaughlin Group is not about details. If you want details, don't watch television. Also, don't read newspapers or magazines and stay off the Internet—buy nonpartisan books about events that happened no less than ten years ago. Modernity is not detail oriented. What *The McLaughlin Group* is about is the abstraction of policy, delivered in the most propulsive way possible. Here's the formula: Take a specific news item, locate its core essence, and then debate its metaphoric significance on the grandest possible scale. Nobody cares if Hillary is up four points in South Carolina; what's compelling is the notion that those four points could somehow represent the potential for how the new American South may (or may not) be rethinking the role of women in society. On CNN, MSNBC, and Fox, all they talk about is politics. On *The McLaughlin Group*, they talk about *political science*. And—yes—I suppose it's the junk science version of political science, but it's still more engaging than the alternative. If you watch *The McLaughlin Group* for a month, you will undoubtedly hear at least one conceptual conversation about the merits of isolationism. If James Monroe were alive today, this is the program he would TiVo.

On the day I attended a *McLaughlin Group* taping, the thrust of the episode was about Mitt Romney's speech on how faith would impact his potential presidency, and McLaughlin's entry query was, "Did Romney dispel doubts about his Mormonism?" In the context of a normal public affairs show, it would seem like this was a question about how religion would impact his likelihood of winning the GOP nomination. But that point was barely mentioned; what actually transpired was an insane debate over the role of secularism and

whether or not the Garden of Eden is located in Missouri, punctuated by Lawrence O'Donnell saying, "Look, Romney comes from a
religion founded by a criminal who was anti-American, pro-slavery,
and a rapist." Oddly, O'Donnell's credibility for making this statement was partially based on his involvement with HBO's *Big Love*.
But at least he was forwarding an *idea*. At least he was talking about
what something means, as opposed to why something might have
happened.

III. Within any random group, the smartest guy is the funniest guy.

While visiting the *McLaughlin Group* set, I was able to talk with
everybody involved . . . except for John McLaughlin. When I arrived
at the studio, he was locked away in a secret room, preparing his bizarre elocutions. The moment the taping concluded, he jumped in a
town car, was driven to Reagan airport, and flew to Florida. Our
only interaction was a handshake, ninety seconds before airtime—he
shook my hand and asked his assistant, "Who's this guy?" It was like
shaking hands with a bipedal owl. It was the best celebrity encounter
of my journalistic career.

McLaughlin's oversight on *The McLaughlin Group* is akin to Vla-
dimir Putin's oversight in Russia: There is no chain of command. He
runs everything. He decides who appears on the show, he decides
what they talk about, and he dictates the dialogue. Buchanan (who
has known him since 1970, when McLaughlin was still a Jesuit priest)
calls him a "benevolent dictator." I never really met the guy, so I can't
say if he's mostly friendly or mostly abrasive. But I do know this:
Now that *Arrested Development* has been canceled and Will Arnett is
off the air, John McLaughlin is the funniest man on television. Has
anyone ever generated so much entertainment from the rudimentary
process of loudly asking questions? Sometimes his material is average,

but his delivery is never in question. He is the best nonsensical talker in contemporary broadcasting.

After shaking my hand, McLaughlin takes his place on the set. The four panelists are already waiting for him. They briefly discuss *The Drudge Report*; for some reason, McLaughlin inexplicably compares himself to a whirling dervish while quasi-flirting with short-skirted conservative talk show host Monica Crowley. This is followed by an exchange between Buchanan and McLaughlin, the latter suggesting that Irishmen were born with web feet because they had to swim to the U.S. from Canada. It appears that this is the normal way they interact. A producer yells at McLaughlin to straighten his tie; her request is completely ignored. He does not seem to care that this conversation will be broadcast on TV. McLaughlin and Buchanan continue talking, first about Jack Germond[2] and then about what time of day the Internet becomes available to the public.[3] Suddenly, the producer starts counting down from five. McLaughlin still ignores her. She silently flashes him three fingers, then two fingers. He does not appear to recognize her efforts. But then—without warning, and with limitless confidence—he swivels his head toward the camera and yells, "Issue One!"

This is how it begins.

—*February 2008*

---

2. Portly, cantankerous Germond was a key component of the show—and often its voice of reason—for its first fourteen years (1982 to 1996). Since his departure, Germond has been critical of *The McLaughlin Group*'s format.

3. !

Use Your Illusion
(but Don't Bench Ginóbili)

L ast week, the Miami Heat defeated the San Antonio Spurs 105–100 in a nationally televised game that people argued over way more than they watched. It spawned one of those pretend controversies we need in order to sustain a twenty-four-hour news cycle: Spurs coach Gregg Popovich elected to not dress four of his best players (Tim Duncan, Tony Parker, Manu Ginóbili, and Danny Green) so that they could rest their legs at the end of a four-game, five-night road trip. This outraged NBA commissioner David Stern, who fined the club $250,000 for committing a "disservice to the league and our fans." The initial debate was straightforward: Is it acceptable for the commissioner to penalize a coach for not playing the players fans want to see? People and pundits[1] were split. And once that split occurred, a bunch of not-so-meaningful mini-arguments were forwarded within the court of public opinion. These smaller, less important debates focused on the following:

---

1. Mostly just pundits, actually.

1. Should it matter that Popovich is the most respected coach in the league (and therefore warrants special treatment)?
2. Would it have made a difference if the Spurs had still won the game (which they almost did)?
3. Is the NBA schedule too taxing?
4. Is Stern unnecessarily draconian?
5. Was Popovich simply trying to poke the bear?
6. Would this have been less problematic if Popovich had warned the league of his decision in advance?
7. Did ticket-buyers in Miami deserve a refund?
8. What responsibility does Popovich have to TNT (the network that broadcast the game and lost viewers because of who wasn't playing)?
9. How is this different from teams that tank games at the end of the year in order to qualify for the draft lottery?

I would respond to those nine questions with the following nine answers: "sort of," "yes," "not really," "usually," "yes," "no," "no," "more than most people realize," and "not at all." But these mini-questions were not the interesting part of this problem. In fact, I suspect those minor issues were mostly being analyzed as a way to avoid the deeper question this conflict demands, because that question is too big to reasonably confront.

The question is this: What are we really doing here?

This is not an existential question about life on earth. This is a question about purpose and utility, applied to a concept intrinsically containing neither. When a dilapidated version of the Spurs plays the Heat in late November, what is actually at stake? What is the central purpose of pro sports, and how much of that purpose is solely tied to entertainment? It's a complicated question that keeps folding back upon itself: In order for a Spurs–Heat game to be entertaining, it has to be competitive; in order for the game to be competitive, the outcome has to matter; in order for the outcome of a regular-season NBA game in November to mean anything, the outcome of the NBA title has to mean a lot. And if we're going to accept the premise that the outcome of the NBA finals is authentically *important* (and that it truly matters who wins), this whole experience needs to be more than mere casual entertainment.

Popovich is a beloved, admired coach who appears unconcerned with the entertainment requirements of basketball (which is how most serious fans insist they want him to behave). He's exclusively concerned with real competition over the long term, particularly in the month of June; everything else is a distraction. Stern's rebuttal is that pro basketball only exists because pro basketball is fun to watch (and if you ignore its entertainment import, the rest of this will all disappear). He's concerned with short-term competition on a night-to-night basis, which translates into an entertaining product overall.

The dissonance between Popovich and Stern is what forces my question. If what makes sports entertaining is the degree to which the games matter, should we value competition above all other factors, even if doing so occasionally makes things *less* entertaining? Because that's what happened in Miami.

ON SUNDAYS, I watch NFL RedZone, so I don't see any commercials. But when I watch college football on Saturdays, I see about two hundred of them on a loop, one of which is an attempt by AT&T to sell me a new phone service. Here is the story this commercial sells: We see a high school football player involved in a marginally crazy play during practice, captured on the phone of an anonymous peer who likes to invent unoriginal catchphrases. The footage goes viral and the player becomes famous—so famous that he gets recruited by Oklahoma football coach Bob Stoops, apparently because Stoops needs more undersized tailbacks who can flip 360 degrees and continue downfield. It's a modern concept, informed by modern values. It has nothing to do with the experience of competition. It's not like the kid wins the city championship and is able to reexperience that victory through his parents' smart phone; it's a celebrity-driven narrative that suggests technology has the power to make a player You-Tube famous from one random moment that didn't even happen in a real game (which, of course, is totally possible). It's the new way to dream about sports.

I hate this commercial. It's glib and insidious. However, I only hate it because it's fiction. I hate that someone at AT&T figured out a way to monetize the fact that high school football players care more about themselves than they care about football (which has probably always been the case, truth be told). And here's what's really stupid: I wouldn't hate it if it happened in reality. If a real kid got a scholarship to Oklahoma because of this type of scenario, I would be charmed. Anytime a real athlete's individual performance outshines the unsophisticated concept of winning or losing, I love it. His or her motives are almost an afterthought. I only find it troubling when the scenario is fake. Fiction is always more real to me.

Just before Thanksgiving, a Division III basketball player for Grinnell College scored 138 points in one game. The player, Jack Taylor, went 52 of 108 from the field; the rest of his team spent the entire game relentlessly feeding him the ball so that he could launch trey after trey after trey (their next highest scorer had 13 points). Grinnell uses a "system" where they full-court press the whole game and concede lay-ups if the press is broken (a player for Grinnell's opponent that night, Faith Baptist Bible College, had 70 points himself). When I read about this game the next day, I was ecstatic. I've often wondered how many points a basketball player could score if that was the *only* goal, and this is the closest we've come; the fact that Taylor shot only 48 percent from the floor makes me think the real number is closer to 175. I didn't see any downside to this event, mostly because (a) it occurred in a game that meant almost nothing, and (b) the statistical absurdity of the total kept the accomplishment from seeming more important than it was. It was fascinating, but nothing more. Personally, I'd be happy if this became a trend in the low end of Div. III basketball. I'd like to see a space race to 200 points.

My reaction, however, was not universally shared. Almost every major news report about this game was tinged with mild distaste: It was cheap, it was galling, it was a gimmick to get on *SportsCenter*, etc. I strongly disagree with those reactions. I don't see why it would have been better for Grinnell and Faith Baptist to play a 54–51 game that would be totally lost to history. I wouldn't want every basketball game to be like this, but that's not a real risk. It strikes me as rather stupid to be upset that some random kid scored 138 points in a basketball game that no one would have known about otherwise. It was a cool explosion. But then I thought about this performance in a different way: What if this game had been an AT&T commercial? What if I saw a commercial where a basketball team sacrificed every traditional, competitive impulse so that one kid could score every single point, and this was celebrated as a brilliant way to demonstrate the power of a 4G network? I'm sure I would hate it. And I would hate it because it would force me to consider what I'm *supposed* to like about sports, as opposed to just watching the games and feeling good.

PERHAPS YOU THINK this is an imaginary problem. Perhaps you say, "Just don't worry about it and the problem will disappear." Maybe so. But the conflict keeps coming up in weird ways. The most consistent trouble spot involves the rise of advanced statistics, and specifically how much we need to care about them.

Right now, in pro football, there is strong statistical evidence that insists teams should punt less often on fourth down (even if it's 4th and 4 and they're at midfield). Some of the merits behind this metric are irrefutable and some are harder to accept.[2] But if you're one who believes that this axiom *must* be embraced for its mathematical veracity, it probably means the reason you're watching football is that you really, really care about the outcome. That's why you're watching the game. It means you believe offensive and defensive coordinators should make all their decisions based on rational probability, almost like they're simulating the game on a computer (and if they make these same rational decisions ten thousand times, they will succeed more often than they fail, which should be the ultimate goal). It means you believe the most important thing about a football game is

---

2. I like when teams go for it on fourth down, and I support any reasoning for doing so. I believe it's (probably) a winning strategy. But there's something about the overwhelming mathematical logic of going for it on 4th and 4 at midfield that doesn't seem complete to me. I'm assuming someone in the comments will explain to me why I'm wrong about this (and I won't disagree if you do), but—as of yet—no one has adequately convinced me of why my counterargument is flawed. Here's my confusion: The reasoning behind going for it on fourth down is built on a specific calculation, designed to amplify the "base rate on success." I do not doubt these calculations. However, isn't part of the reason the numbers suggest going for it on fourth down at least partially due to the fact that almost no one regularly does so? Statistics aren't predictive; they can only show us what happened in the past. So if going for it on 4th and 4 at midfield is still a relative rarity, isn't the available data for its rate of success questionable? And isn't it buoyed by the specific situations in which it occurs? I mean, what kind of team tends to go for it on 4th and 4 from midfield? It generally seems like teams who are desperate (and sometimes facing a prevent defense) or teams who feel confident that they have the personnel and the play-calling acumen to succeed (most notably the Patriots). But let's say *every* team started doing this, all the time (which appears to be what the stat-heads want). Won't the base rate of success drastically change in potentially unexpected ways? Or let's say only three NFL teams suddenly decide they're going to apply this theory wholesale, but those three teams are the Browns, the Chiefs, and the Jaguars. Wouldn't this wreck the metric? Or would it somehow prove it? Why do I find myself suspecting that if absolutely everyone started going for it on fourth down, advanced statisticians would respond by telling teams they should consider punting?

who wins and who loses, which is fine. Except that it makes the whole endeavor pointless and a little sad. For sports to matter at all, they have to matter more than that; they have to offer more cultural weight than merely deciding if Team A is better than Team B. If they don't, we're collectively making a terrible investment of our time, money, and emotion.

This is why the recent Spurs-Heat situation mattered—it raises real questions regarding what we're supposed to care about when we watch thirty-year-old millionaires participating in a schoolyard game with made-up rules. What matters is not the outcome of Miami–San Antonio, but how important that outcome was to begin with.

So within this debacle, who was justified? Who was on the right side?

My natural, nonthinking inclination is to side with Gregg Popovich. It seems like a head coach should have autonomy over how he runs his team. If Popovich believes the Spurs' likelihood of winning an NBA title is better served by resting Duncan and Ginóbili in November, I believe he's probably right. I am emotionally motivated to side with him, because his reasoning makes it seem like sports are more important than the people watching them on TV (which is what I want to feel).

Yet—in my head—I know that David Stern is right.

There was a period in my life when I thought Stern was a genius, and then another period when I thought he was hurting basketball more than he was helping it. I suspect he'd be a terrible person to work for, or with. But now that he's a year from retirement, I've come to realize his primary achievement represents the most important thing any sports commissioner can do—he always made it clear that someone was in charge. His edicts are sometimes infuriating, but they're always enforced for the same motive. He sees the biggest possible picture. Stern holds an inflexible vision of how the NBA should operate, and he's never wavered. And though he would (probably) never admit this directly, his vision of how the league is supposed to exist can be understood through his fining of the Spurs for insubordination: The NBA will always provide the *illusion* of competitiveness, which fans will unconsciously accept as viable entertainment. If you turn on an NBA game, you will see the game that you expect (and you will be able to pretend that it's exactly the game you desire). You will get what you think you want, and any question about what that should (or should not) be will not factor into the equation. And if it does, somebody will get fined $250,000.

So that's what's really going on here.

—*December 2012*

The Drugs Don't Work
(Actually, They Work Great)

Shawne Merriman weighs 272 pounds. This is three pounds less than ex–Cincinnati Bengal Anthony Muñoz, the most dominating left tackle of all time. Shawne Merriman also runs the 40-yard dash in 4.61 seconds. When Jerry Rice attended the NFL draft combine in 1985, he ran a 4.60. Rice would go on to gain over 23,000 all-purpose yards while scoring 207 career touchdowns.

You do not need Mel Kiper's hard drive to deduce what these numbers mean: As an outside linebacker, Shawne Merriman is almost as big as the best offensive tackle who ever played and almost as fast as the best wide receiver who ever played. He is a rhinoceros who moves like a deer. Common sense suggests this combination should not be possible. It isn't. Merriman was suspended from the San Diego Chargers for four games last season after testing positive for the anabolic steroid nandrolone. He argues this was the accidental result of a tainted nutritional supplement. "I think two out of ten people will always believe I did something intentional or still think I'm doing something," Merriman has said. If this is what he believes, no one will ever accuse him of pragmatism. Virtually everyone who follows football assumes Merriman knowingly used drugs to turn himself into the kind of hitting machine who can miss four games and still record 17 sacks. He has been caught and penalized, and the public shall forever remain incredulous of who he is and what he does.

The public knows the truth.

And knowing that truth, the public will return to ignoring this conundrum almost entirely.

The public will respond by renewing their subscription for the NFL Sunday Ticket, where they will regularly watch dozens of 272-pound men accelerate at speeds that would have made them Olympic sprinters during the 1950s. This, it seems, is the contemporary relationship most people have with drugs and pro football: unconditional distrust of anyone who tests positive, balanced by an unconscious willingness to overlook all the other physical impossibilities they see all the time. This is understandable; socially, sports serve an escapist purpose. Football players are real people, but they exist in a constructed nonreality. Within the context of any given game, nobody cares how a certain linebacker grew so big while remaining so fast. When a tailback breaks 77 yards for a touchdown, nobody says, "That was an incredible run. I wonder how he became the person who he is?" Part of what makes football successful is its detachment from day-to-day life—for three hours, it subsists in a vacuum. However, that detachment is going to become more complicated in the coming years, mostly because reality is evolving (and becoming harder to block out). And the Evolved Reality is this: It's starting to look like a majority of the NFL is on drugs.

As a consequence, you will have to make some decisions.

Not league commissioner Roger Goodell.

You.

IN 2006, a Pittsburgh physician named Richard A. Rydze purchased $150,000 of testosterone and human growth hormone over the Internet. This is not against the law. However, Rydze is a team doctor for the Pittsburgh Steelers. He says he never prescribed any of those drugs to members of the Steelers, and I cannot prove otherwise. But the Steelers' relationship with performance enhancers has been complicated for a long time; linebacker Steve Courson (now deceased) admitted using steroids in 1985, and former Saints coach Jim Haslett said he did the same when he played for Pittsburgh during the 1980s.

Shortly after going to the Super Bowl in 2004, several members of the Carolina Panthers were implicated in a steroid scandal involving Dr. James Shortt. One of these players was punter Todd Sauerbrun. Do not mitigate the significance of this point: *The punter was taking steroids*. The punter had obtained syringes and injectable stanozolol, the same chemical Ben Johnson used before the 1988 Olympics. This is not to suggest that punters are not athletes, nor I am overlooking how competitive the occupation of punting must be; I'm merely pointing out that it's kind of crazy to think punters would be taking steroids that defensive tackles somehow don't want. We all concede that steroids, human growth hormone, and blood doping help people ride bicycles faster through the French Alps. Why do we even *momentarily* question how much impact they must have on a game built entirely on explosion and power?

"People may give a certain amount of slack to football players because there's this unspoken sense that, in order to play the game well, you need an edge," USC critical studies professor Todd Boyd told the *Los Angeles Times* last month. Boyd has written several books about sports, race, and culture. "That's what people want in a football player: Someone who's crazy and mean." It's a subtle paradox: People choose to ignore the relationship between steroids and the NFL *because* it's unquestionably the sport where steroids would have the biggest upside. But what will happen when such deliberate naiveté becomes impossible? Revelatory drug scandals tend to escalate exponentially (for proof, look at Major League Baseball and American track and field). It's possible that Merriman, Sauerbrun, and the other thirty-three players suspended by the NFL since 2002 are the exceptions; it seems far more plausible that they are not. We are likely on the precipice of a bubble that is going to burst, and everybody claims to know this. But if this is what we know, how are we supposed to feel? Does this invalidate the entire sport, or does it barely matter at all?

This is where things become complicated.

THE MOST IMPORTANT DATE in the history of rock music was August 28, 1964. This is the day Bob Dylan met the Beatles in New York's Delmonico hotel and got them high.

Obviously, a lot of people may want to disagree with this assertion, especially if they are teaching junior high health class. But the artistic evidence is hard to ignore: The introduction of marijuana altered the trajectory of the Beatles' songwriting, reconstructed their consciousness, and prompted them to make the most influential rock albums of all time. After the summer of 1964, the Beatles started taking serious drugs, and those drugs enhanced their musical performance. They just thought they were having a good time, but the results were astonishing. Though it may not have been their intent, the Beatles took *performance-enhancing drugs*. And this is germane to sports for one reason: Absolutely no one holds this against them. No one views *Rubber Soul* or *Revolver* as "less authentic" than the band's earlier albums, despite the fact that they would not (and probably could not) have been made by people who weren't on drugs.

Jack Kerouac wrote *On the Road* on a Dexedrine binge, yet nobody thinks that makes his novel less significant. Wall Street stockbrokers get jacked up on cocaine before going into the trading pit, but nobody questions the merit of their business acumen. Kindergartners eat Ritalin like candy, but nobody discounts the validity of their Candy Land performance. It's entirely possible you take 20 milligrams of Ambien the night before a difficult day at the office and then drink 32 ounces of coffee when you wake up (possibly with a mind-sharpening cigarette). Anytime a person takes drugs for purposes that aren't exclusively recreational (i.e., staring at a ceiling fan, renting *Planet of the Apes*, etc.), he or she is using them to do something at a higher level. And—yes—I realize there is a difference between caffeine and HGH. They are not the same. But there's an even greater difference between a morning of data processing and trying to cut block Shawne Merriman.

My point is not that all drugs are the same, or that drugs are awesome, or that the Beatles needed LSD to become the geniuses they already were. My point is that sports are unique in the way they're retrospectively colored by the specter of drug use. East Germany was an Olympic force during the 1970s and '80s; today, you can't mention East Germany's dominance without noting that its athletes were pumped full of Ivan Drago–esque chemicals. That relationship changes the meaning of their achievement. You simply don't see this in other idioms. Nobody looks back at Pink Floyd's *Dark Side of the Moon* and says, "I guess this music is okay, but it doesn't really count. Those guys were obviously high in the studio."

Now, the easy rebuttal to this argument is contextual; it's not as if

Roger Waters was shooting up with Anadrol in order to strum his guitar strings *harder*. Unlike songwriting or stock trading, football is mostly physical, so it seems like there needs to be a different scale for what endangers competitive integrity. But how do we make that distinction? In all of these cases (sports-related and otherwise), people are putting foreign substances into their bodies in the hope of reaching a desired result. The motive is the same. What's different (and sometimes arbitrary) is how much people care. Baseball fans were outraged when Rafael Palmeiro took steroids; they remain generally indifferent to the fact that most of Major League Baseball regularly took amphetamines for forty years. A major steroid scandal would undoubtedly hurt the NFL, and fans would freak out; as a member of the Philadelphia Eagles in 1994, Bill Romanowski electively received two trauma IVs to help recover from injuries. Trauma IVs are what emergency room doctors connect to people dying from car accidents. In his autobiography, Romanowski claims one of his teammates received *six* trauma IVs in the span of a single season. This is natural?

I am told we live in a violent society. But even within that society, football players are singular. Another former Eagle, strong safety Andre Waters, committed suicide last November at the age of forty-four. A post-death examination of his brain tissue indicated that he had the neurological tissue of an eighty-five-year-old man with Alzheimer's, almost certainly the result of using his skull as a weapon for eleven seasons. Announcers casually lionize pro football players as "gladiators," but that modifier is more accurate than most would like to admit: For the sake of entertainment, we expect these people to be the fastest, strongest, most aggressive people on earth. If they are not, they make less money and lose their jobs.

It seems hypocritical to hate football players for taking steroids. We might hate them more if they did not.

AROUND THIS TIME LAST YEAR, I wrote an essay for ESPN about Barry Bonds, and specifically how steroids made his passing of Babe Ruth on the career home run list problematic. I still believe this to be true, just as I believe the notion of 40 percent (or whatever) of the NFL performing on juice is 80 percent (or whatever) bad. It would be easier to be a football fan if none of this had ever happened. But—since rewriting the passage of time is not an option—we will all have to decide how much this Evolved Reality is going to bother us. Over time, we won't be able to separate Merriman from the rest of the puzzle (which MLB has successfully done with Bonds). It won't be about the guilt of specific players. This will be more of an across-the-board dilemma: We will have to publicly acknowledge that the most popular sport in the country has been kinetically dictated by drugs, probably for the past twenty-five years. I have no idea if the NFL will ever accept that view, and I have no idea how they would respond if they did. In many ways, the league's reaction barely matters. What matters more is how fans will attempt to reconcile that realization with their personal feelings toward the game. The question, essentially, is this: If it turns out that the totality of the NFL is unnatural, does this make the game less meaningful?

The answer depends on who you are. And maybe how old you are.

In 1982, I read a Herschel Walker photo essay in *Sports Illustrated* titled "My Body's Like an Army." It explained how—at the time— Walker didn't even lift weights; instead, he did 100,000 sit-ups and 100,000 push-ups a year, knocking out twenty-five of each every time a commercial came on the television. This information made me worship Herschel. It made him seem human and superhuman at the same time. "My Body's Like an Army" simultaneously indicated that I could become Herschel Walker, but that I could *never* become

Herschel Walker. He was beyond who I was, even though his physical perfection was self-generated and pure. He had made himself better than other mortals, and that made me love him.

But I was ten years old.

There comes a point in every normal person's life when they stop looking at athletes as models for living. Any thinking adult who follows pro sports understands that certain owners are corrupt and that the games don't really matter and money drives everything. It would be stranger if they did *not* realize these things. But what's equally strange is the way so many fans (and seemingly all sportswriters, myself included) revert back to their ten-year-old selves whenever an issue like steroids shatters the surface. Most of the time, we don't care what football players do when they're not playing football. On any given Wednesday, we have only a passing interest in who they are as people or how they choose to live. But Sunday is different. On Sunday, they are supposed to be super-fast, super-strong, super-entertaining, and—weirdly—super-ethical. More ethical than the rest of us. They are supposed to be pristine 272-pound men who run 40 yards in 4.61 seconds, simply because they did sit-ups during the commercial breaks for *Grey's Anatomy*. Unlike everybody else in America, they cannot do "whatever it takes" to succeed; they have to fulfill the unrealistic expectations of ten-year-old kids who read magazines. And this is because football players have a job that doesn't matter at all, except in those moments when it matters more than absolutely everything else.

It may be time to rethink some of this stuff.

—Summer 2007

The City That Time Remembered (Tulsa, Oklahoma)

All my life, I've wanted to stop time. I see no value in the future, and I suspect every technological advance since the advent of the gramophone has been—on balance—detrimental to the human race.[1] Our slow erosion of authentic consciousness will never stop, and there is nothing we can do about it.

Of course, this opinion is based on anecdotal evidence. I can't prove any of it, and I wouldn't even know how to try.

As such, it's possible that my opinion is wrong. I certainly hope that it is. If I have learned anything from existence, it is (probably) this: It is more lucrative to write about why things are good than about why things are bad, chiefly because the former is so much more complicated than the latter. Moreover, I cannot deny my perpetual enslavement to the very elements of modernity that I bemoan; for the purposes of my own psychological security, it would be nice to believe that "progress" is actually *progress*, even though it (usually) is not.

This is a story about slowly flying to Tulsa and not seeing a car.

---

1. A key exception: air-conditioning.

Getting There

In June 1957, the community of Tulsa buried a Plymouth Belvedere in a downtown concrete bunker beneath the Oklahoma topsoil. The car would act as the public vortex for a time capsule that would be unearthed five decades later. It would also be the grand prize in a stridently futuristic contest: During the summer of its entombment, various local citizens were given the opportunity to guess what the population of Tulsa would be in 2007.[2] Whoever was closest (and was—presumably—still alive) would win the (now classic) car, along with several barrels of gasoline and oil. It appears that people in 1957 weren't sure if gas and oil would still be popular half a century later. This is how optimistic Americans used to be: We used to imagine that cars of the future would probably run on uranium, potato peels, and distilled water.

It was this optimism that drew me to Tulsa. The motive behind any time capsule is inherently positive—at worst, it suggests some kind of (non–robot dominated) future will, at the very least, exist. Cynics don't bury cars in the ground. The excavation was scheduled for June 15 of this year; it was the linchpin for an event unironically titled "Tulsarama." I left for Tulsa on June 14. Unfortunately, I elected to travel via Northwest Airlines. The problems start immediately: My plane out of LaGuardia Airport sits motionless for almost an hour, causing me to miss a connecting flight in Detroit. The airline redirects me to Minneapolis, but that flight is also delayed; when I arrive in Minnesota, I miss another connection and find myself forced to stay overnight. I return to the airport the following morning for a 5:58 flight (to Memphis!), but the plane doesn't take off until 7:40.

---

2. 382,457, roughly triple what it was in '57.

No explanation is given. This causes me to miss another connection, so I sit in the Memphis airport[3] for four hours. My ultimate flight to Tulsa is also late, so I miss the excavation entirely. That fucking car was in the ground for fifty fucking years, and I still couldn't get there on time. It's too bad the 9/11 terrorists did not patronize Northwest Airlines; they undoubtedly would have been stranded in Logan International Airport until they all collectively renounced Islam.

When I finally arrive in Tulsa, the city is abuzz over Tulsarama, at least judging from the front page of the *Tulsa World*. Almost every hotel is filled to capacity. However, there's now a shared grimness regarding the condition of the Plymouth Belvedere: Several feet of water have seeped into the vault, coating the vehicle in rust and grime. They remove it from its watery tomb, but there is no possible way the engine will turn over. Still, people are trying to stay positive. "This is nobody's fault," a seventy-three-year-old man named Jim Sosebee tells me as we share a cab ride downtown. Now living in Texas, Sosebee had been an Oklahoma Marine when he attended the car's funeral in 1957. "Back in those days, nobody knew nothing about waterproofing a concrete vault."

I assume this man knows what he's talking about, but I'm still a little surprised by this revelation. Waterproofing a concrete vault seems *exactly* like something people would have understood fifty years ago.

Being There

Having missed everything except Saturday night's Tulsarama Sock-Hop (Fabian, Bobby Vee, and the Chiffons are scheduled to

---

3. Excellent pork ribs there, though. I could gain a lot of weight in this airport.

perform), I decide to find a bar and drink until my situation improves. This is harder than one might anticipate; taverns don't seem to exist here. I have lived in some of the least exhilarating cities in America, but Tulsa is almost like urban sarcasm. Tulsa makes Akron seem like Las Vegas (and I lived in Fargo, so I can say this). It's Friday night, but every downtown street is a reenactment of the opening ten minutes from *28 Days Later*. All the avenues have names like "Denver" and "Detroit" and "Cincinnati," as if those cities are theoretical, unattainable utopias. The townsfolk are incredibly nice, but the emptiness is relentless (and kind of terrifying). I can't fathom what things are like here when they're *not* having a festival.

After forty-five minutes of meandering, I finally find a restaurant called Tsunami Sushi, just up the street from a dive bar called Dirty's and another called 1974. There is a super-thin kid outside the sushi restaurant, wearing an apron and smoking a cigarette. His name is Eli, he's nineteen, he sports an undecided beard, and he's on break from his job as a cook. We talk a little about the '57 Belvedere and the town that buried it.

"I hate Tulsa, but only because I live here," says Eli, the kind of sentiment anyone who comes from anywhere can instantly understand. "Still, there are some good things about living here. I love working at Tsunami's, for example. The people who work here are hella cool. And Tulsa has some awesome underground tunnels. Huge, train-sized tunnels. They're amazing."

I don't know what this means,[4] so I ask him how he views the future. I ask him what he thinks the world will be like in 2057.

"I'm pretty pessimistic," he says. "The way America spends its money, the way we are hated around the world . . . I don't know if

---

4. It is speculated that these tunnels (now used for tourism) were originally used by bootleggers during Prohibition.

there will ever be an all-out war,[5] but people are walking around angry."

I ask him when (or how) America went wrong. Curiously, he says, "Disco." Considering that this kid was born eleven years after the release of *Saturday Night Fever*, I find his thesis intriguing. "It was terrible music," he explains. "And it was all flash. It was just something to make stupid people happy. And after that, things only got worse." Eli finishes his cigarette and we shake hands. He goes back inside to work. I continue to sit on a bench outside the restaurant, staring at a barren street.

Two minutes later, a different nineteen-year-old comes outside for five minutes of smoking.

This kid's name is Levi.[6] He's a busboy with a ponytail. And unlike Eli, he *adores* Tulsa. He will never leave. "I love it here," says Levi. "In my opinion, it's the world's biggest little city. I know they say that about Reno, but they should say it about Tulsa. This is kind of a hard thing to explain, but there is so much action here—it's just that there's nothing to do."

I know exactly what he means by this (like I said, I used to live in Fargo). When I ask Levi about his vision for the future, he insists that he's very optimistic. But when I ask him why, his reasoning is confusing: He starts talking about how high the per capita murder rate is,[7] and about all the problematic issues with Tulsa's exploding Hispanic population. He tells me, "Every street in this town is dangerous at one a.m. Every single one." Why, I ask, would these things make him enthusiastic? "Tulsa is growing like crazy," he says. "It's headed in the

---

5. I think he means a nuclear war.
6. I have not made these names up. For whatever the reason, employees of Tsunami Sushi have names like *Deadwood* characters.
7. Tulsa had fifty-six murders in 2006. This was actually a slight decrease from 2005, when they had sixty-four.

right direction." And then his cancer stick is extinguished, and Levi returns to busing tables.

Obviously, these are just two nineteen-year-olds, chosen in a manner that's less than random. Neither is a metaphor for anything. But I want to point something out: One of these teenagers was pessimistic about the future, even though he was enjoying the present and despondent about the past. The other was optimistic about tomorrow, despite the fact that his description of today was terrible.

It took me a while to figure out which person I could relate to more. I'm still not sure.

Leaving There

Not wanting to be on any street after one a.m., I find a taxi to take me to my hotel. The driver is forty-nine years old and resembles vampire novelist Anne Rice. I mention what Levi had said about the murder rate.

"That's all true," she says as her car radio plays "Escape (The Piña Colada Song)" and a track off the second Bad Company album. "I don't feel safe in my own home. They will come right into your house and kill you. I wish they would all just kill each other off, because that's all they know." At first, I'm pretty sure I know who *they* are supposed to be, so our conversation becomes a little uncomfortable. But then she starts talking about attending a recent Kool and the Gang concert at a casino, so who knows? I am in no position to judge this woman.

Up in my hotel room, I turn on the television. It appears I have missed the first eight minutes of the local news, so—once again—I don't see any footage of the goddamn rusted Belvedere. Its existence mocks me, even as I consume room service pasta. I notice that

Showtime is airing *Basic Instinct 2*, and Sharon Stone suddenly strikes me as the human equivalent of the '57 Plymouth: an iconic creation that was once glamorous and futuristic, but who now only reminds us of a slightly better, slightly weirder past (particularly during those moments when we try to jam her back into the living present). Stone was born less than one year after the burial of this Belvedere. All things considered, I suppose she's held up considerably better than the car. No water damage, at least.

I don't know why I believe the world is getting worse. It seems like it obviously must be, but I've been wrong before. If "nostalgia" is remembering the past as better than it actually was, what word is its opposite? What word describes inaccurately imagining a future that will be worse than logic dictates? Whatever it is, I need less of it. And Northwest Airlines needs more.

—October 2007

But What If We're Wrong?
(Drink the Acid,
Swallow the Mouse)

I t has been brought to my attention that Mountain Dew can dissolve a mouse.

This information comes not from some rival beverage critic, but from PepsiCo itself: In an attempt to get out of a lawsuit, the manufacturers of Mountain Dew are suggesting that—if a mouse were somehow trapped inside a bottle of Dew—the rodent would be turned into a gelatinous, unrecognizable blob. If true, such evidence would contradict the accusation of Ronald Ball, a Wisconsin man who claims to have purchased a Mountain Dew at a vending machine and found a dead mouse inside the bottle.

As someone who's consumed 32 to 64 ounces of Mountain Dew almost every single day for the past twenty-one years, I found this news unnecessarily salacious. I've experienced no ill effects whatsoever from my Mountain Dew consumption, except that I'm kind of fat and pretty crazy and I can never sleep (even though I'm always tired). I'm sipping one right now, and it's making me invincible. I'm not gonna lie—I feel awesome. I feel more awesome than you, in all probability. Which prompts me to consider a counternarrative to this atypical Mountain Dew controversy: How do we know it's *not* good for us to drink mouse-dissolving acid?

If you're a serious Mountain Dew drinker, you're probably also the eater of many processed, nonorganic foods. Perhaps you're also a compulsive worrier and a functioning alcoholic. Maybe you sometimes eat things that aren't technically food, like napkins (a surprisingly easy mistake to make, particularly when eating a hot dog inside an unusually dark movie theater in suburban Atlanta). There's just no way the natural gastric acid inside your stomach can compete with today's ultra-aggressive, hypermodern "super foods." Your tummy needs a supplement. And that's where Mountain Dew thrives. With its advanced mouse-eroding electrolytes, Mountain Dew can destroy what your body cannot. You know what I never get? I never get food poisoning. Ever. I don't get food poisoning *when I eat poison*. And there's no way this is a coincidence. There's something sloshing around inside me that generates a secret kind of power, and that something is green and sweet and designed for extreme skateboard enthusiasts. I will never stop drinking Mountain Dew. I don't care if it starts dissolving the very aluminum cans that house its existential refreshment. I will live forever, or at least until I'm forty-five.

Also, semi-related: Fuck you, Ronald Ball. Maybe liquefied mice are delicious?

—January 4, 2012

Never Love Anyone
Who Treats You Like
You're Ordinary

Times change, and you have to change with them, even when the changes are dumb.

Something you may notice in the following 2015 feature on Taylor Swift is that I never describe what she looks like or how she was dressed, even though I almost always do that with any celebrity I cover. Around the same time my piece was published in *GQ*, two other high-profile articles on female pop stars ran in *The New York Times*: a Nicki Minaj feature by Vanessa Grigoriadis and a reported magazine essay on Rihanna by Miranda July. Grigoriadis noted that Minaj has "a shockingly beautiful and complex face, with a wide, high forehead [and] dark, almond-shaped eyes." July literally describes sniffing her own blouse hours after the interview in order to relish the remnant scent of Rihanna's perfume. These are visceral, vivid details. They're excellent details. But I would no longer write anything close to those passages, assuming the person I was profiling was female. If I did, it would be reframed as creepy misogyny and proof that I didn't take the woman seriously as an artist. It would derail everything else about the story. It would *become* the story.

This is part of the reason it's so much easier to write about old white guys: nobody gives a shit how you describe them.

Owner of a Lonely Heart

That's a pap," she says as we leave the restaurant, pointing toward an anonymous gray car that looks like the floor model in an auto dealership specializing in anonymous gray cars. Her security detail suggests that it's probably not a paparazzo and that there's no way a paparazzo could find us at a place so unglamorous and conventional. But, as with seemingly every other inference she has ever made, Taylor Swift is ultimately proven right. The guy in the gray car is taking her picture. This annoys her, but just barely.

It's August in Southern California. We crawl into the back of a massive Toyota and start driving to Swift's West Coast residence, located in a rural enclave of Beverly Hills. The gray car trails us through Franklin Canyon. Swift whips out her phone and starts showing me images from the video shoot for "Wildest Dreams," including a clip of a giraffe licking her face. She has more photos on her phone than any person I've ever met. "I wanted this video to be about the making of a 1950s movie being filmed on location in Africa," she explains. Swift came up with the concept after reading the semi-unauthorized biography of Ava Gardner *The Secret Conversations*. Her premise for the video (costarring Clint Eastwood's son) is that— since social media did not exist in the '50s—it would be impossible for actors not to fall in love with each other if they were isolated together in Africa, since there would be no one else to talk to.

We chat a little about Ryan Adams and a little about books. Swift mentions that she wrote a nonautobiographical novel when she was fourteen, titled *A Girl Named Girl*, and that her parents still have it. I ask her what it was about, assuming she will laugh. But her memory of the plot is remarkably detailed (it's about a mother who wants a son but instead has a girl), and if she released it today, it would immediately be the best-selling YA novel in the nation. When she was around that same age, Swift's family moved from Pennsylvania to Nashville, ostensibly to jump-start her music career. I ask what she imagines might have happened if they'd never moved and if she'd never become an artist. "I would still be involved with music in my spare time," she says. "But I would have gone to college and I would probably be involved with a form of business where words and ideas are at the forefront. Such as marketing." She returns to her phone and starts scrolling for an old voice memo she sent to Jack Antonoff of the band Bleachers while they were cowriting songs for *1989*. Antonoff's nickname for Swift is "Dead Tooth," a reference to a minor dental mishap. Just as she tells me this, her cell phone rings. The display panel says the incoming call is from J TIMB. "Oh my God. Justin Timberlake?" Her surprise does not seem artificial. "Can I take this?"

She takes the call. The volume on her phone is loud enough for me to intermittently hear both sides of the conversation. Swift explains that she's driving to her house, but that she can't actually stay there because contractors are renovating almost every room. "Have you ever seen the movie *The Money Pit*?" asks Timberlake. She has not, so Timberlake provides a capsule review. He has a four-month-old baby at home and is constantly tired, yet he can't fall asleep. He asks Swift for advice on sleeping. Swift tells the driver to pull over to the shoulder of the road, since she keeps losing reception as we drive through the canyon. The paparazzo in the gray car casually passes, having not-so-casually followed us for at least five miles.

The conversation lasts almost fifteen minutes (which is a little weird, since I'm just sitting there beside her, openly taking notes). "You're never going to get old," Swift assures Timberlake. "That's scientific fact. That's medical." Even her sarcasm is aspirational. Eventually J.T. tells her the reason he's calling is that he wants to perform the song "Mirrors" with her on the last night of her upcoming five-date stand at Staples Center. (Late in every concert, Swift brings a surprise guest onstage.) She reacts to this news the way a teenage girl in Nebraska would react if suddenly informed that a paternity test had revealed Taylor Swift was her biological sister.

When she ends the call, Swift looks at me and says, "This is so crazy. This is so crazy." She repeats that phrase four times, each time with ascending volume.

Now, inside my skull, I am thinking one thought: This is not remotely crazy. It actually seems like the opposite of crazy. Why *wouldn't* Justin Timberlake want to perform with the biggest entertainer in America, to an audience of twenty thousand people who will lose their collective mind the moment he appears? I'd have been much more surprised if he'd called to turn her down. But then I remember that Swift is twenty-five years old, and that her entire ethos is based on experiencing (and interpreting) how her insane life would feel if she were exactly like the type of person who'd buy a ticket to this particular concert. She has more perspective than I do. Every extension of who she is and how she works is (indeed) "so crazy," and what's even crazier is my inability to recognize just how crazy it is.

So Taylor Swift is right again.

IF YOU DON'T TAKE Swift seriously, you don't take contemporary music seriously. With the arguable exceptions of Kanye West and Beyoncé Knowles, she is the most significant pop artist of the modern age. The scale of her commercial supremacy defies parallel—she's sold 1 million albums in a week three times, within an era where most major artists are thrilled to move 500,000 albums in the span of a year. If a record as comparatively dominant as *1989* had actually existed in the year 1989, it would have surpassed the sales of *Thriller*. There is no demographic she does not tap into, which is obviously rare. But what's even more atypical is how that ubiquity is critically received. Swift gets universally excellent reviews, particularly from the most significant arbiters of taste (a 2012 *New Yorker* piece conceded that Swift's reviews are "almost uniformly positive"). She has never gratuitously sexualized her image and seems pathologically averse to controversy. There's simply no antecedent for this kind of career: a cross-genre, youth-oriented, critically acclaimed colossus where the success is exclusively based on the intuitive songwriting merits of a single female artist. It's like if mid-period Garth Brooks was also early Liz Phair, minus the hat and the swearing. As a phenomenon, it's absolutely new.

And this, somewhat predictably, creates a new set of problems.

Even within the most high-minded considerations of Swift's music, there is inevitably some analysis (or speculation) about her personal life. She's an utterly credible musician who is consumed as a tabloid personality. Very often (and not without justification), that binary is attributed to ingrained biases against female performers. But it's more complicated than that. Swift writes about her life so directly that the listener is forced to think about her persona in order to fully appreciate what she's doing creatively. This is her greatest power: an ability to combine her art and her life so profoundly that both spheres become more interesting to everyone, regardless of their emotional investment.

Swift clearly knows this is happening. But it's something she can't directly admit, because it's the kind of thing that only works when it seems coincidental. She's careful how she describes the process, because you don't become who she is by describing things carelessly.

Even the most serious critics inevitably discuss the more tabloid aspects of your life. Is this valid? Does the fact that you write about yourself in such a confessional style require intelligent people to look at your music through that lens?

I don't feel there is any injustice when people expand beyond my music and speculate on who certain songs might be about. I've never named names, so I feel like I still have a sense of power over what people say—even if that *isn't* true, and even if I don't have any power over what people say about me. The fact that I've never confirmed who those songs are about makes me feel like there is still one card I'm holding. So if you're going to look at your life and say, "I get to play sold-out football stadiums all over the world. I get to call up my favorite artists and ask them to perform with me, and most of the time they say yes. I get to be on the cover of this magazine"—this is all because I write songs about my own life. So I would feel a little strange complaining about that.

But I'm not asking if it's fair or unfair, or if the downside is worth the upside. I'm asking from an aesthetic perspective: Is thinking about your real life an essential part of appreciating your music? Could your music be enjoyed the same way in a vacuum, even if no one knew anything else about you?

"Shake It Off" is one of my most successful songs, and that has nothing directly, intricately, pointedly personal in it. No one really says I stay out too late. I just thought it sounded good.

Have you ever stopped yourself from writing a fictional lyric because you feared it would be incorrectly applied to your literal life?

No. Some of the things I write about on a song like "Blank Space" are satire. You take your creative license and create things that are larger than life. You can write things like, "I get drunk on jealousy but you'll come back each time I leave, because darling I'm a nightmare dressed as a daydream." That is *not* my approach to relationships. But is it cool to write the narrative of a girl who's crazy but seductive but glamorous but nuts but manipulative? That was the character I felt the media had written for me, and for a long time I felt hurt by it. I took it personally. But as time went by, I realized it was kind of hilarious.

It's impossible for an artist to control how she is perceived. But an artist can anticipate those perceptions, which is almost as good. "A nuanced sense of humor does not translate on a general scale," Swift says, "and I knew that going in. I knew some people would hear 'Blank Space' and say, *See, we were right about her.* But at this point, if you don't get the joke, you don't deserve to get the joke."

THERE'S A LONG TRADITION of musicians expressing (or pretending to express) a degree of disinterest in how they are metabolized by the culture. They claim to ignore their own reviews while feigning a lack of discernment about what their audience wants or expects, since these are things that cannot be controlled. Swift is not like this. She has an extrinsic focus that informs her creative process. From her perspective, not tracking how people view your work feels stranger than the alternative.

"I went through a few years when I just never went online and never looked at blogs. This was around 2013, when the only thing anyone wanted to write about me was about me and some guy," she recalls. "It was really damaging. Doesn't everyone go on dates when they're twenty-two? Nope. Not when you're in my situation, and everything you do is blown out of proportion and commented upon. And all of a sudden, there's an overriding opinion about who you are that doesn't reflect how you actually live your life. So I didn't go online for a year and a half. I actually forgot my Instagram password. But now I check in and see what's happening. In 2015, that stuff does matter. Because if enough people say the same thing about me, it becomes fact in the eyes of the general public. So I monitor what people say about me, and if I see a theme, I know what that means. I've had it happen twice before. In 2010, it was, *She's too young to get all these awards. Look how annoying she is when she wins things. Is she even good?* And then in 2013, it was, *She just writes songs to get revenge. She's boy crazy. She's a problematic person.* It will probably be something else again this year."

How you view this level of consciousness is proportional to how you feel about Swift as a public figure. There is a perpetual sense that nothing about her career is accidental and that nothing about her life is unmediated. These are not unusual things to think about young mainstream stars. But what's different with Swift is her autonomy. There is no Svengali directing her career; there is no stage mother pushing her toward the spotlight. She is in total control of her own constructed reality. If there was a machine that built humans out of millennial stereotypes, Swift would be its utopian creation.

"I used to watch *Behind the Music* every day," she says. (Her favorite episode was the one about the Bangles.) "When other kids were watching normal shows, I'd watch *Behind the Music*. And I would see these bands that were doing so well, and I'd wonder what went wrong. I thought about this a lot. And what I established in my brain was that a lack of self-awareness was always the downfall. That was always the catalyst for the loss of relevance and the loss of ambition and the loss of great art. So self-awareness has become such a huge part of what I think about. It's less about reputation management and strategy and vanity than it is about trying to desperately preserve my self-awareness, since that seems like the first thing to go the moment people achieve success."

The upside of this self-focused fixation is clear. Swift is allowed to make whatever record she wants, based on the reasonable argument that she understands her specific space in the culture more deeply than anyone around her. The making of *1989* is a prime example: She insists everyone at her label (the Nashville-based Big Machine) tried to convince her not to make a straightforward pop album. She recounts a litany of arguments with various label executives over every possible detail, from how much of her face would appear on the cover to how cowriter Max Martin would be credited in the liner notes.

As far as I can tell, Swift won every one of these debates.

"Even calling this record *1989* was a risk," she says. "I had so many intense conversations where my label really tried to step in. I could tell they'd all gotten together and decided, 'We gotta talk some sense into her. She's had an established, astronomically successful career in country music, and shaking that up would be the biggest possible mistake.' But to me, the safest thing I could do was take the biggest possible risk. I am confident that I can write a song. I'm not confident about a lot of other aspects of my life, but I know how to write songs. I'd read a review of [2012's] *Red* that said it wasn't sonically cohesive. So that was what I wanted on *1989*: an umbrella that would go over all of these songs, so that they all belonged on the same album. But then I'd go into the label office, and they were like, 'Can we talk about putting a fiddle and a steel guitar solo on "Shake It Off" to service country radio?' I was trying to make the most honest record I could possibly make, and they were kind of asking me to be a little disingenuous about it. 'Let's capitalize on both markets.' No, let's not. Let's pick a lane."

LIKE ALMOST ALL FAMOUS PEOPLE, Swift has two ways of speaking. The first is the way she talks when she's actively shaping the interview—optimistic, animated, and seemingly rehearsed (even when that's impossible). The second is the way she talks when she cares less about the way the words are presented and more about the message itself (chin slightly down, brow slightly furrowed, timbre slightly deeper). The first way is how she talks when she's on television; the second is more unequivocal and less animatronic. But she oscillates between the two styles fluidly, either because (a) this dissonance is less intentional than it appears or (b) she can tell I'm considerably more interested in anything delivered in the second style.

Late in our lunch, I mention something that happened several years ago: By chance, I'd found myself having dinner with a former acquaintance of Swift's who offhandedly described her as "calculating." This is the only moment during our interview when Swift appears remotely flustered. She really, really hates the word "calculating." She despises how it has become tethered to her iconography and believes the person I met has been the singular voice regurgitating this categorization. As she explains these things, her speech does not oscillate from the second mode.

"Am I shooting from the hip?" she asks rhetorically. "Would any of this have happened if I was? In a sense, I do think about things before they happen. But here was someone taking a good quality—the fact that I think about things and that I care about my work—and trying to make that into an insinuation about my personal life. Highly offensive. You can be accidentally successful for three or four years. Accidents happen. But careers take work."

Here we see Swift's circuitous dilemma: Any attempt to appear less calculating scans as even more calculated. Because Swift's professional career has unspooled with such precision, it's assumed that her social life is no less premeditated. This even applies to casual, non-romantic relationships. Over the past three years, Swift has built a volunteer army of high-profile friends, many of whom appear in her videos (for free) and serve as special guests at her concerts (for free). In almost any other circumstance, this would be seen as a likable trait; Leonardo DiCaprio behaved similarly in the '90s and everyone thought it was awesome. But it's somehow different when the hub of the wheel is Swift. People get skeptical. Her famous friends are marginalized as acquisitions, selected to occupy specific roles, almost like members of the Justice League ("the ectomorph model," "the inventive indie artist," "the informed third-wave feminist," etc.). Such perceptions perplex Swift, who is genuinely obsessed with these attachments. "I really think my lack of female friendships in high school and middle school is why my female friendships are so important now," she says. "Because I always wanted them. It was just hard for me to have friends."

It's not uncommon for popular people to claim they were once unpopular, so I ask Swift for a specific example. She tells a story about junior high, when she called several of her peers on the phone and asked if they wanted to go shopping. Every girl had a different excuse for why she couldn't go. Eventually, Swift's mother agreed to take her to the local mall. When they arrived, Swift saw all of the girls she had called on the phone, goofing around in Victoria's Secret. "I just remember my mom looking at me when this happened and saying, *'We're going to King of Prussia Mall, right now.'* Which is the biggest mall in Pennsylvania, forty-five minutes away. So we left and went to the better mall. My mom let me escape from certain things that were too painful to deal with. And we talked about it the whole way there, and we had a good time shopping."

This incident appears to be the genesis for a verse in her 2008 song "The Best Day," a connection she doesn't note when she tells me the story. A cynical person could read something into this anecdote and turn it into a metaphor about capitalism or parenting or creativity or Pennsylvania. But in the framework of our conversation, it did not seem metaphoric of anything. It just seemed like a (very real) memory that might be more internally motivating than ordinary logic would suggest.

So is it unfair to categorize Swift as "calculating"? Maybe, and particularly if you view that term as exclusively pejorative. But calling her "guileless" would be preposterous. Swift views her lyrics as the most important part of her art ("The lyrics are what I want you to focus on," she asserts), so we spend some time parsing specific passages from specific songs. Here is how she dissects that conjecture over "Bad Blood," a single universally assumed to be about Katy Perry.

You never say who your songs are about, but you concede that if enough people believe something it essentially becomes fact. So by not saying who you're writing about, aren't you allowing public consensus to dictate the meaning of your work? If everyone assumes that "Bad Blood" is about a specific person, aren't you allowing the culture to create a fact about your life?

You're in a *Rolling Stone* interview, and the reporter asks, "Who is that song about? That sounds like a really intense moment from your life." And you sit there, and you know you're on good terms with your ex-boyfriend, and you don't want him—or his family— to think you're firing shots at him. So you say, "That was about losing a friend." And that's basically all you say. But then people cryptically tweet about what you meant. I never pointed a finger in any specific direction, and I can sleep at night knowing that. I mean, I knew the song would be assigned to someone, and the easiest mark would be someone that song was definitely not about. It was not a song about heartbreak. It was about the loss of friendship.

But nobody thinks that song is about a guy.

But they would have. I didn't care who they thought that song was about. I just needed to divert them away from the easiest target. Listen to the song. It doesn't point to any one person or any one situation. But if you'd listened to my previous four albums, you would assume it was about a guy who broke my heart. And nothing could be further from the truth. It was important to show that losing friendships can be just as damaging to a person as losing a romantic relationship.

Now, there are more than a few molecules of bullshit in this response. When Swift says, *"And that's basically all you say,"* she's neglecting to mention she also told the reporter that the disharmony stemmed from a business conflict, and that the individual in question sabotaged an arena tour by hiring away some of her employees. These details dramatically reduce the pool of potential candidates. Yet consider the strategy's larger brilliance: In order to abort the possibility of a rumor she did not want, she propagated the existence of a different rumor that offered the added value of making the song more interesting.

Swift can manufacture the kind of mythology that used to happen to Carly Simon by accident.

SPEAKING OF ACCIDENTS, here's some breaking news: They happen to Taylor Swift, too. She believes the most consequential accident of her professional life was when Kanye West famously stormed the stage during her acceptance speech at the 2009 MTV Video Music Awards. I'm surprised when she brings this up unprompted, because she hasn't addressed the incident itself in five years, outside of the (comically undisguised) song "Innocent." But fences have been mended and feelings have been felt. At this summer's VMAs, Swift warmly presented West with the Video Vanguard trophy. She'll probably serve as secretary of the interior when he becomes president.

Swift was lauded for handling West's '09 intrusion with grace and composure. But her personal memories of the event dwell on the bewilderment. When West first jumped onstage, Swift halfway assumed he was about to make a special presentation, honoring her for being the first country artist to ever win a VMA. She truly had no idea what was transpiring. "When the crowd started booing, I assumed they were booing because they also believed I didn't deserve the award. That's why I was hurt. I went backstage and cried, and then I had to stop crying and perform five minutes later. I just told myself I had to perform, and I tried to convince myself that maybe this wasn't that big of a deal. But that was definitively the most hap-penstance thing to ever happen in my career. And to now be in a place where Kanye and I are friends—that was one of the *best* moments of my career."[1]

Swift references friendship so frequently that I eventually ask what seems like an obvious question: Does she ever feel lonely? She responds by literally talking about *Friends*. "I'm around people so much," she says. "And massive amounts of people. I do a meet-and-greet every night on the tour, and it's a hundred fifty people. Before that, it's a radio meet-and-greet with forty people. After the show, it's thirty or forty more people. So then when I go home and turn on the TV, and I've got Monica and Chandler and Ross and Rachel and Phoebe and Joey on a *Friends* marathon, I don't feel lonely. I've just been onstage for two hours, talking to sixty thousand people about my feelings. That's so much social stimulation. When I get home, there is not one part of me that wishes I was around other people."

This is understandable. Still, I note something any musician obsessed with self-awareness would undoubtedly recognize: In the retrospective context of a hypothetical *Behind the Music* episode, this anecdote would be framed as depressing. It would paint the portrait of a super-famous entertainer spending her day emoting to thousands of strangers, only to return home to an empty house and the one-way company of two-dimensional characters.

Does she not see the irony, I wonder?

---

1. Swift said this a year before West released "Famous," a song that strongly implied Kanye could still potentially have sex with her, supported by a video that included a nude wax mannequin of Swift (alongside mannequins of other naked celebrities like Donald Trump and Bill Cosby). This was followed by West's wife, Kim Kardashian, releasing a secretly recorded audio clip of Swift and West talking on the telephone, a private conversation that contradicted things Swift had expressed in public. The phone incident incited a curious media backlash against Swift that is still happening in 2017, although I doubt it will continue forever. Either way, it can be safely assumed this alleged friendship is over.

Oh, she sees it. But that doesn't mean it's real.

"There is such a thing as having enough," she says in her non-TV voice. "You might think a meet-and-greet with a hundred fifty people sounds sad, because maybe you think I'm forced to do it. But you would be surprised. A meaningful conversation doesn't mean that conversation has to last an hour. A meet-and-greet might sound weird to someone who's never done one, but after ten years, you learn to appreciate happiness when it happens, and that happiness is rare and fleeting, and that you're not entitled to it. You know, during the first few years of your career, the only thing anyone says to you is, 'Enjoy this. Just enjoy this.' That's all they ever tell you. And I finally know how to do that."

Taylor Swift is twenty-five. But she's older than you.

I can't think of another human who's had a career quite like Kobe Bryant's. He was introduced in 1996—a brilliant, selfish prodigy who didn't seem to care about anything except winning. He evolved into a complicated superstar—arguably the best player in the NBA while still the second most important member of his own team. He desperately wanted to be cool, which (of course) had the opposite effect. He was a hard man to understand . . . and then he was accused of sexual assault. By day, he sat through his trial. By night, he averaged 24 points a game. The charges were eventually dropped (he lost a lot of money, but not his freedom or his skills). Again, he reinvented himself: This new Kobe was an autodidactic maniac, driven by an unquenchable desire to dominate. He emotionally abused his own teammates. He presented himself as a hoop historian, better suited for a bygone era. He scored 81 points in a single game, but that didn't make people love him; people only started to love him when he reached the cusp of retirement and began saying whatever the fuck he felt like. He adopted still another persona, wiser and more introspective than all of his peers. And then, in 2016, in his final (and wholly irrelevant) NBA moment, he took 50 shots and scored 60 points—a brilliant, selfish old man who seemed to care about absolutely everything, except who won the game.

Very often, in the first moments after an interview, I stroll back to my rental car and wonder, "Was that conversation even interesting? Does this person's experience really warrant a story? What am I possibly going to write about?" When I walked away from Bryant, I had no such concerns. My only thought: "Well, that one worked."

The Enemy of My Enemy Is Probably Just Another Enemy

I know who I am," is among the first things Kobe Bryant tells me, which is the kind of statement made only by people who are very, very right or very, very wrong. He tells me this in a breakfast café called Haute Cakes, tucked inside a strip mall in Newport Beach, Calif. We're fifteen minutes from his house, but I nonetheless mention that this is not the kind of place I expected to meet him. "What did you expect," he asks, "a dungeon?"

It's the first Monday of 2015. Last night, Bryant hit a floater with 12 seconds on the clock to beat the struggling Indiana Pacers; tonight his team is in Portland, but he's not traveling, in order to rest his aging bones. Two days from today, he'll go 2 of 12 against the Clippers as the Lakers fall 18½ games out of first place in the Western Conference; two weeks after that, he'll suffer a rotator-cuff injury that will end his season completely. This will be the most disheartening campaign of his nineteen-year career—he just doesn't know it yet. I mentally prepare myself for a justifiably surly, potentially uncommunicative sociopath.

My assumptions are wrong.

He walks through the door at 8:40 a.m. Bryant, who has already been awake for three hours, is a few minutes late for our meeting (broadcaster Stuart Scott had died the day before, so Bryant needed to provide a eulogistic response for ESPN Radio). He sits with his back to the wall, expressionless. My first question is unrelated to sports: On behest of *GQ*, I'm supposed to get Bryant's feelings on the attention rivals like Russell Westbrook and Dwyane Wade receive for their fashion choices. Mildly amused, he notes that he now tries to be "less fashion forward" (he's wearing camouflaged pants as he says this) and that if he dressed like Westbrook ("skinny pedal pushers and low-cut sneakers with a polka-dotted shirt and glasses and a backpack") it would be received as a practical joke. This spills into a banal discussion over branding, which is not a subject I want to talk about.[1] Knowing that Bryant has to leave the café by ten o'clock, I decide to take a calculated risk: I tell him that there is no point in pretending we're about to have a normal conversation, because nothing about this meeting is remotely normal. I just want to directly ask him all the things I've always wondered about his life. And from the moment I say this, I can tell that this is what he wants, too.

LET'S START IN THE MIDDLE: Bryant won five titles with Phil Jackson as his coach and three with Shaquille O'Neal as his teammate. Despite that success, both relationships are largely defined by their complexity. It is widely assumed Shaq and Bryant are not friends, particularly after a 2008 incident in a New York nightclub when O'Neal performed an impromptu freestyle rap requesting that Kobe describe the flavor of his anus. Bryant's trajectory with Jackson has

---

1. Bryant views branding as a modern form of "storytelling." I note that this comparison is only partially accurate, since branding is a form of storytelling with a conscious commercial purpose. "For some," he concedes. "But that's not a universal thing. That's like saying every wizard within Slytherin House is a villain." I pretend like this makes sense to me.

been more nuanced, but deeper and (at times) more painful. Though Jackson has said he views Bryant "like my son," he's also written damaging things about Kobe in multiple books, once classifying him as "uncoachable" and expressing a curious lack of surprise when Bryant was accused of rape in 2003.

Why do you think Jackson would write such negative things about you? Was he trying to psychologically motivate you, or is he just kind of a weird, arrogant person?

Well, most successful people are a little arrogant . . . I was very stubborn. I was like a wild horse that had the potential to become Secretariat, but who was just too fucking wild. So part of that was him trying to tame me. He's also very intelligent, and he understood the dynamic he had to deal with between me and Shaq. So he would take shots at me in the press, and I understood he was doing that in order to ingratiate himself to Shaq. And since I *knew* what he was doing, I felt like that was an insult to my intelligence. I mean, I knew what he was doing. Why not just come to me and tell me that? Another thing was that I would go to him in confidence and talk about certain things, and he would then use those things to manipulate the media against me. And from that standpoint, I finally said, "No way. I'm not gonna deal with that anymore." This was during our first run, during those first three championships. So when he'd come out in the press and say those things about me, I was finally like, "Fuck it. I'm done with this guy. I'll play for him and win championships, but I will have no interaction with him." Yet at the same time, it drove me at a maniacal pace. Because either consciously or unconsciously, he put a tremendous amount of pressure on me to be efficient, and to be great, and to be great *now*.

When this was happening, did you actively dislike him?

Yeah. (*pause*) Yeah. I was like—fuck him. I'm out here busting my ass. I'm killing myself. And it became insulting. Because I chose to extend my deal with the Lakers to play with Shaquille O'Neal and win championships. I knew what I could have done individually. I could have gone to another team and averaged 35 points a game. I could have gone anywhere and *destroyed* people. I gave that up to win championships. So it was infuriating to hear people say I was selfish. It was very, very maddening.

Do you feel like Shaq was publicly rewarded for not working hard? Somehow, the fact that he was a little lazy always came across as charming.

Well, he was [charming]. The perception of him was exactly that. Now it's not. The city of L.A. knows *me* now, and they know who I am. But at the time, the perception was that Kobe was trying to break up the team. That was wrong. I am a maniacal worker, and if you're not working as hard as I am, I am going to let you know about it. That's why Shaq and I still have a good relationship: He knows I have zero fear of him. I would tell him what he was doing and what he wasn't doing. And vice versa. There were times when we absolutely could not stand each other. We could not be in the same room together. But we challenged the shit out of each other.

So would you say the perception of him being lazy was inaccurate?

He had years where he was lazy. But during those three championships we won? To say he was a beast would be an understatement. To say I didn't learn things from him that I still use to this day would be a disservice. To be fair, I think what happened is that—as you get older—your body starts breaking down and you have to really love the process in order to get through that. Like, right now, I hurt. My ankle joints, my knee joints. My back. My thighs are sore. But for him, with his big toe and his knee, it became very hard for him to get up in the morning and push through those things. He might not have been as willing to do those things at the time, and I wasn't thrilled about that.

THE IMAGE OF BRYANT being less than "thrilled" with the not-so-maniacal work ethic of a teammate has become the center of his persona. Though he will never usurp the greatness of Michael Jordan within the public consciousness, he has likely already surpassed MJ in terms of the terror and antipathy he instills in those who play alongside him. His legacy is littered with the corpses of slackers who could not match his commitment, particularly underachievers of unusual size (Dwight Howard, Andrew Bynum). It has become popular to suggest that his ego—and his two-year, $48.5 million contract—are now actively hurting the franchise. The perception has become so universal that *ESPN The Magazine* published a story implying the Lakers cannot sign top-flight free agents as long as Bryant controls the system. Most of the story's sources were anonymous and Bryant claims he didn't read the article. But he also said he has been asked about it enough to "grasp what it was conceptually," and he certainly doesn't dispute the takeaway.

"Does my nature make me less enjoyable to play with? Of course," he says. "Of course it does. Is it possible that some top players in the league are intimidated by that? Yes. But do I want to play with those players? Does the Laker organization want those specific players? No.

Magic. Jordan. Bird. We all would have been phenomenal team-mates. This organization wants players who will carry this franchise to another five or six championships. The player who does that has to be cut from the same cloth. And if they're not cut from that cloth, they don't belong here."

This self-perpetuating image of Bryant as an unyielding worka-holic has become so integral to his ethos that it reflexively informs every other detail about his life. He has become The Last Hard Man, the realest of the real, the lone remnant from a Precambrian NBA era when players still hated each other and the only people who cared about AAU basketball were actual eighth-graders. Yet people forget that this was not always the case. As crazy as it now seems, there was a long stretch in the '90s when the principal knock on Bryant was his alleged insincerity. He smiled constantly, spoke Italian, and took Brandy to the prom. He adopted a "plain vanilla" persona modeled after Julius Erving, despite a transparent aspiration to embody the most conventional definition of urban cool; it often came across like Grant Hill trying to impersonate Allen Iverson.

"It wasn't that people thought I was *soft*," he says, slightly wincing at the implications of the word. "It was more of a street credibility thing: 'He grew up in Italy. He's not one of us.' But what I came to understand, coming out of Colorado, is that I had to be me, in the place where I was at that moment."

Which brings us to the hinge-point in the career of Kobe Bryant: the night he checked into a Colorado hotel room, had sex with a woman who worked there, and was subsequently arrested on a sexual assault charge. A year later, the charges were dropped and Bryant apologized. But the incident will (obviously) never go away. When Bryant dies, the accusation will probably appear in the second para-graph of his obituary. And he knows this.

"I started to consider the mortality of what I was doing," he says.

At the time, he was twenty-four. "What's important? What's not important? What does it mean when everybody loves you, and then everybody hates your guts for something they *think* you did? So that's when I decided that if people were going to like me or not like me, it was going to be for who I actually was. To hell with all that plain-vanilla shit, just to get endorsement deals. Those are superficial, anyway. I don't enjoy doing them, anyway. I'll just show people who I actually am . . . the [losses of the] endorsements were really the least of my concerns. Was I afraid of going to jail? Yes. It was twenty-five to life, man. I was terrified. The one thing that really helped me during that process—I'm Catholic, I grew up Catholic, my kids are Catholic—was talking to a priest. It was actually kind of funny: He looks at me and says, 'Did you do it?' And I say, 'Of course not.' Then he asks, 'Do you have a good lawyer?' And I'm like, 'Uh, yeah, he's phenomenal.' So then he just said, 'Let it go. Move on. God's not going to give you anything you can't handle, and it's in His hands now. This is something you can't control. So let it go.' And that was the turning point."

THE REASON Bryant needs to leave at ten a.m. is that he's working on a documentary for Showtime titled *Kobe Bryant's Muse*. He seems exceedingly interested in filmmaking at the moment, so I ask if he's seen *Whiplash*. "Of course," he replies. *Whiplash* is about a psychotic music instructor (J. K. Simmons) who physically abuses and emotionally manipulates a self-driven jazz drummer (Miles Teller) until the teenage musician both collapses and succeeds. Thematically, the film suggests an idea that has been mostly erased from modern popular culture: the possibility that inhumane, unacceptable treatment is sometimes essential to the creation of genius. I ask Bryant what he thought of *Whiplash*. "That's me," he says, although I can't tell if he means the Simmons character or the Teller character. He might mean the entire movie. In any case, he's acutely aware of the draconian strangeness of his own personality and of the downside to his ambitions, two characteristics he views almost interchangeably.

Do you ever think that the qualities that make you great are actually problems?

Oh, yeah. But the things that make a person average are also problems. The things that make someone not good at anything at all are a problem. If you want to be the greatest of all time at something, there's going to be a negative side to that. If you want to be a high school principal, that's fine, too—but that will also carry negative baggage.

So how much are you willing to give up? Have you given up the possibility of having friends? Do you have any friends?

I have "like minds." You know, I've been fortunate to play in Los Angeles, where there are a lot of people like me. Actors. Musicians. Businessmen. Obsessives. People who feel like God put them on earth to do whatever it is that they do. Now, do we have time to build great relationships? Do we have time to build great friendships? No. Do we have time to socialize and to hang out aimlessly? No. Do we want to do that? No. *We want to work.* I enjoy working.

So is this a choice? Are you actively choosing not to have friends?

Well, yes and no. I have friends. But being a "great friend" is something I will never be. I can be a *good* friend. But not a *great* friend. A great friend will call you every day and remember your birthday. I'll get so wrapped up in my shit, I'll never remember that stuff. And the people who are my friends understand this, and they're usually the same way. You gravitate toward people who are like you. But the kind of relationships you see in movies— that's impossible for me. I have good relationships with players around the league. LeBron and I will text every now and then. KG and I will text every now and then. But in terms of having one of those great, bonding friendships—that's something I will probably never have. And it's not some smug thing. It's a weakness. It's a weakness.

Do you miss the idea of having a great friendship?

Of course. It's not like I'm saying, "I don't need friends because I'm so strong." *It's a weakness.* When I was growing up in Italy, I grew up in isolation.[2] It was not an environment suited to me. I was the only black kid. I didn't speak the language. I'd be in one city, but then we'd move to a different city and I'd have to do everything again. I'd make friends, but I'd never be part of the group, because the other kids were already growing up together. So this is how I grew up, and these are the weaknesses that I have.

PART OF WHAT MAKES interviewing athletes difficult is the way they purposefully misunderstand questions, and the way they ignore

---

2. Bryant's father, Joe "Jellybean" Bryant, played pro basketball on four different Italian teams from 1984 to 1991.

certain questions, and the inflexibly straightforward manner in which they answer the handful of queries they perceive as relevant. This is not the case with Kobe. "Me sitting here, doing this interview—I don't have to do this," he says. "Ever since Colorado, I control my shit. If I don't want to do something, I don't fucking do it. Nobody is going to control my career or my life." He is wildly discursive, but never without purpose. At one point, I ask him how the aesthetics of basketball have changed due to the rise of advanced metrics, a trend that has devalued the mid-range jump shot (which, for Bryant, remains a strength). He starts his response by comparing the mid-range game to grunge fashion, arguing that all trends are cyclical and that the mid-range game will eventually return to prominence, just as grunge fashion eventually will ("and *GQ* and *Vogue* will have an absolute shit fit" when it does). This drifts into a meditation on popular metrics like "plus-minus," which Bryant sees as a way to measure shifts in momentum without explaining why those shifts occur. He concludes by noting that "guys like Henry Abbott actually are on to something," which is mostly interesting because Henry Abbott is (coincidentally) the same guy who wrote the aforementioned ESPN article about free agents not wanting to go to Los Angeles (the article that Bryant supposedly did not read). A few minutes earlier, I'd asked how Bryant feels about those who think he shoots too much. He responded by comparing himself to an eighteenth-century Austrian.

"I've shot too much from the time I was eight years old," Bryant says. "But 'too much' is a matter of perspective. Some people thought Mozart had too many notes in his compositions. Let me put it this way: I *entertain* people who say I shoot too much. I find it very interesting. Going back to Mozart, he responded to critics by saying there were neither too many notes nor too few. There were as many as necessary."

Assuming he spends the rest of this season in rehab, Bryant will finish his nineteenth year in the league with 32,482 points, roughly 6,500 fewer than the league's all-time leader, Kareem Abdul-Jabbar. He expresses no interest whatsoever in that record. "I could play for five or six more years if I wanted to. But I don't. This year and next year is enough. If my goal had been going after Jabbar, I would have done that. I would have gone to a different team and scored thirty-seven points a game. But that was never my goal.[3] My goal is to sit at the table with Michael and Magic, having won the same number of titles."

That sentiment, of course, raises an inescapable conflict: If Bryant's only goal is winning championships, it makes no sense for him to continue playing in Los Angeles. The team is objectively terrible. But Bryant thinks this is a temporary condition. And while his argument seems implausible, his reasoning is as sublime as it is conspiratorial.

The Lakers are not going to make the playoffs this year, and it seems unlikely that they will challenge for a title next year. So if titles are your only goal, why even play these last two seasons?

I know what Mitch [Kupchak, the Lakers GM] tells me. I know what Jim and Jeanie [Buss, the team owners] tell me. I know that they are hell-bent about having a championship-caliber team next season, as am I.

---

3. I find it amusing that—earlier in the conversation—Bryant had said he could have averaged 35 points a game if he'd gone to a different team. Twenty minutes later, the number he gives is 37. Somehow, he managed to increase his hypothetical nightly average by a basket, just by giving this interview.

***But how could that possibly be done? Doesn't the league's
financial system dictate certain limitations?***

Well, okay: Look at the [2011] lockout. That lockout was made to
restrict the Lakers. It was. I don't care what any other owner says.
It was designed to restrict the Lakers and our marketability.

The Lakers specifically, or teams like the Lakers?

There is only one team like the Lakers. Everything that was done
with that lockout was to restrict the Lakers' ability to get players
and to create a sense of parity, for the San Antonios of the world
and the Sacramentos of the world. But a funny thing happened,
coming out of that lockout: Even with those restrictions, the
Lakers pulled off a trade [for Chris Paul] that immediately set us
up for a championship, a run of championships later, *and* which
saved money. Now, the NBA vetoed that trade. But the Lakers
pulled that shit off, and no one would have thought it was even
possible. The trade got vetoed, because they'd just staged the
whole lockout to restrict the Lakers.[4] Mitch got penalized for
being smart. But if we could do that . . .

Bryant is arguing that the Lakers will just *manufacture* a competitive roster, through sheer intellectual creativity. Unrestricted free
agent LaMarcus Aldridge[5] may be in play. Rajon Rondo[6] (who Bryant recently had dinner with) might be on the table. It all seems

---

4. The official reason given as to why then-commissioner David Stern vetoed the Paul trade was
"basketball reasons." Stern was acting on behalf of Paul's former team, the Hornets (then playing
in New Orleans), who did not have an owner at the time of the proposed deal.
5. He ended up in San Antonio.
6. He signed with Sacramento and was later traded to Milwaukee.

hopeless, but stranger things have happened. Now, do I totally believe Kobe on this? I'm not sure if I totally believe Kobe. But I know
that I want to, and I know that he believes himself. He believes he
can do anything, simply through the power of will.

In 2011, Bryant's wife, Vanessa, filed for divorce, citing irrecon-
cilable differences. Yet those differences *were* reconciled, thirteen
months later. They remain a married couple. "I'm not going to say
our marriage is perfect, by any stretch of the imagination," Kobe
says. "We still fight, just like every married couple. But you know,
my reputation as an athlete is that I'm extremely determined, and
that I will work my ass off. How could I do that in my professional
life if I wasn't like that in my personal life, when it affects my kids? It
wouldn't make any sense." The logic is weirdly airtight: If we concede
that Kobe would kill himself to beat the Utah Jazz, we must assume
he'd be equally insane about keeping his family together. And he
knows that we know this about him, so he uses that to his advantage.

He knows who he is. He really, really does.

My recollection of meeting Jonathan Franzen in 2010 fixates on a perpetual sense of clinical oddness. I came into the interview assuming Franzen had no idea who I was, and I don't think he did—except when he'd toss random details into the conversation that almost felt like pointed, scolding references to things I had written in the past. I could never tell if he hated being interviewed or if he was trying to hide the fact that he kinda liked it. He had a warm smile but a clumsy laugh. It was a formal interaction, even when we talked about the Mekons. I was never particularly comfortable. Maybe he wasn't, either? No idea.

Part of my discomfort was a product of our theoretical similarity and practical imbalance. We are both working writers with vaguely similar lives. He, however, is more talented, more successful, and significantly more respected. We're doing the same thing but getting different results. There was a power imbalance, recognized by both of us.

When I interview people like Taylor Swift or Kobe Bryant, I never internalize their greatness or their success, or their public perception. It doesn't have anything to do with me, so I feel nothing. My curiosity is impersonal. But that's not how it was with Franzen. The whole time I was with him, I felt like his subordinate. I felt vaguely embarrassed to be there, wasting his time. Which says more about me than it says about him.

A Road Seldom Traveled
by the Multitudes

mportant" is a problematic word, particularly when prefaced by the modifier "most" and especially when prefaced by the modifier "only." To classify a man as "important" is different from merely calling him great, because an important person needs to matter even to those who question what he's doing.

Within the literary sphere, there are at least four ways an author can become semi-important: He (or, of course, she) can have massive commercial success. He can be adored and elevated by critics. He can craft "social epics" that contextualize modernity and force op-ed writers for *The New York Times* to reevaluate How We Live Now. He can even become a celebrity in and of himself, which means whatever that man chooses to write becomes meaningful solely because he was the one who made that choice. There are many, many writers who fulfill fractions of those criteria. However, only Jonathan Franzen hits for the cycle. Only Franzen does all four, and he does them all to the highest possible degree. This is why Franzen is the most important living fiction writer in America, and—if viewed from a distance—perhaps the only important one. He's the most complete. But the deeper explanation for Franzen's import is something that's hard to quantify but easy to feel: For whatever reason, people just care about him *more*. They love him more, they criticize him more, and they think about him more. They can tell he's different and they want him to be different. They want that difference to matter. And Franzen understands this, which is both how it happened and why it's less implausible than it should be.

"I think there is a space in our culture—in the living memory of people over forty, and probably in the collective memory of people under forty—for the American novelist," Franzen says, sounding exactly how you'd expect him to sound. "And for various reasons, after Mailer and Updike and maybe Anne Tyler went into eclipse, there was a wish to have some new people in that position. But culture had changed so much that it became hard for someone to fulfill that role. So when someone came along who could be easily mistaken for that type of novelist, there was a hunger to latch on to that person. And that's what happened. I had an interest in being that kind of novelist and I worked at it for thirty years, even during periods when I didn't think it was possible for that position to exist."

Now, the depth and language of that response forces a question that was asked to me every single time I mentioned (to anyone) that I'd just interviewed Jonathan Franzen: *Is he arrogant?* That's the first thing people always want to know, and Franzen is the only author who engenders this kind of emotional conflict from the public at large. People want to understand what he's like as a person, even if they haven't read his multi-perspective, 576-page masterwork *Freedom* or 2001's National Book Award–winning *The Corrections*. Somehow, this personality question matters. And here's the answer: He's a little arrogant. But he's not remotely unlikable, and there's no element of his self-perception that seems inflated or misplaced. He knows why all this has happened. At one point, we talk about his appearance on the cover of *Time* magazine, something that hasn't happened to a novelist in almost a decade. He casually mentions how the profile in *Time* was mostly good. But he also laughs and says this: "I think of myself as an ordinary person with a lot of friends, and the picture that came out of that article was of a monastic person who's incredibly focused on writing. My favorite line of the piece was that I'm supposed to be 'spectacularly bad' at managing my public image. Well, if that's true, maybe they should look at the cover of their own magazine."

In fiction, there are no accidents. And maybe not in nonfiction, either.

I MEET FRANZEN in the Philadelphia train station; we will both ride the Acela to Washington, D.C., where he's completing the last U.S. stages of his *Freedom* book tour before another four weeks of touring through Europe. He looks like himself: unshaven, gray sport coat, dark jeans, modest luggage. He enjoys touring about as much as I thought he would, which is to say "not much." He mentions how the crowd at last night's reading at the Philadelphia library was oddly confrontational, both with him and with each other (the discourse unraveled after someone asked an adversarial question about Oprah). The only part of going to Europe he seems excited about is the opportunity for some UK bird-watching, and even that excitement is muted. The only time he shows a spike of emotion is when he correctly predicts exactly where the café car will stop on the train platform. "My father was a railroad man," he says as the mechanical doors slide open.

We end up sitting in regular business-class seats. Franzen sits by the window. He answers my questions slowly and deliberately, looking at the passing scenery while silently composing his answers. To suggest that Franzen is some kind of unknowable sphinx would not be accurate; he's written a memoir, he's published a lot of personal nonfiction, his girlfriend wrote about the complexity of his success (the 2003 *Granta* essay "Envy"), and he's conducted many interviews with many persistent people for more than ten years. A complete record of Franzen's autobiographical details already exists. But these artifacts might be misleading, at least to those interested in deconstructing how Franzen views the universe. One example: We touch briefly on his literary influences, and he mentions Thomas Pynchon. But we're not really talking about the content of Pynchon's books; we're actually talking about how the reclusive Pynchon has a different kind of notoriety from Franzen, and that Pynchon's smaller audience is closer to "the audience that counts." I ask him what that phrase means. This is his response, which feels simultaneously true and incomplete.

"I'm not talking about the grad students with unwashed hair who might actually stalk Pynchon," he says. "I'm talking about people who want to have an ongoing relationship with interesting books, and I've realized there are more people like that in America than I used to believe, even just ten years ago. And those types of people are different from the people who only care about me because I was on the cover of *Time*. Those people don't want a book signed. They want a magazine signed. And it seems ridiculous that a writer like me could become that person, even for a moment."

Here's the reason I view that answer as incomplete: Franzen is so utterly cautious about his image that he never says exactly what he thinks, which is why certain critics read his tone as detached and condescending. Yet when he speaks in person, you can immediately tell his unedited thoughts are both hyperpresent in his consciousness and embedded in the subtext of his delivery. There's a point in our conversation where he declines to answer the only question I ask that he classifies as "astute." In order to satisfy my own curiosity (and against my better judgment), I allow him to give his answer off the record. During the three minutes my recorder is off, he provides one of the most straightforward, irrefutable, and downright depressing answers I've ever experienced in an interview. His posture changes and his language simplifies. Nothing is unclear. But once the red light returns, he rematerializes into the same truthful-but-withholding person I met at the train station. It's easy to understand why Franzen's literary characters are so rich and fully realized; he understands himself better than most people I've encountered, which is always the first step toward understanding people who aren't you.

THERE ARE FLEETING PASSAGES in *Freedom* that discuss music, and one gets the sense that Franzen both loves and distrusts the concept of rock 'n' roll. The first band he ever liked was the Moody Blues, followed by a period in high school where he listened to the Grateful Dead without smoking pot. He enrolled at Swarthmore College in 1977 and became obsessed with all the rock you'd expect a bookish college kid to obsess over in '77, particularly the Talking Heads. Today, he mainly listens to music at the gym. He offers to show me the iTunes playlist he's created for the elliptical machine. The track list is up-tempo and inscrutable: The Jackson 5, M.I.A., Grace Jones, Ted Leo, the Rolling Stones, Steely Dan's "My Old School," and Mission of Burma's "Academy Fight Song." It does not serve as a means for unpacking anything essential about its creator.

"My favorite band is the Mekons," he tells me. "That tells you everything you need to know about me."

The Mekons are a prolific, righteous, highly credible punk band from Britain. But this description doesn't tell us much either, because—even though he *does* love the Mekons—when Franzen adds, "That tells you everything you need to know about me," he's completely joking.

This, it seems, is where many people get confused.

"It's not my responsibility if some people are tone deaf to irony," he says. "The lead book reviewer for *The New York Times* [Pulitzer Prize winner Michiko Kakutani] is utterly tone deaf when it comes to irony. She just can't hear it. Which you'd think would disqualify her from reviewing books for a blog in Kansas City, let alone *The New York Times*. But there you go. There's always going to be a percentage of the populace who doesn't get irony and will therefore not get seventy-five percent of good literature."

When Franzen talks, it's difficult to tell which are the ironic parts and which are the real parts. That, I suppose, is what makes him interesting.

What's the least accurate thing anyone has written about you?

I don't read much about myself. I learned my lesson after spending ninety ill-advised minutes googling myself once in the fall of 2001. I think the whole "Franzen is a spoiled elitist" thing was wrong, although not without a kernel of truth. I do lead a privileged life. I do believe some books are better than others. I do think that mere popularity does not indicate greatness. In those respects, I suppose I'm an elitist. But I think what was meant by the term "elitist" at the time was the antithesis of what I've tried to do as a writer, which is to reach the largest possible audiences and exclude the smallest number of people. I've worked so long—and in such a conscious way—to not exclude people. So that was galling.

What do you worry about? What would be the worst-case scenario for your career?

Global pandemics. I do worry about global pandemics. But I'm not a compulsive hand washer or anything.

How would a global pandemic impact your career?

I don't really worry about my career. I suppose the worst thing that could happen would be if someone would be so nasty as to harass my ex-wife. We don't have an ongoing close relationship, and she wants to be left alone. So if someone would bother her and ask her a bunch of questions about me, that would be a very unfortunate consequence of this book.

Do you think about your ex-wife very much?

(*pause*) Let's move on.

THE FIRST TIME I ever saw Franzen was at the Brooklyn Book Festival in 2008, the day after news of David Foster Wallace's suicide had become mainstream information. Backstage, various writers (many of whom had never met him before) were coming up to Franzen to express awkward condolences over the loss of his close friend; I remember how Franzen looked like the least shocked person in the room. To my surprise, he brings up DFW before I do, always referring to him as "Dave Wallace." It reminds me of how actors who've worked with Robert De Niro always make a point of referring to him as "Bobby."

"At various points we both envied the kind of attention the other person received," Franzen explains. "Dave envied my mainstream attention, and I envied the very intense critical attention he received. Which is part of the reason it makes it so hard to go on without him."

To classify the Franzen–Wallace relationship as "complex" would be like saying the relationship between Israel and Palestine is "contentious." They met in the early '90s when Wallace wrote Franzen a fan letter about his debut novel, *The Twenty-Seventh City*; soon after, Wallace become recognized as the next great American genius with the 1996 publication of *Infinite Jest*, only to have Franzen shoot past him (at least in terms of recognition and readability) with *The Corrections*. When Wallace killed himself, his literary reputation exploded a second time, and countless obituaries noted the Franzen–Wallace friendship. Now they are linked forever. Immediately after DFW's death, Franzen consciously adopted Wallace's habit of chewing tobacco, similar to how Michael Jordan started playing baseball and doing crossword puzzles following his father's murder. Though it technically took nine years, the vast majority of *Freedom* was written in a rush of inspiration in the aftermath of Wallace's hanging, and one of the novel's central characters displays many Wallace-like affectations: Richard Katz (the narrative's mercurial rock musician) chews tobacco, prefers working in a dark room (as did DFW), and speaks with grains of Wallace's syntax. But Franzen insists the fictional character is not based on the literal man, and I have no grounds to disprove this.

Weirdly (or perhaps predictably), it turns out that one person who knew both Franzen and Wallace during their formative writing years was Elizabeth Wurtzel, the confessional author of the 1994 bestseller

Prozac Nation, who now works with David Boies as a lawyer in Manhattan. When I reach Wurtzel on the telephone, she immediately tells me she's not going to read *Freedom* on principle ("I don't like what he did to Oprah"). She tells me she always found Franzen and Wallace's joint obsession with literary greatness "a little obnoxious," that she hasn't spoken to Franzen since the late '90s, and that maybe she never *really* knew him at all. I assume this is her way of saying she's in no position to comment, so I start to apologize for wasting her time. But it turns out she really, really wants to talk about him.

"I have a unifying theory about this," says Wurtzel, her guard dog compulsively barking in the background. "I think that when Dave died, everyone said Dave was the greatest writer of his generation. And that really got to Franzen. I don't think he could stand the thought of Dave Wallace being the greatest writer of his generation, so he wrote this new book. And now people say those same things about him. You know, in '96 he wrote an essay ["Perchance to Dream," first published in *Harper's*] about how to write a readable novel, and then he went out and did exactly that. That's what he does. I admire his determination, and I relate to that determination. If he'd gone to Wall Street, he'd have made a million dollars. I feel no ill will toward him. I just wonder if he still remembers who he used to be."

But who is the person he used to be?

And how does that negate the person he is now?

And wouldn't it be far more troubling if he were the *exact* same person he was fifteen years ago, unchanged by the life he's lived and the books he's created?

These questions could be asked of any middle-aged novelist, I suppose. It's a present-day problem: There's just no escaping the larger, omnipresent puzzle of "reality." Even when people read fiction, they want to know what's *real*. They want to know if who the writer is dictates how his work should be taken. But this, it seems, is not Franzen's concern. He disintegrates the issue with one sentence.

"Here's the thing about inauthentic people," he says on the train, speaking in the abstract. "Inauthentic people are obsessed with authenticity."

LESS THAN TWO HOURS after leaving Philly, our train hits the outskirts of D.C. I try to whip a few more questions at Franzen before we depart; I ask if he found it difficult to write about sex, and he grins so uncomfortably that the query is never addressed. I ask if he has any recurring dreams, knowing that people talk about their dreams in order to tell secrets about themselves they want other people to know. He says that he does. In fact, it seems like the question he enjoys answering the most.

"I've even written about one dream that still happens occasionally. I wrote about it briefly in *The New Yorker* after 9/11, but I've had the dream my whole life," he says. "It's a dream of flying, but I'm not a human flying—I'm an airplane, flying with great maneuverability at high speed, very low to the ground, usually in an urban environment, always at risk of having my wings ripped off and crashing into a fireball . . . I think it's probably about the difficulty of being myself on my own terms, and trying to be myself in a world that doesn't automatically accommodate that."

I ask him to define his own terms.

"I try not to lie, and I try to interact with others as full people, even if they're strangers. And I want to write fiction with those two premises."

As we exit the train, a man in a three-piece suit who's been sitting behind us (and eavesdropping on the interview) interjects himself into our closing conversation. He tells Franzen that he regularly has that exact same dream. "I know exactly what you're talking about," he says.

Franzen smiles at the man, but says nothing. He probably gets this a lot, which is why he is the writer that he is. People know what he's talking about, and the feeling is mutual.

What follows is not a profile of a person, but of an organization. That organization is the Cleveland Browns. And it's a good thing the Browns are not a person, because that person's life would be miserable.

During the nineties, there was a popular Fox TV show called *Beverly Hills, 90210*. One of the lead characters was a woman named Kelly Taylor, portrayed by Jennie Garth. Over the course of ten seasons, Kelly Taylor was raped, became addicted to cocaine, had a miscarriage, was shot with a firearm, had a mother who was an alcoholic, had a brother who was a meth addict, briefly got amnesia, was unsuccessfully murdered by a woman who'd become obsessed with her haircut, and was trapped inside a burning building after joining a cult. Obviously, this has nothing to do with football. But if the writers of *90210* had somehow created a storyline where Kelly Taylor became the first woman to enter the NFL, I'm certain she would have been drafted by the Browns. Any other scenario would seem implausible.

I spent a week inside the Browns compound during the summer of 2013. Part of the reason I was invited was to see how the franchise was allegedly reinventing itself. It was supposed to be a new beginning, defined by an embrace of innovation. In the subsequent years since my visit, the Browns have won 15 games and lost 49, including a humiliating 1-15 campaign in 2016. Read in retrospect, this article makes that destiny seem inevitable. Most of the people mentioned in the story are now employed elsewhere.

Brown Would Be the Color
(If I Had a Heart)

Four men sit around a wood table, watching three televisions simultaneously. They are talking among themselves, but only sporadically; they spend more time gazing at the wall of TVs, glancing down at speculative lists on laptop computers, checking their text messages, and then returning their eyes to the televisions. There is moderate to heavy sighing. It's 2:30 p.m. on the last Thursday in April: In about six hours, these four men will officially decide that a relatively large, uncommonly quick man from Louisiana State named Barkevious Mingo will be the person they shall hire to jump-start an NFL franchise that has been relatively awful for the past fifteen years. This verdict has already galvanized in their collective brain: Mingo is absolutely the man they want to draft. They describe him as "always relentless." They identify him as the type of player who "represents everything" they aspire to as a franchise. But—right now, as they make those remarks casually—it's still the middle of the afternoon. The future remains unwritten. Maybe they will get Mingo and maybe they will not; all they can do right now is write his name on a dry-erase board and periodically stare at the letters, whenever they grow bored of staring at the TV or staring at the computer or staring at each other.

At one end of the wood table sits Rob "Chud" Chudzinski, the new head coach of the Cleveland Browns. He wears a visor and coach's shorts, almost like a character from a Kevin Costner movie about who the Cleveland Browns should draft (which, as it turns out, is a movie that's actually going to exist). Sitting next to Chud is Joe Banner, the Browns' new CEO, who has come to the club after twenty years with the Eagles (he wears a hoodie promoting an Alaska-based brewery and drinks a Pepsi). Next to Banner is Ray Farmer, a former Eagles linebacker now serving as the assistant to the team's new general manager, Mike Lombardi, the fourth man in the room. Lombardi wears a suit and sometimes circles the table like a half-hungry hammerhead shark. Lombardi talks the most. Chudzinski talks the least. Banner runs the room. Farmer is the equilibrium (he rarely speaks first but provides the most balanced insights). None of these men worked for the Browns in 2012, which is why this particular draft is unusually meaningful: For all practical purposes, Cleveland is rebooting their entire franchise. Everything is completely new—the ownership, the front office, the coaching staff. This first-round draft decision, at least symbolically, signifies the beginning of yet another new era for professional football in Northeast Ohio, a geographic region that cares about football a little too much.

The war room is tense. Its ambiance falls somewhere in between a maternity waiting room and an East Berlin safe house. Sometimes the cable cuts out and all three televisions flicker in unison—but before an IT worker is allowed to enter the room and check the connection, Lombardi hastily erases Mingo's name from the whiteboard. This IT worker is a Browns employee who (I assume) works in the facility every single day. He's nobody. Yet he still can't be trusted. It seems a little crazy, but that's how this world operates. It's crazy on purpose. I think they like it that way.

Watching the war room is like watching grown men play *Risk!* without a board. Every so often, something happens. But it's difficult to tell what's *really* happening. Here's an example: The Browns have the sixth overall pick in this draft. They do not have a pick in the second round, having forfeited it after the selection of wide receiver Josh Gordon in the NFL's supplemental draft last summer (this, it is widely felt by the organization, was still the right move—Gordon is the best WR the Browns currently possess). Like most 5-11 teams, Cleveland is desperate for talent at almost every position. They'd like to trade down and get more manpower. This is complicated by the fact that almost every low-end team wants to trade down in this particular draft (the conventional wisdom is that the difference in quality between the fifteen best players and the thirty picks who'll follow is negligible). What the Browns want to do is swap the #6 pick for a later selection in the first round and another selection in the second (a conventional two-for-one exchange). At 2:30, such a deal is already in place. The St. Louis Rams are willing to surrender the sixteenth overall pick and their second-round selection (plus a throw-in seventh-rounder) in order to move up to #6. However, the agreement has caveats. The Browns will only agree to the deal if Mingo is no longer available at #6, and the Rams will only make the swap if the specific guy they want (dynamic West Virginia WR Tavon Austin) is still available at #6. Everything depends on Mingo being gone and Austin sticking around, which is impossible to anticipate this far in advance. In other words, this theoretical deal can only happen during the fleeting ten-minute window that will follow the fifth overall selection, so nothing can be etched in stone.

Here's something else that's transpiring: math. There's a lot of low-level math happening. When not contemplating Mingo, the Cleveland front office considers the possible acquisition of Davone

Bess from the Miami Dolphins.[1] Bess was fourteenth in the league in receptions last season, but it looks like he's being phased out of the Dolphins' future (particularly after the signing of free agent Mike Wallace for $60 million). Miami doesn't particularly need Bess, so they're willing to give him up for the simple transposition of middle-round draft picks. The Browns offer Miami the 104th overall selection and the 164th overall selection in exchange for Bess, the 111th pick, and the 217th pick. This requires an objective discussion about the mathematical value of average draft prospects and a subjective (and seemingly less essential) debate about what Bess offers on the field. Later that afternoon, an even crazier hypothetical spontaneously emerges: The Browns consider trading tonight's #6 pick to a marquee franchise, in exchange for a second-round pick tomorrow, a first-round pick in 2014, another first-round pick in 2015, and two other future selections. This would mean Chudzinski would start his coaching career with a 5-11 team that doesn't even have a first-round draft option; it would also mean the Browns would be extremely well-positioned over the next three years. Ultimately, the blockbuster does not happen. It's possible that it was never close to happening. But this is how you rebuild a franchise that's made the playoffs once in fourteen years: You look at what the team has always done, and then you try to do the opposite.

THE LAST TIME the Browns won an NFL championship was 1964. This feels distant to everyone in America, except those living in Northeast Ohio. To them, it seems like last weekend. If you try to annoy a Browns fan by noting how Cleveland has never won a Super

---

1. The first attempt at this trade collapses. However, it does go through the next day, after I leave town. Results were mixed. Bess had 42 receptions in 2013, but the Browns released him in March 2014. He is now under indictment for a litany of felonies in Arizona.

Bowl, they will tell you that they've actually won four titles (1950, '54, '55, and '64) and that the only problem is that the term "Super Bowl" had not yet been invented. They will go on to tell you that the greatest football player who ever lived was a Brown, and that his *name* was literally "Brown," and that the greatest player who ever lived is still only the second most important person named "Brown" in the history of the franchise. They will tell you that they'll always root for the Browns, under any circumstances, no matter what happens, forever.

And then they will proceed to tell you how much the Browns suck.

This is the central dichotomy of Cleveland football: No rival fan base is so deeply loyal and so self-consciously negative at the same time. Locally, there just seems to be a universal belief that—somehow, either by human error or random chance—the Browns will fail at whatever they try. Longtime fanatics have code words for all the moments that have crushed their souls. "Red Right 88" denotes the fatal play call from the 1981 divisional playoffs against the Oakland Raiders, when—trailing 14–12 with less than a minute to play, inside the red zone—the Browns tried to pass instead of running the ball and attempting a field goal.[2] The ensuing end zone interception ended the season. That '81 squad was (arguably) Cleveland's best team of the modern era, unless you consider the '86 Browns (who were killed by John Elway and "The Drive") or the '87 Browns (whose hopes were dashed by "The Fumble" in the AFC championship). There are no code words for things that went right, because those things never

---

2. There is, of course, a little more to this story: The weather was insane (the wind chill was –36), the Browns kicker was hurt (and had already missed two field goals and a PAT), and the Browns quarterback was Brian Sipe, who'd just been named AFC MVP. If the play had succeeded, it would have exemplified the gambling style the team had employed all season. But it did not, because this is Cleveland.

happen. In 1996, owner Art Modell moved the franchise to Baltimore, a move so devastating to the community that many citizens openly expressed glee when Modell died in 2012. For three seasons in the nineties, there was no football team in Cleveland, although the nonexistent Browns remained just as popular as the Indians and more popular than the Cavaliers. (This three-year stint was actually an excellent era for Browns fans, since nothing bad could possibly occur.) The club was reintroduced in 1999, showcased by a new $300 million downtown stadium and the first overall pick in the draft, Kentucky quarterback Tim Couch. In the fourteen years that have since passed, the team's record is 73-151.

Still, the team sells out virtually every home game. This is not Jacksonville. When it comes to football, Ohio is just a colder version of Texas. The Browns are always the biggest story in town: Two days before the draft, the Cavs rehired Mike Brown as their head basketball coach for $20 million; among the local media, the move received roughly the same amount of attention as the imaginary possibility of the Browns drafting E. J. Manuel. Such single-minded obsession creates a unique problem for the Browns front office: How do you appease a fan base that is both highly critical and eternally infatuated? It's like dating a woman who hates you so much she will never break up with you, even if you burn down the house every single autumn.

I pose this question to Alec Scheiner, the team's new president and my de facto liaison during the three days I spend in Cleveland. "My feeling is that we need to present a different picture of this organization," he says. "It's been stale. It has not done well. I don't think people view the Browns in a positive light. My perception from the outside was that the Browns just weren't successful. They weren't energetic or forward-thinking."

Scheiner is forty-three. A native of Pennsylvania, he comes to Cleveland from Dallas, where he spent eight years as a senior vice president and team counsel (essentially, he assisted Cowboy owner Jerry Jones and was heavily involved with the legal negotiations during the construction of the new Texas Stadium). "We have a long-term vision. And I realize that sounds simplistic, but a lot of teams don't have that. They take shortcuts. Our long-term vision is sustained success over a long period of time. When you look at organizations like San Francisco and Philadelphia and New England and Baltimore and Pittsburgh, what you see are organizations that stayed consistent with their ideals. If you look at other teams, you can see where they took shortcuts. You can see where they gave up three assets for one guy, because they thought they were one player away. But you're never just one player away."

At this point, Scheiner goes off-the-record and gives examples of franchises who (in his opinion) have done this incorrectly. Over the next three days, he tells me many interesting things, but virtually none of them are eligible for attribution. He's a very nice guy and a nuanced sports thinker, but his level of caution is profound (almost to the point of comedy). Most of my direct queries are answered with either banal business-speak or a nondescript chuckle. He ultimately tells me only two "on the record" anecdotes that are worth mentioning here. One involved his failed attempt in Dallas to play Radiohead in the Cowboys weight room ("All the guys were like, *What* the *fuck* is *this*?"). The other is that—upon his graduation from Georgetown law school—he almost became a diplomat.

"I wanted to be a diplomat in Latin America," he tells me. "I had lived in Costa Rica and Nicaragua. I guess I was more idealistic back then. I was working down there, right after El Salvador had finished a civil war. I thought I could make the world a better place. But then I realized all I was really doing was helping rich people get richer than they already were. I figured if that was all I was doing, I might as well work in professional sports."

BACK IN THE WAR ROOM, the four aforementioned fellows continue to watch ESPN, ESPN2, and the NFL Network. I'm a little surprised by how much they rely on mainstream media outlets as a means for gathering information. I had always assumed there was an under-reported intelligence gap between normal civilians and NFL executives, but that chasm is connected by the same rumor mill. Their personal reactions to the TV are not dissimilar from those of casual football fans: When the face of one high-profile draft analyst appears on the screen, Banner immediately says, "That guy is clueless." Later, one of the channels runs a three-minute puff piece about Manti Te'o's family in Hawaii. For reasons that remain unexplained, they all wordlessly watch the segment with genuine interest.

At 3:30 p.m., the likelihood of trading the #6 pick still seems high. The discussion veers toward who they might end up taking if they fall back into the middle of the first round, a problem complicated by the utter impossibility of knowing who will still be available. On his laptop, Chudzinski is rewatching tape of a lineman he likes a little more than he probably should. He keeps watching footage from the same game, the single best performance the player had all year. Chudzinski knows the kid is flawed, but he remains intrigued by his physical frame. Banner is less bullish. "What does a bust look like before it happens?" he asks rhetorically. "It looks like four guys sitting in a room, trying to convince each other that some guy is better than we think he is."

The main reason this deficient lineman is even being considered is that he happened to play his best game against an opponent from the Southeast Conference, the most secure pedigree any potential pick can offer. That partially explains why the Browns are so enamored with Barkevious Mingo. "The SEC is a whole different animal," says Lombardi. "If all we did was take guys from Alabama and LSU, we'd be fucking great."

Lombardi has a long relationship with Grantland (he's been a guest on numerous podcasts with Bill Simmons), but this is the first time I've ever spoken with him. He's a polarizing figure in Cleveland, solely because he's worked there in the past (he was the director of player personnel with the team in the '90s, right before they escaped to Baltimore). His name gets mentioned a lot on local talk radio, sometimes pejoratively (it's endlessly noted that—while working as an analyst for the NFL Network in 2012—Lombardi criticized the Browns' first-round selection of twenty-eight-year-old Brandon Weeden, the man now positioned as the team's starting QB). One gets the sense the Browns want to lower Lombardi's public profile. This strikes me as a mistake. Lombardi is very good at talking. He's a detail freak and a polymath, or at least a person successfully attempting to impersonate one. At one point, he engages me in a meticulous conversation about LBJ biographer Robert Caro, including what kind of typewriter Caro uses, his research methods, what clothing he wears while working, and the geographic location of Caro's Manhattan office (I know almost nothing about Robert Caro, so the dialogue is pretty one-sided). He asks me what specific font I will use when I write this story. He nonchalantly talks about "the candle problem," a hypothetical puzzle devised by Gestalt psychologist Karl Duncker in 1945. The takeaway from all this is the import of "divergent thinking," a cognitive system that focuses on solving problems by exploring nontraditional modes of assessment. Before it became a cliché, people called this process "thinking outside the box." It's a hard philosophy to disagree with, because nobody likes the box. That said, drafting an edge rusher from LSU doesn't exactly qualify as divergent thinking. That's not outside the box. It might be the box itself. But when you're twenty-fifth in the league in yards allowed, the box is what you need.

"I'M NOT AFRAID of transparency," says Scheiner as he leads me around the Browns' semi-renovated practice facility, pointing at metal beams and temporary flooring and exposed electrical wiring. "Most of what we do here—there's no secret to it."

Well, what can I say? That statement is totally inaccurate. During the three days I visit the Browns organization, I hear the phrase "This is off the record" more often than I've heard it during the past ten years of my career. The team told me I would have unprecedented access to their workplace, which (I suppose) was *technically* true. I could walk around the halls and peer inside the empty offices. I could hang out in the weight room and use the locker room lavatory. The only problem was that almost none of the 150 people who work in this facility were allowed to answer any specific questions pertaining to football. It was a little like being allowed inside Willy Wonka's chocolate factory but being informed that no one in the building was allowed to discuss the manufacturing of candy.

Cleveland's practice facility exists in the suburb of Berea, a community of nineteen thousand people that's five minutes from the airport. The community was built upon a bed of sandstone and looks like an industrial park; the atmosphere suggests an unglamorous version of the '80s. But the Browns' refurbished headquarters on Lou Groza Boulevard is nice (and getting nicer). There is a statue of deceased former owner Al Lerner outside the main entrance. The staff is friendly. In three months, all the major offices will be located on the facility's second floor, overlooking the practice field. Unlike traditional NFL franchises, the Browns are not going to silo their football operations separately from their business operations. The head coach's office won't be isolated from the marketing department or the legal division. This is a group effort. All goals are unilateral.

I try to schedule an interview with Joe Banner,[3] but it never happens (although I guess I can understand why he might be busy during the week of the draft). After a five-hour wait on Wednesday afternoon, I do get a chance to interview Chudzinski, a jovial, cherubic man who doesn't say anything revealing or divisive (the closest he comes is this: "I know this sounds abstract, but we need to define a vision").[4] Most of my days in Berea are spent waiting in the facility's brand-new cafeteria, the one aspect of the organization everyone insists has been legitimately reinvented. Judging from how the previous dining center is unanimously described, the Browns used to feed everyone slop. "This place is unreal," says Spencer Lanning, a punter from South Carolina competing for a job. "For breakfast, you used to just get a greasy breakfast sandwich. It made you feel worse. Now we have all this great cereal." When CEO Banner came to the Browns from Philadelphia, he hired the same caterers the Eagles employed, a company called Flik. I must admit: The food is borderline delicious. On the day of the draft, they serve prime rib for lunch and crab legs for dinner. It seems curious that the concept of nutrition had never

---

3. Though I never directly spoke to the diminutive, sixty-year-old Banner, I was impressed watching him work. He might not be the warmest guy in the world, and I suspect he's a demanding boss. He's a little more sarcastic than necessary. But you can just tell he's hypercompetent. It's weirdly obvious. He seems like the kind of man who could effectively run any kind of business, regardless of what it did or what it sold.

4. This may be partially my own fault. I had a theory going into my interview with Chudzinski about who the Browns might draft: Chudzinski was a collegiate tight end at the University of Miami, and the Browns' new offensive coordinator is Norv Turner, a man who's had major success with tight ends in the past (Antonio Gates, Jay Novacek, et al.). This led me to suspect the Browns might take Notre Dame tight end Tyler Eifert. But when I mentioned this possibility aloud, Chud looked at me like I had no idea what I was proposing, which is probably true. Eifert ended up going to the Bengals at #21.

occurred to the Browns until 2013, but maybe that explains a lot about what was broken here.

For most of Tuesday and virtually all of Wednesday, I just sit in the cafeteria and look at my iPhone, waiting for interviews that are habitually canceled. For a couple of hours, a fledging Browns publicist named Brian Smith sits at the same table and tries to make innocuous conversation. I ask him if he's doing this to be friendly or if he was specifically instructed to make sure I don't wander around asking questions to random employees. "Both," he replies.

I don't think they're building chemical weapons in Berea. But they might be. I can't say for sure.

Another person I try to interview is a boyish thirty-five-year-old named Ken Kovash, the Browns' analytics guru (his official title is "director of football research and player personnel"). Kovash is the kind of guy who only needs to shave once every ten days and is mercilessly teased by everyone in the building when he unexpectedly shows up wearing a suit on draft day. I suspect he's the kind of guy who has been teased his whole life, simply because he's smarter than most normal people (he used to work with Steven Levitt, the Chicago economist who published *Freakonomics*). Moving forward, the Browns intend to amplify their emphasis on statistical analytics. They intend to be mathematically progressive. Kovash will be key to this, so he seems like a useful person to talk to. But my interview request is denied. I am not allowed to talk to Ken Kovash in any official capacity (we have dinner in a Mexican restaurant, but I have to agree beforehand to print nothing we discuss).

In so many ways, this denial represents the grand irony of the Browns organization (and, I would assume, every other organization in the NFL). The Browns live in a state of perpetual war, endlessly convincing themselves that every scrap of information they possess is some kind of game-changing superweapon that will alter lives and transmogrify the culture. They behave like members of a corporate cult. Yet what do these cultists watch on the day of the draft? They watch ESPN. They log onto the Internet and scan Pro Football Talk. The comments they make about college prospects are roughly identical to whatever your smarter friends might glean from *The Plain Dealer*. I've never witnessed this level of institutional paranoia within a universe so devoid of actual secrets. I don't even know what they don't want me to know.

BY 5:15 P.M. on Thursday, the sensation of chaos is starting to subside. All the war room occupants have changed into formal attire (Banner goes with a red sweater). The Browns are fixated on taking Mingo, assuming he's still there at #6. There is a strong rumor that the Kansas City Chiefs have already informed Central Michigan left tackle Eric Fisher that they'll take him with the first overall selection, which means early favorite Luke Joeckel, the left tackle from Texas A&M, will fall to the second slot.[5] Lombardi suspects the Oakland Raiders may use the third overall pick on Houston Cougar cornerback D. J. Haden, a player who suffered a bizarre (and nearly fatal) heart injury late in his senior season. His inferior vena cava is scaring many teams away. The Raiders, however, are comfortable with the risk (and though they ultimately trade the #3 pick to Miami, they'll still get Haden with the twelfth selection, a relative steal).

The draft officially starts at 8:00 p.m. I'm intrigued by how the war room[6] atmosphere will change when the picks start happening,

---

5. The 2013 draft was deepest at left tackle, which was good for the Browns. Joe Thomas, the incumbent Browns left tackle, is the only irrefutably great player on the entire Cleveland roster. It's the only position they don't have to worry about, so—since they have no applicable interest in Fisher or Joeckel—it's almost like the Browns were actually selecting fourth overall.

6. For the record, I would like to note that the term "war room" is kind of silly. But it's the term everyone uses.

and I'm curious about the number of last-minute trades that will be offered and rejected. I feel like I'm about to see something few people ever see. But I'm totally wrong. I don't see anything. Because at exactly 5:30, the owner of the Cleveland Browns steps into the war room, and I am immediately kicked out.

This, of course, contradicts the entire reason I went to Cleveland in the first place. As far as I was concerned, the machinations of draft night were pretty much the whole story. But something else is going on here—something a little more serious. It's possible the Browns never intended to let me see the draft, and that this carrot was only offered as a way to make the story happen. It's equally possible I somehow misunderstood our original agreement. However, I suspect my ejection from the draft room had more to do with the owner himself. Jimmy Haslam III purchased the Browns franchise last October for $1 billion. His brother is the governor of Tennessee. But Haslam has been in the news all week, for reasons that are unrelated to football. It's due to a possible conspiracy involving the company Haslam owns, Pilot Flying J. According to the FBI, Haslam's company has been defrauding "unsophisticated" diesel fuel customers for the past five years. Investigators believe Pilot Flying J—one of the largest truck stop chains in the country—was offering trucking clients substantial fuel rebates that were never honored. Taken at face value, it doesn't sound like the crime of the century. But on April 15, FBI agents raided the Pilot Flying J headquarters in West Knoxville, Tennessee. Draft night was held a scant ten days after this raid. Haslam's personal role in the fraud remains unclear, but it's easy to understand why he might not be thrilled by the concept of spending an evening in the same room as a reporter, regardless of what the story is supposed to be about.

Scheiner escorts me out of the room without explanation (although he does apologize the next morning, via text). The rest of the night becomes a massive anticlimax. I spend the remainder of the evening with the other media members in the end zone of the team's indoor practice field, watching the draft on television. The Browns do select Barkevious Mingo and make a point of referring to him as "Kiki." In a press conference following the pick, Banner says, "This is the outcome we were hoping for."

That's true. For Banner, it probably was. But it wasn't the outcome I was hoping for. I was hoping to see the unseen. I wanted to understand how you turn a losing franchise into a winning franchise. I wanted to be inside the inside. But that proved impossible, and perhaps it always was. At least in suburban Cleveland, the future remains a burnt-orange shade of opaque.

The following profile of James Murphy ran in *The Guardian* in 2010. It's the reason I was later cast in the 2012 documentary *Shut Up and Play the Hits*, a film allegedly chronicling the "final" show of Murphy's band LCD Soundsystem. The directors of the movie asked if I would be willing to interview Murphy again, on camera, so that our conversation could serve as interstitial interludes in between the concert footage. They said they liked the interview in *The Guardian* and wondered if I could do it again. What I did not realize is that they literally wanted me to do the *exact same interview*. They were hoping I would ask all the same questions so that Murphy could answer them in the same way. This, as it turns out, didn't really happen (partially because I couldn't precisely remember what I had asked originally). But if you happen to see this movie, you're definitely not seeing a normal interview. You're seeing a fake version of me, attempting to conduct a fake interview for purposes unrelated to journalism.

I did a pretty bad job of pretending to be myself. But the rest of the film is quite good.

LCD Soundsystem reunited in 2016, four years after making a movie about how they would never perform again. Many people have since asked if I was annoyed by this, as I'm now a central character in a nonfiction film that was utterly unreal. My lazy answer is, "A little." But you know what? Nobody promised me anything. It was a job. The directors said, "Come to this location, sign this paperwork, conduct this interview, and we will pay you $5,000." I received what I was owed and got what I deserved.

I Hear That You and Your
Band Have Sold Your Guitars

James Murphy is the kind of guy who knows a little bit about a lot of hazily connected subjects—making music, selling music, fashion, drugs, electronics, mixed martial arts. But the thing he understands most is the unifying concept of *cool*. He's spent an inordinate chunk of his life thinking about what being cool signifies, and it's something his band LCD Soundsystem dissects and refigures in almost every song they produce. This May, LCD will release their third (and last) album, *This Is Happening*. And what appears to be "happening" is that Murphy has reached the apex of his (mostly real) persona: He now understands coolness so intimately that it's become an almost academic pursuit. He thinks about it more than he feels it.

"I was a lot cooler ten years ago." Murphy is saying this at a restaurant near his home in the Brooklyn neighborhood of Williamsburg, North America's hipster utopia. He immediately explains the difference between being in LCD now and his early days with Death From Above, the record label he helped create in 2001 with two like-minded associates. "New York likes art stars. When I was in DFA, we were seen as these crazy guys throwing these drug parties connected to some fashion show. That was cool to people. Now I'm just a guy in a band. I suppose what happened is that I spent my whole life wanting to be cool, but eventually came to recognize the mechanism of how coolness works. So it's not really that I don't want to be cool anymore—it's more like I've come to realize that coolness doesn't exist the way I once assumed."

People continually mention how Murphy doesn't look like a conventional pop star, but he doesn't look like a conventional forty-year-old adult, either—he's six-foot-one with an XXL torso, and his bangs protrude forward like the shelf of a cliff. His hands are enormous and he (somehow) always seems to have exactly two days' growth on his jowls. He wears a designer Yves Saint Laurent T-shirt to our interview, and he's still wearing it when he performs in front of 1,400 dance-punk nerds twelve hours later. Much like his lyrics, Murphy's conversation style toggles between low and high culture: He brings up arcane philosophies, undercuts his own ideas with self-deprecation, and then tries to reconcile the middle ground between them. Even when he talks about other people, it sounds like self-analysis.

"There are some people who are just plain great at making music. That's not who I am," he says. "However, I can succeed at making music that works as dumb body music, but that can also meet someone in the middle if they want to investigate our songs in a deeper way. I know the things I can do: I understand music and I trust my taste. And taste is important." What this essentially means is that LCD tries to make sophisticated music within the simplest possible parameters. Some might call such a goal pretentious; if they did, Murphy would not mind.

"I actually want to write a treatise in defense of pretension," he says. "I think the word 'pretension' has become like the word 'ironic'—just this catch-all term to distance people from interesting experiences and cultural engagement and possible embarrassment. Pretension can lead to other things. You know, the first time I read

Gravity's Rainbow, I did so because I thought it would make me seem cool. That was my original motivation. But now I've read it six times, and I find it hilarious and great and I understand it. You can't be afraid to embarrass yourself sometimes."

BECAUSE HIS LYRICS are often sardonic (the first single off the new record is titled "Drunk Girls") and because Murphy has a reputation for living hard (he often swigs a concoction of whiskey and champagne onstage), LCD appeals to a lot of people who just want to get stoned and jump in place. But the real reason it works is that Murphy understands the nature of sound; he uses repetition and tempo to dictate how the listener emotively responds to his work. I ask him if he can remember the first specific sound that moved him.

"Oh, yeah. *Revolver*, when I was six," he says immediately. "It was the song 'Tomorrow Never Knows.' The hum on that song. The other sound that really affected me was the hum from our refrigerator. I used to lie on the kitchen floor and put my head next to the vent on the refrigerator and sing these weird melodies in my mind. I've always sung to machines."

Twenty-five years later, he heard that hum again—but this time he was on Ecstasy. And in many ways, that was the embryonic moment when LCD Soundsystem was born.

"I was at a club not dancing, because I didn't dance. For years, I never danced," Murphy says. "I was on Ecstasy and I was peaking, and then the DJ played 'Tomorrow Never Knows' and I lost my marbles. But I also had a very important revelation, which was that the way I was feeling was actually *me*. It wasn't the drug. It was *me*. But you know, I never took Ecstasy until I was thirty. That's important. When it comes to drugs, I'm a big proponent of the boat-sails-wind analogy: Your life is a boat, the sails are your emotions, and drugs are the wind. When you're a kid, your boat is small and your sail is huge, and drugs are like a hurricane. So you need to get to a point in life where you have a big enough boat to navigate the weather."

IT SHOULD NOT BE DIFFICULT to imagine Murphy as a teenager, but it is. When he describes the younger version of himself, he sounds like a person who only exists in unrealistic teen movies—an idealistic counterculture badass who listened to krautrock while kickboxing. Yet when he tells these stories, the details are so rich and oblique that they must be at least partially true: Within the world of his rural New Jersey high school, Murphy was a very interesting, periodically terrifying kid.

"I used to get in fights a lot in high school," he says. "I was sort of fixated on fairness when I was fifteen, and I sort of looked wussy—I wore a lot of Smiths shirts and I had skater bangs. But I would often get into fights whenever things seemed unfair, and I was notorious for being a really, really crazy fighter. I hurt a few kids pretty bad. I broke one kid's orbital bone. I broke one person's arm. Broke some ribs. I was the kind of person who would sit on a guy's chest and just keep hitting him. I just got very upset anytime someone would antagonize me to the point of fighting, and I wanted to teach them a lesson. I kind of got psychotic, actually."

The inherent ambiguity of "fairness" is still present in a lot of Murphy's music. On the 2007 song "New York, I Love You," he fixates on the phrase *"Maybe I'm wrong and maybe you're right."* On the new track "Pow Pow," he keeps reconstructing and rewording the sentiment, *"From this position, I can see both sides. There's advantages to each."* Some of this obsession may have been inherited from Murphy's (now deceased) father. When James was eighteen, he got hassled by a police officer. Murphy's dad responded by saying, "Well, what do you expect? Look at how you're dressed." James countered that such a stereotype was "unfair." His father was not sympathetic to his plight.

"You're not even Irish. You're just *white*," the elder Murphy told him. "Fairness only matters when you're in a position of power and you're trying to make things fair for someone else. Life is not fair. You're a white, upper-middle-class male in the United States of America. The world is insanely unfair, and 99.9 percent of the time it's unfair in your favor. You've actively marginalized yourself, and that's your choice. I respect that. But tomorrow, you can cut your hair and become like everybody else. Try being black."

Murphy later attended New York University (he got mostly A's). In another weird example of fairness (or the lack thereof), Murphy almost became a writer for a television sitcom in 1992. A friend had submitted Murphy's prose writing to a TV executive who was looking for someone who understood New York. Murphy passed on the opportunity; he absentmindedly thought the offer had come from someone involved with *It's Gary Shandling's Show*, an esoteric comedy that ran on the fledgling Fox network from 1986 to 1990. A decade later—while looking through storage boxes in his parents' home after they'd both died—he found the old business correspondences from that period of his life. The show he had actually been offered a writing job with was *Seinfeld*, which would become the most popular sitcom in U.S. history.

"I didn't think much about it at the time. I was twenty-two. I just went back to New York to smoke pot and play guitar," he says. "But even knowing what I know now, I'm happy I didn't do it."

Recorded in drug-friendly Los Angeles, *This Is Happening* is very much in the vein of LCD's previous work: long, euphoric, rhythm-conscious songs that are only slightly more funny than depressing. Murphy writes exceptionally well about friendship and self-identity, and he deftly captures the aphoristic interior monologues of smart, problematic people (on the album's first cut, he sings about a person who finds himself *"Talking like a jerk / Except you are an actual jerk / And living proof that sometimes friends are mean"*). This was a central reason director Noah Baumbach tapped Murphy to score *Greenberg*, a film about a former musician who loathes the world almost as much as he loathes himself. Of course, the clearest illustration of LCD's identity will always be 2002's multidimensional "Losing My Edge," the best song ever written about liking music too much.

"Almost all of my songs are perspective songs. People are complicated, and they're different on different days. To me, 'Losing My Edge' was the perfect narrative song that could have ever come from me," Murphy explains. "Everything had a layer behind it. Was it making fun of other people? Sure. Was it making fun of myself for making fun of other people? Sure. But it was also about me kind of *believing* the things I was saying, and it was also about being a little embarrassed for being the kind of person who would believe those kinds of things."

But now, the "kind of person who would believe those kinds of things" is (apparently) going to stop being that person; Murphy says *This Is Happening* will be the final LCD album (he'll still make music, but not with this same band and not in this same way). To some, the timing of this seems strange. But not to the man making the decision. He is still losing his edge, but this time it's on purpose.

"It seems simple to me," he says. "It just feels like this should be the last one. For one thing, I always told myself I wouldn't do LCD past the age of forty. For another thing, I don't know if EMI would put another record out by us. They've been very good to me and they've never tried to force me to create a hit, and everything people have told me about signing with a major label has proven untrue. But the way the industry is going, EMI might not even exist in three years. And a third factor is that I really want to do a good job, and I want to do everything myself. Now, I could have other people do some of those things for me, but then it's not really the band I want. The only reason I would do that is that this is a business, and that's not a good enough reason . . . It seems like something I didn't want to have happen *did* happen: I see this band as pure evidence that having a decent idea is more important than being talented."

That final statement is only half true. But that fact that Murphy can comprehend the part that *is* true is precisely why he'll never be uninteresting, even if LCD Soundsystem disappears forever.

The opening line of the subsequent feature is, "I probably don't need to tell you who Royce White is." I then spend the next two hundred words pedantically explaining who, in fact, Royce White is (because that's how journalism works). But it's a good thing I did, because he's pretty much evaporated from the popular culture. The average basketball fan has already deleted him from memory.

White was the sixteenth pick in the 2012 NBA draft. Two years later, he played 56 seconds for the Sacramento Kings in a game they lost by 20 points. That is the totality of his NBA career. He never made a single basket or snared a single rebound. But the reason White did not fulfill his potential is mesmerizing, as are many of the things he says in this interview. Someday, people may look back on the failure of Royce White and conclude that he was the first athlete to talk about a problem everyone else pretends isn't there: the strong possibility that many, many successful people are mentally ill (and precariously insulated by their notoriety).

On the day this article was published, White loved it and saw it as an objective, positive description of who he was and how he felt. He called my cell phone and left a super-excited voice mail about how much he appreciated the story. A few days later, other people convinced him that the profile was condescending and anti-labor, so White decided he liked it less.

White's Shadow

I probably don't need to tell you who Royce White is. He's already received about as much attention as any professional basketball player can, assuming that player has never played one minute of professional basketball.

This is, in fact, the second feature Grantland has published with White as the subject, along with a ten-minute *30 for 30* documentary filmed on the day he was drafted. *Sports Illustrated* sympathetically profiled White around that same time that summer, only to criticize him in a back-page essay the following winter. Last week, he appeared on both HBO's *Real Sports* and ESPN's *Pardon the Interruption* and made the same argument in both venues. As with the coverage of any cult of personality, there's a handful of biographical factoids that appear in virtually all of these profiles: One is that White led his college team, the Iowa State Cyclones, in all five major statistical categories as a sophomore (the only Div. I player in the country to do so). Another is that he's terrified of air travel. Another is that he's a self-styled twenty-one-year-old eccentric who plays the piano and writes screenplays about windmills. But the main thing everyone knows about Royce White is that he's locked in a contractual, philosophical dispute with the Houston Rockets, hinging on a mental illness that everyone accepts to be real.

White wants the Rockets to implement what he calls a "mental health protocol," a medical curriculum that essentially hinges on White having his own personal psychiatrist decide when he's mentally fit to play. The Rockets feel they've already done enough (including agreeing to drive him to away games so he won't have to fly). They want him to accept their compromise and show up for work. And for most people, this is the whole argument. If you side with White, you believe that his anxiety disorder is no different from a physical injury, and that his mental health advocacy is warranted and overdue; if you side with the Rockets, you suspect that White is something of a con man whose adversarial attitude is an affront to his $3 million contract and the calculated risk Houston took by drafting him sixteenth overall. It's a clash between labor and management, and his supporters and detractors tend to split down those preexisting lines.

But that practical dichotomy tends to deemphasize something that's considerably more complex: Royce White's radical (but not absurd) belief about mental illness as a whole.

I spoke to White last Wednesday, the night after his appearance on *Real Sports* debuted. Before examining anything else, I want to cut straight to the most interesting part of our conversation, which happened within the first ten minutes of dialogue. Here are the circumstances: I'd just landed in Houston and driven to my hotel downtown. At 4:56 p.m., I get a text from White, instructing me to meet him at the Cheesecake Factory near First Colony Mall, a shopping complex in Sugarland, Texas (roughly forty-five minutes away on US-59) at 5:50.[1] When I get there, he's seated in the outside patio with two African-American associates; one is a large fellow who declines to give his name ("That's irrelevant," he says when asked) and the other

---

1. Not 6:00 p.m., 5:50 p.m.

is someone named Bryant (who's wearing a faux-vintage 1956 letterman's jacket and constantly checking his phone). The roles these individuals play are nebulous. The 6-8 White is relaxed. He's wearing a backwards Obey Propaganda hat and shoes that resemble (and may actually function as) house slippers. He's built like a double helix of panther sinew—whenever he adjusts his left arm, the biceps bulges so dramatically that it's distracting. We make no chitchat. We immediately start talking about all the things we're expected to talk about. I mention a statistic: According to the National Institute of Mental Health, 26 percent of Americans over the age of eighteen suffer from a diagnosable mental disorder in any given year. I ask White if he thinks that stat carries over into the NBA. This was the subsequent interaction (make sure you read all the way to the end, when the conversation shifts unexpectedly) . . .

Do you believe 26 percent of the league is dealing with a mental illness, or does mental illness prompt those dealing with it to self-select themselves out of the pool? Are you the rare exception who got drafted?

The amount of NBA players with mental health disorders is *way* over 26 percent. My suggestion would be to ask David Stern how many players in the league he thinks have a marijuana problem. Whatever number he gives you, that's the number with mental illness. A chemical imbalance is a mental illness.

So, wait . . . if somebody has a drinking problem, is that—

That's a mental illness. A gambling addiction is a mental illness. Addiction is a mental illness.

Then what's the lowest level of mental illness? What is the least problematic behavior that still suggests a mental illness?

The reality is that you can't black-and-white it, no matter how much you want to. You have to be okay with it being gray. There is no end or beginning. It's more individualistic. If someone tears a ligament, there is a grade for its severity. But there's no grade with mental illness. It all has to do with the person and their environment and how they are affected by that environment.

Okay, I get that. But you classify a gambling addiction as a mental illness. Gambling is incredibly common among hypercompetitive people. The NBA is filled with hypercompetitive people. So wouldn't this mean that—

Here's an even tougher thing that we're just starting to uncover: How many people *don't* have a mental illness? But that's what we don't want to talk about.

Why wouldn't we want to talk about that?

Because that would mean the majority is mentally ill, and that we should base all our policies around the idea of supporting the mentally ill. Because they're the majority of people. But if we keep thinking of them as a minority, we can say, "You stay over there and deal with your problems over there."

Okay, just so I get this right: You're arguing that most *Americans have a mental illness.*

Exactly. That's definitely correct.

But—if that's true—wouldn't that mean "mental illness" is just a normative condition? That it's just how people are?

That doesn't make it normal. This is based on science. If there was a flu epidemic, and 60 percent of the country had the flu, it wouldn't make it normal . . . the problem is growing, and it's growing because there's a subtle war—in America, and in the world—between business and health. It's no secret that 2 percent of the human population control all the wealth and the resources, and the other 98 percent struggle their whole life to try and attain it. Right? And what ends up happening is that the 2 percent leave the 98 percent to struggle and struggle and struggle, and they eventually build up these stresses and conditions.

So . . . this is about late capitalism?

Definitely. Definitely.

It is not that Royce White thinks he has a unique problem. It's more that Royce White believes society has made everyone slightly insane. And this helps and hurts his argument at the same time.

THE MORNING after I meet White, the Houston hip-hop station 97.9 KBXX interviews White on the air. He has been reinstated by the Houston franchise and intends on reporting to the Rockets D-league franchise, the Rio Grande Valley Vipers, on February 11 (he did not mention this the night before, although he did vaguely suggest he'd be on the Rockets roster "soon").[2] Maybe this will happen exactly as planned. Maybe he'll just become a conventional rookie, and maybe this controversy will evaporate. But that seems unlikely. For one thing, it's hard to deduce the level of White's current focus on basketball. In a theoretical universe, there's no question he could contribute to just about any team in the league: He's an ultra-physical point forward who can consistently get to the rim.[3] He's a deft passer[4] and an intelligent rebounder. Yet when I ask how much basketball he's been playing during this long stretch of inactivity, his answer is that he's hardly been playing at all. "I work out very sparingly, to be honest," White says. "I probably shoot once a week."[5] He's also currently experiencing the short-term reward of untested potential: As long as White doesn't play (and as long as his weaknesses remain unexposed), his reputation as a game-changer can only grow.

However, there's a much larger issue at play here, and it's unrelated to the game of basketball. It has to do with White's wider view on how mental illness—both his own, and that of others—is destroying the fabric of modern living. He's obsessed with the idea that no one wants to accept the "reality" of a profound social crisis he sees everywhere, infiltrating every aspect of culture and killing us softly.

"At the end of the day, we don't associate mental health disorders with having severe health risks. And they do," he explains. "In that

---

2. I also spoke with Daryl Morey, the Rockets' general manager. He declined to make any on-the-record statements, but seems to have a pretty reasonable view on White's potential future. Morey also mentioned that the true risk of selecting White was not as severe as many people think, since only about 20 percent of players drafted sixteenth overall end up having major NBA careers, anyway.
3. One comparison might be something in between James Harden and Roy Tarpley.
4. White partially credits his exceptional court vision directly to his anxiety disorder: "I'm always scanning for threats. I'm always watching everything. It's almost like a superpower. I'm ultra-aware . . . as a passer, and as a player who likes to play on the break, I see things before they happen. I can do things with the ball because I can anticipate what other people are going to do."
5. In some ways, this was the most unexpected thing White said to me. Maybe he was exaggerating to seem diffident—but why would he do that? I suspect he was just being straight.

Real Sports piece, they only touched on the addictive traits and the suicidal and homicidal behaviors [associated with mental illness]. But there are other elements that no one wants to talk about. Stress is one of the number-one killers of human beings. Stress hardens your arteries. And that's scary for a lot of humans, so they don't want to talk about it. It's like—what is the pollution in the air really doing to us? We'd rather just tiptoe around that idea and argue that it's the food that's killing us. But the reality is that stress is a killer of humans, and if we don't support mental health in the right way, the nature of the illness causes people to become overly stressed. And that's serious."

White's language is intense and discursive. Though usually well delivered, his statements toggle between progressive common sense and difficult-to-decipher, contradictory aphorisms. For example: The crux of White's demand to the Rockets is that he needs his own personal doctor to decide whether he's in the right mental mind frame to play a game or attend practice. That seems reasonable—until you consider what would happen if all 400+ players in the NBA made the same request (for both mental *and* physical ailments). It would reinvent the power dynamic, effectively allowing players to dictate when they were healthy enough to participate.

But White doesn't see it like that.

Except that he does.

"My request was to have an addendum to *my* contract," he begins. "Now, would that set a precedent? That's not really my thing. I asked for something to be put into *my* contract. Not something for all players to use."

But then he continues talking. And this is where it becomes difficult to see how White and the Rockets will ever find real common ground, even if he eventually ends up on their roster.

"But if you want to talk about it through that lens, every player *should* have their own doctor. The reality is that American businesses are built on the idea of cutting overhead. And how do we cut overhead?" White points to the door that leads from the patio to the main restaurant. "Why do restaurants put exit signs over every exit? I bet if Cheesecake Factory didn't have to do that, they wouldn't. Because it would cost less to do nothing. They have to be forced to do that. So if a team or a business can save money by making things less safe, they're going to do that. They don't care. It's a conflict of interest to have the team doctor paid by the team. What we need is a doctor who can look at a situation and say, 'Listen, I know the team wants you to do this, and I know their doctor is saying you should do this. But as a non-biased doctor with no interest in how you perform athletically, I recommend differently.' Right now, you have players pushing themselves back in three weeks who have three-month injuries."

I ask him if he understands why NBA owners might be reticent to give players that level of input into when they're ready to play basketball, particularly for a disease that's invisible and subjective.

"I'm always going to run into problems with people who think business is more important than human welfare," he replies.

PART OF WHAT MAKES WHITE so baffling (and so infuriating to his detractors) is the degree to which he seems normal. He concedes this is part of the problem, perception-wise; he says he's thought about his condition so much that he can now control it, most of the time. But that control makes it difficult for him to illustrate how he's different from any normal person who tends to get more nervous than necessary. For instance, it's not that White cannot bear to step on an airplane; he's taken dozens and dozens of flights throughout his short career, including one to Italy to play an exhibition for Iowa State. He just deeply hates the experience of flying (and says that he's racked with anxiety for several hours before takeoff, which is worse than the flight itself). White also hates driving and constantly scans the road for "threats," but that doesn't mean he *can't* drive (in the *Real Sports* segment, we see him calmly operating a vehicle with only one hand on the wheel). When I spoke with him at the Cheesecake Factory, he seemed more composed than many other celebrities and athletes I've interviewed in the past. But this, he insists, proves nothing except the complexity of his dilemma. "Everything is tied to my mental illness," he tells me. "It's like when you have arthritis: Even when you're not hurting, you're worried about when you will hurt next. It's always related."

White's problems began at age sixteen, in a cabin outside of Minneapolis, on the first (and only) day he ever smoked marijuana. The episode may superficially seem like a standard case of weed-induced paranoia, but that's not how it felt to White. "I think it was in Forest Lake, Minnesota," he recalls. "I had an out-of-body experience. It felt like I was watching myself have the experience. It was so traumatic for me, and I had such a bad reaction, I started having panic attacks for the next two or three months, in rapid succession. Sometimes two or three a day."

The son of a cosmetologist and a social worker, White was prescribed Prozac at the age of eighteen (he's still on it today). Having won Minnesota state titles with two different teams in high school, he initially attended the University of Minnesota but never played a game for the Gophers, transferring in the wake of two off-the-court incidents (the latter being an accusation of theft that was eventually dropped). He announced his "retirement" from the sport on You-Tube but eventually transferred to Iowa State, where he flourished under coach Fred Hoiberg (a man White clearly admires).

Somewhat surprisingly, White does not deny that he could play for Houston right now, if that were his decision. He could handle the travel, at least in the short term. "I probably could do it," he says. "But what would the effect be? What would I have left at the end of the season? How good would I be for the team during the season?"

His argument, in essence, is that just being able to *withstand* something does not mean it's reasonable and healthy. He doesn't think that a person's mere ability to manage stress detracts from its corrosive nature. That's undeniably true. But here again, a conflict emerges from the specific lifestyle White is involved with: The demands of his chosen profession are utterly abnormal. Which leads to another unusual exchange . . .

What if stress is just part of it?

What does that mean, "It's just part of it"? That's like saying people getting killed is just part of war.

But people getting killed is part of war. That's the downside of war.

It doesn't have to be, though. We choose that. When you say, "That's just part of it," it implies that this is natural. Volcanoes don't kill human beings. Volcanoes kill human beings because human beings build houses right next to them.

Yes. But when I ask, "What if stress is just part of it?" I'm really asking, "What if it's just part of the choice that society has made?" It may be problematic, but what if we've all agreed that this problematic thing is part of the experience of being involved in a rarefied profession?

That's fine. But don't act like this wasn't a choice.

So what would you have done if, upon drafting you, the Rockets had said this: "Look—this is going to be hard for you. It might, in fact, be detrimental. But that is just part of competing at this sport at this level."

You can't do that, though. You can't discriminate against somebody, because that's ADA[6] law. People say I'm getting special treatment, but it's the NBA who wants special treatment. They want to say they're this rarefied profession where laws don't apply. But ADA law is federal. I've always said the NBA should have a mental health policy. I didn't know they didn't have one, until I got drafted. But the NCAA doesn't have one, either . . . I had to sit my first year at Iowa State, because there was no mental health protocol. I transferred on the basis of mental health issues. Both my doctor and my psychiatrist wrote letters to the NCAA that said my staying at Minnesota would not be healthy, because I'd just been through a three-month case where I was targeted by police for a crime I was not guilty of, and that I needed a fresh start. Because I have a mental illness. But the NCAA denied my waiver.

What was the NCAA's argument?

They didn't really have one. They said it was my choice to transfer.

THERE ARE TIMES when White seems like a brilliant ninth-grader who just wrote a research paper on mental illness and can't stop talking about it. He's arrogant, and perhaps not as wise as he believes himself to be. But sometimes he offers genuine insight into the mediated

---

6. Americans with Disabilities Act.

discomfort of modernity, such as when we discuss Twitter.[7] White is the type of celebrity who likes to retweet messages that are sent to him directly. This makes (a little) sense when the content of the tweet is positive and uplifting. But it comes across as unlikable when he retweets messages that are negative and crazy (because it makes it seem like the attention is its own reward). I ask him why he does this. He gives two reasons. The first is banal and abstract (something about "neutralizing negativity with positivity"). But his second reason is worth considering: He views social media as "the greatest census of our era." And the census data he's collecting is really, really dark.

"As much as we want to think that these are just people behind computer screens, those people are living next door to you," he says. "They are people behind computer screens in schools. In hospitals. Working in Washington, D.C. These are real people. How many times does this stuff have to happen before we admit something really disturbing is going on here? I think *one* person tweeting *'Fuck you, go kill yourself'* is disturbing. But when you get into the hundreds of those tweets? The thousands of those tweets? I see a lot of people out there with really volatile mental disorders that are not getting help. Because I go to their own Twitter pages, and I can see they're not just sending those messages to me. They're sending them to a bunch of people. I mean, if you tweet at me five times in seven minutes, because I'm not playing for a team you have no real connection to? That is not good. That suggests mental illness. And even if you say, 'But I love this team to death,' it means you've put too much investment into entertainment. It's probably not good for you."

Because White sees mental illness everywhere, his goal as an activist is the creation of free mental health clinics in every major urban

---

7. When I originally wrote this story, White had about 144,000 Twitter followers. By late 2016, that number approached 500,000.

area, modeled after the system currently used by Planned Parenthood. It's a valid idea, particularly if you accept White's insistence that pretty much everyone needs help. We talk about his cultural heroes, and he detects shades of mental illness in all of them: John Lennon, Frank Sinatra, Michael Jordan. "[Jordan] definitely had a mental illness," he argues. "He was obsessed. He was obsessed with being great. Now, is that bad? It would be, if everybody else wasn't already telling him that he was." His dedication to this cause is sincere; he tells me he's "literally willing to die" for human welfare. I don't doubt that he would jeopardize his career over this principle, and when he casually notes that basketball does not "define" who he is, it doesn't sound like cliché posturing. This is a man who wants his cultural footprint to be deep. I ask how he felt when the *Real Sports* reporter (Bernie Goldberg, who is also a correspondent for Fox's *The O'Reilly Report*) referred to him as either courageous or "insufferable." White's initial response was confusion. His real response was unflinching.

"I think it's a very true statement. At the end of the day, we all stand on one side of a line, and it's always going to be opposed by somebody else," he says. And then he really goes to the rack. "I don't like to compare myself to other great people.[8] But I'm sure Gandhi was insufferable to some people. Martin Luther King was insufferable. JFK was certainly insufferable. Galileo was insufferable. It's always tough to tolerate people who say the things that other people don't want to say."

First they ignore you, then they laugh at you, then they fight you, then you win. In the coming weeks, we shall all see where Royce White fits into that continuum (or if he fits there at all).

---

8. I realize people who read this article will exclusively dwell on the segment of the quote that follows this particular sentence. But I want to remind people that he did start with, "I don't like to compare myself to other great people." Granted, phrases that start in that manner rarely reflect positively on the speaker. But he was talking to a reporter who was asking him about his own self-perception, and—though I did not ask him to compare himself to anyone—I certainly did not dissuade him from doing so.

I wrote a Gnarls Barkley feature for *The New York Times Magazine* in spring of 2006, right before the band got huge. That hugeness lasted slightly more than one summer. As I reread this story a decade later, I'm mostly struck by all the things that now seem incorrect. The story dwells on one member of a two-man band, even though the other guy ultimately became more conventionally famous. The whole premise of the profile operates from the perspective that rock music would remain popular throughout the twenty-first century. And most notably, the article doesn't have a proper conclusion. In the original version, I had a hokey, tacked-on ending that made very little sense. Before it ran in the magazine, my editor and I came up with an alternative ending that was more sensible, but also boring. Looking at it now, I think it's better with no ending at all. The story just stops. But that was going to happen anyway.

I'm including it in this anthology because (a) it accidentally captures the awkward cultural atmosphere of 2006, and (b) Danger Mouse—who doesn't grant many interviews—said several smart things about how art works.

House Mouse
in the Mouse House

North Hollywood sounds like a place that could be glamorous, or perhaps mildly attractive. It is not. At least it's not on Hinds Ave., where dirty one-story buildings look semi-deserted and many of the local "beautiful people" appear to have jobs that involve (a) ripping apart used cars, and (b) selling those individual parts to less beautiful people whose cars are even more used. Nobody on this North Hollywood avenue looks famous, and a few of them look terrifying. But it just so happens that 7325 Hinds Ave. is the geographic location of Power Plant Studios, and—inside those nondescript walls—a human named Danger Mouse is talking about an album that has just sold 91,000 copies in England within the span of seven days. Danger Mouse doesn't look famous, either; he also doesn't look dangerous, or even rodent-esque. And even though I am asking him about music, he is (kind of) talking about movies. But that doesn't mean he isn't answering my questions.

"What changed everything was when I got into Woody Allen," says Danger Mouse, whose real name is Brian Burton. He is sitting on a couch in the Power Plant lounge, eating two different kinds of pizza and drinking Vitamin Water; his legs and arms are folded like a mantis. There is a massive flat-screen TV in the room that's tuned to the TV Guide network, but the volume is off. "When I got to college, I saw *Manhattan* and *Deconstructing Harry*. I thought to myself, 'Why do I relate so much to this white sixty-year-old Jewish guy? Why do I understand his neurosis?' So I just started watching all of his movies. And what I realized is that they worked because Woody Allen was an auteur: He did his Thing, and that particular Thing was completely his own. That's what I decided to do with music. I want to create a director's role within music, which is what I tried to do on this album."

If you know who Danger Mouse is (which is totally possible, considering the commercial potentiality of the record we're discussing and the illegal things he's done in the past), these sentiments probably make sense immediately. If you have no idea who Danger Mouse is (just as plausible, considering the nature of pop music), they will require *a lot* of context before it becomes apparent how a record producer's greatest musical influence is the same man who made *Hannah and Her Sisters*. But here's the bottom line, regardless of how much you know (or don't know) about Brian Burton: The musical object in question, *St. Elsewhere* by Gnarls Barkley, was constructed differently from the vast majority of mainstream rock 'n' roll albums. And if *St. Elsewhere* succeeds over the long haul, that success will be a direct result of the way it was made, a blueprint that contradicts the conventional way in which rock bands are supposed to create music.

When Gnarls Barkley performs live, there are fourteen people on-stage. However, Gnarls Barkley is technically just two people: Danger Mouse (the aforementioned Burton) and an Atlanta-based singer/ rapper named CeeLo (born Thomas Calloway). But in a larger sense, Gnarls Barkley is really just *one* person, and that person is Burton. CeeLo is essential, but essential in the same way Diane Keaton was essential to *Annie Hall*: He is the voice that incarnates Burton's vision, so he serves as the frontman. On the surface, CeeLo looks like the vortex—he wrote the lyrics and sings the vocals on "Crazy," a single on the cusp of becoming the demographically limitless song of the summer (i.e., a 2006 version of OutKast's "Hey Ya!"). Yet even while "Crazy" is CeeLo's song, it's still Burton's *design*. It's the product of a singular vision, which is (more or less) the whole idea. The music of Gnarls Barkley is collaborative, but not in a creative sense; the goal of this collaboration is to reproduce the music that already exists inside Burton's skull.

"A song like 'Crazy' is a great example. I brought in a song that I felt was a complete Ennio Morricone rip-off," says Burton, referring to the definitive composer of countless spaghetti western scores. "But CeeLo and I started talking, and I somehow got off on this tangent about how people won't take an artist seriously unless they're insane. And we were saying that—if we *really* wanted this album to work—the best move would be to just kill ourselves. That's how audiences think. It's retarded. So we started jokingly discussing ways in which we could make people *think* we were crazy. We talked about this for hours, and then I went home. But while I was away, CeeLo took that conversation and made it into 'Crazy,' which we recorded in one take. That's the whole story. The lyrics are his interpretation of that conversation."

On the surface, such a methodology might make Danger Mouse sound like egocentric taskmaster (and accused murderer) Phil Spector, the studio genius who (allegedly) threatened musicians with firearms when they did not perform songs to his liking. This would not be accurate. A better comparison might be Brian Eno, the British engineer/musician who used various bands and artists to generate the myriad musical concepts he imagined. However, there's at least one crucial difference: Even though Eno was the intellectual force behind groups like Roxy Music and albums like *"Heroes,"* he was never the star; the star was always someone like Bryan Ferry or David Bowie. The star was someone else. What's atypical about Gnarls Barkley is that the star is Burton, even though he's barely visible onstage and—during the performance—plays only one instrument (the xylophone, and only when the band covers a specific Violent Femmes song). Burton has the kind of paradoxical personality that's weirdly familiar among creative types: He's simultaneously confident and insecure, and he's a natural introvert who elected to become a public figure. More significantly, he's a highly focused dude, and that focus is clear—Danger Mouse wants musical autonomy. He wants to be the first modern rock auteur, mostly because he understands a critical truth about the creative process: Good art can come from the minds of many, but great art usually comes from the mind of one.[1]

"I don't make a band's next album," he says. "I don't like making someone else's songs better. I'm not interested in that. This is where the Woody Allen thing comes back in. I have to be in control of the project I'm doing. I can create different kinds of musical worlds, but the artist needs the desire to go into that world. I won't fight with people to try and make the sounds I hear inside my head. What I want is for the leader of a group to come to me, and then I lead *that* person. Because even with my favorite bands, I only like thirty or forty percent of what they do. I'd want to make that thirty percent into the whole album."

I ask if there is anyone he considers to be a model for this paradigm, or if there is any producer whose career he would like to emulate.

"Musically, there is no one who has the career I want. That's why I have to use film directors as a model," Burton says. "But I think there are other people who could do what I do, and maybe *St.*

---

1. This kind of belief in the sublime vitality of auteurism has been widely dismissed over the past ten years, replaced by the belief that everything of value is inherently collaborative (and that amplifying the creative role of a lone individual enforces an ingrained form of social privilege). I believe this new thinking is mostly wrong and misses the point. I will, however, concede that the argument exists.

Elsewhere will open things up. Like, Jack White was able to take control of Loretta Lynn, and the result [2004's *Van Lear Rose*] was a great record. And that's cool. That's the goal."

THE COACHELLA VALLEY Music and Arts Festival is the hottest weekend in American popular music. This designation is literal: It takes place in the arid California desert, and it feels like watching MTV2 inside a blast furnace. Set on an expanse of polo fields twenty-five miles west of Palm Springs, Coachella annually hosts around eighty disparate musical acts and forty thousand highly disparate fans; I was told that one of the people in attendance at this year's event was Francis Ford Coppola, spotted wearing unmatched socks and sitting in the VIP area with his daughter, Sofia, checking out a Sunday-afternoon performance by Sleater-Kinney.

There were three acts at the 2006 Coachella that most of its forty thousand guests seemed to be talking about. The first was Madonna, arguably the most important female musician of the twentieth century (she was curiously performing inside a tent, far away from the main stage). The second was the prog-metal band Tool, a reclusive, hypercredible volume machine performing live for the first time in four years. The third act was Gnarls Barkley. The combined record sales of Madonna and Tool exceed 100 million; during the weekend of Coachella, Gnarls Barkley had yet to release a record in America. This, somehow, did not seem strange.

Gnarls would play Sunday afternoon; on Saturday, Burton and CeeLo conducted backstage interviews with a succession of random journalists (this was four days before I would talk with Burton privately in North Hollywood). Because it's an outdoor festival, the backstage area of Coachella is merely a collection of couches shaded by tents, hidden on three sides by trailers. There were no throngs of pretty girls, although there were several girls dressed as if they thought they were pretty; there was no backstage debauchery, unless you count roadies eating hummus. When I first saw Burton and CeeLo, they were talking to a reporter from *Rolling Stone*. Burton was dressed plainly and wearing sunglasses. CeeLo was eating Lay's potato chips. CeeLo's head is bald and his limbs are freakishly huge; his wristwatch looked as large as a wall clock. He is covered with tattoos. One is the familiar symbol of yin and yang. Another is the logo of the Green Bay Packers. Another is the word "blood." I asked him if the BLOOD tattoo means he is a gang member, and he said it does not. However, his denial was not particularly convincing.

"I am not gang-affiliated," said CeeLo, "but I am gang-*associated*. I'm not the least bit active, but—*coincidentally*—a lot of my homies are Bloods. *A lot* of them."

CeeLo is a clever guy with a diverse career: Before Gnarls Barkley, CeeLo was best known as a member of Goodie Mob, one of the first significant hip-hop acts to emerge from the Deep South (he would eventually quit the group, citing his peers' unwillingness to expand musically). He was a backup singer on TLC's #1 single "Waterfalls" and the writer and producer of "Don't Cha," a club hit for the Pussycat Dolls (and a track currently used in a Heineken commercial, the beverage CeeLo—perhaps coincidentally—drinks during our conversation). He was also in an episode of the MTV reality program *My Super Sweet Sixteen* with his sixteen-year-old stepdaughter Sierra (it is important to note that Sierra is his stepdaughter, as CeeLo is only thirty-one years old).

CeeLo classifies himself as a soul singer and a writer, but not as a rapper (he says "rap is just a cadence"). When he talks, CeeLo sounds like a preacher, which might be a product of his upbringing; both his parents were ministers. However, his father died when he was two and his mother passed when he was eighteen. It sounds like CeeLo's youth was not tranquil.

"I was reckless," he said. "I was a bully. I was a violent guy, and I was a pyromaniac. I almost burned down our house once. We were moving into this house in College Park, Atlanta; we had just moved in, and the heat wasn't turned on yet. I was sprinkling gasoline on a fire to keep warm, and the fire jumped up through the nozzle. I panicked. I threw the whole gas can into the fire. It burned up a side of a wall."

After he told this anecdote, I mentioned that this did not sound like the actions of a teenage pyromaniac; it sounded more like an accident.

"Yeah, except that I liked it," CeeLo responded. "I liked the fire I was causing."

Before they ever met, Burton knew who CeeLo was. This was primarily because he liked Goodie Mob, but partially because Burton's sister married a guy who had gone to CeeLo's high school ("My brother-in-law told me he was a thug," he recalls). They first interacted in the mid-'90s, on a rainy night in Athens, Ga., back when Burton was still an unknown telecommunications student at the University of Georgia. Goodie Mob was playing a show with Out-Kast, and there was a local talent contest to see who would serve as the opening act. Burton enlisted a few friends and created an ad hoc group dubiously called Rhyme & Reason. They placed second in the contest, but they still got to perform. After the show, Burton gave CeeLo a CD of music he had been working on, because he knew CeeLo's tastes went outside the normal parameters of rap.

"He knew I liked Portishead," said CeeLo. "That was our unspoken bond. When he told me he dug Portishead, that was all I needed to know."

Considering the consciously genre-defying construction of *St. Elsewhere*, it might seem almost paradoxically predictable that the druggy, suicidal soundscapes of a white British trip-hop act served as foundation for a musical relationship between two black guys in Georgia. "When I played my music for CeeLo," says Burton, "he moved his body in the way I imagined this music was supposed to make people react. So I thought, 'Maybe I've found the singer for these songs.'" The pair eventually began work on *St. Elsewhere* in the fall of 2003, starting with a demo called "Storm Coming" that would eventually make the final LP. However, something happened in between then and now, and that something probably needs to be explained before we go any further: In 2004, Danger Mouse released the most popular album in rock history that virtually no one paid for.

"AH, *THE GREY ALBUM*," says Burton, sighing dramatically. We are back in North Hollywood, where Danger Mouse is still consuming pizza. I had a suspicion this was a subject Burton might find troubling, and I assumed he would not want to talk about it. I am half right. "*The Grey Album* is so misunderstood. I didn't even call it *The Grey Album*. If you look at my original files for those songs, they're labeled 'The Black-White Album.' And the thing is, most people who have that record think the way it sounds is the way I *wanted* it to sound. And that's not the case at all."

Timing isn't everything, but it's close. Sometimes interesting things happen and nobody cares; sometimes interesting things happen and everybody cares. *The Grey Album* exists in that second category. In early 2004, Burton was working on albums with a couple of uncommercial indie rappers; he had already released three well-regarded (but widely ignored) electronic albums under the moniker Pelican City, and he'd earned some money making bumper music for the Cartoon Network. He was unknown to the world at large, but mildly established within a specific, insular faction of the music industry. And in 2004, that industry was being reinvented against its will. The concept of downloading music had suddenly become normative; because of Napster (and the lawsuits that had shut it down), everyone understood what downloading was, even if they weren't doing it. That process raised new questions about who owned music, and about what that ownership meant. Meanwhile, technology had accelerated, making it possible for anyone with a computer to manipulate existing music and copy it instantaneously. The entire sonic landscape teetered on the precipice of wholesale evolution.

It was at this point that Burton decided to straighten up his bedroom.

"One day I was cleaning my room and listening to the Beatles' *White Album*," he says. "I was kind of bored, because the other hip-hop work I was doing was really easy. Somebody had sent me an a cappella version of *The Black Album*, but I was already doing stuff with CeeLo and Jemini and Doom, so I didn't want to waste my beats on a remix record." *The Black Album* is a 2003 release by Jay-Z. Jemini and Doom are two rappers who Burton was collaborating with. The Beatles are the Beatles. "So I'm listening to *The White Album* and I'm putting *The Black Album* away, and I suddenly have this idea: I decide to see if I could take those two albums and make one song, just because of the names of the two albums and because they're perceived as being so different and because I've always loved Ringo Starr's drum sound."

Despite the avalanche of publicity that eventually surrounded *The Grey Album*, the first part of Burton's explanation for its creation is consistently overlooked: This was mainly a linguistic coincidence. If everyone referred to the Beatles' 1968 double album by its proper eponymous name (*The Beatles*), none of this would have ever happened.

"I sat down and tried to make one track, and it happened really fast," Burton recalls. "Then I tried to make a second song, and it took *a lot* longer, but it still worked. And I thought, 'Wow. What if I can do the whole album?' It was almost this Andy Warhol moment, where I made a decision to do something artistically without a clear reason as to why, except to show people what I *could* do. I could never do an album like that again. I still don't know where I found the patience to make those songs. It took me about twenty days in a row, and those were all twelve- and thirteen-hour days. And the whole time I was doing it, I was terrified someone else would come up with the same idea, which would have ruined everything. Because really, the idea is pretty simple."

This is true; it's simple to anyone who's played *The Grey Album* even once. But if you haven't, here's what it sounds like: Imagine every musical element of *The White Album* chopped into separate parts (every individual drum fill, the bridge from "Helter Skelter," the intro to "While My Guitar Gently Weeps," etc.). Burton then reconstituted those dissected parts into loops and patterns and samples, which were then placed underneath Jay-Z's rapping (Jay-Z had officially released an a cappella version of *The Black Album*, so the acquisition of the words was easy). Some of those combinations melded remarkably well, and it all seemed like such a clever idea, and it was the perfect moment for something like that to happen, and people just went nuts for it. Burton now assumes the album has gone multiplatinum, although (of course) he has no way of knowing for sure. *Entertainment Weekly* named it album of the year, and the record label EMI sent Burton a cease-and-desist letter for unlawful use of the Beatles catalog. And it was all because some shadowy, enigmatic figure called DJ Danger Mouse burned three thousand CDs to impress a handful of people nobody has ever heard of.

"I thought it would be a weird, cultic record for techies to appreciate, because they would be the only people who would understand how much work was involved," he says. "But then it was taken into this whole different world, where a million people were downloading it at the same time. At best, that record is just quirky and odd and really illegal. I never imagined people would play those songs in clubs. I also think the people who love it tend to love it for the wrong reasons, and the people who hate it tend to hate it for the wrong reasons. I think some people love it for what it supposedly did to the music industry, which was not my intent. I did not make *The Grey Album* for music fans. I made it to impress people who were really into sampling."

That is probably true. However, there's a metaphoric relationship between *The Grey Album* and the person who made it, and that relationship feels relevant. To unsuspecting consumers, *The Grey Album* seemed like the union of two cultures that were not only different, but ideologically opposed; it made people realize musical connections they never knew existed. That is more or less the story of Burton's life.

His childhood was spent in a predominantly Jewish neighborhood in Spring Valley, New York, where his was one of only two black families. "My parents didn't tell me anything about why I was different," he insists. "I think that was good. I had no idea why I looked the way I looked, so I had to use my imagination." It was the 1980s, so Danger Mouse listened to Poison. When he became a teenager, his parents moved to Georgia. Everyone there was black. He listened to RZA. By the time he got to college, he had become deeply obsessed with hip-hop; for a long while, it was the only genre he consumed. But then he decided to have a beer in public, and everything changed at once.

"I remember hearing Pink Floyd's 'Wish You Were Here' in a bar," Burton says. "This was around 1995. And I remember thinking it was so beautiful. It just put me in a daze. I asked someone what it was, and they were like, 'You don't know? This is Pink Floyd.' Now, I had heard of Pink Floyd, but I never really knew what they sounded like.

I had never actually played Pink Floyd records. And I suddenly found myself wondering, 'Why have I spent all these years never listening to this music?' And the reason was that I was afraid to do anything that would have seemed socially unacceptable. I was afraid that people wouldn't think of me as this hip-hop guy, because hip-hop was my Thing. So then I went out and bought every Pink Floyd record."

WHEN GNARLS BARKLEY finally takes the Coachella stage at 6:42 p.m. on Sunday, the band opens with the intro to "Breathe" off Pink Floyd's *Dark Side of the Moon.* This is not because Burton had a beer in 1995; this is because all fourteen group members are dressed like characters from *The Wizard of Oz,* a movie that so-called synchronicity buffs like to play simultaneously with *Dark Side of the Moon* (you hit "play" on the CD player when the MGM lion roars for the third time, just before the opening credits, and all kinds of weird coincidences pop up as you watch and listen). The stage is populated with numerous flying monkeys, two Dorothys (one black, one white), two Scarecrows, a bunch of witches, and six laptop computers. Burton portrays the Tin Man and hides at the rear of the stage. CeeLo is out front as the Cowardly Lion, sporadically asking the crowd if they have ever "seen freedom" and if they "want to rock" (he makes it very clear that Gnarls Barkley is supposed to be a *rock* band).

CeeLo's voice is octaves higher than his physical appearance indicates, so it soars above the unconventional tempos of the music; one of Burton's pet interests is presenting melodies at unorthodox, inconsistent speeds. All the songs are short, often under three minutes. Considering that this show was nine days before the U.S. release of *St. Elsewhere,* it was surprising to note how much of the audience was already familiar with the material, but perhaps that should be expected; the songs have been in the electronic ether for weeks. "Crazy" went to #1 in the UK solely on the strength of download sales.[2]

None of the twelve musicians added to the Gnarls Barkley touring lineup played on *St. Elsewhere*, but they're generally polished veterans; most have more professional experience than Burton. The drummer (Chris Vrenna) was in Nine Inch Nails. The bassist (Justin Meldal-Johnsen) plays with Beck. One of the backup singers (Res) has her own record deal with Universal. When the *St. Elsewhere* songs are performed live, they sound a little like funk songs; when I later mention that to Burton, he gets a little bummed out. ("Yeah, I know," he says, mildly annoyed. "We kept saying, 'Too funky. This is too funky.' It's a problem.") During the early days of the *St. Elsewhere* sessions, CeeLo and Burton had no intention of touring at all, or at least no notion of how such a tour would operate. The only goal was to make a certain kind of album, which *St. Elsewhere* may or may not be.

"What I was originally trying to do was make a psychedelic record that sounded liked psychedelic records from the late 1960s and early '70s. Basically, anyone who was copying the Beatles," Burton says. "I suppose bands like the 13th Floor Elevators and the Prunes are the ones people have heard of, but that was really nameless music; there were thousands of those groups. And what I liked about those bands was that the musicians made crazy decisions. They would play a normal melody for thirty seconds and then throw in something completely uncommercial and insane. Why did they do that? It blew my mind. I wanted to make experimental music that still had melody."

The degree to which *St. Elsewhere* succeeds as psychedelia is open

---

2. I'm sure some people will read this sentence and think, "Well, why is that remotely remarkable? How else would a song go to #1, if not for downloads?" But in 2006, downloadable music was still viewed as an unserious commercial force. It almost felt like a novelty that was only of interest to college kids and technocrats obsessed with their iPods. At the time, even Danger Mouse was way more concerned with selling physical CDs.

to debate; at first exposure, it doesn't seem especially trippy or mind-altering. Burton claims there is a "steep learning curve" to the album, because the unorthodox tempos and cinematic elements can be lost on casual listeners. But this does not seem to be the case with the ultra-accessible "Crazy." The learning curve on that single was ridiculously low, which is probably why it exploded. "To have a record go to number one, you have to appeal to people who have no idea who you are or what you do," says Burton. "That's just the way it is."

There are several espoused mysteries surrounding Gnarls Barkley, some of which the duo seems to perpetuate on purpose. They usually refuse to explain why they named the band "Gnarls Barkley," prompting many writers to assume they must love former NBA power forward Charles Barkley. This is not the case. Burton was in a café with several friends in Silver Lake, Calif., and everyone at the table started making up fictional celebrity names like "Prince Gnarls" and "Bob Gnarley." When someone came up with "Gnarls Barkley," Burton wrote it down. That's the whole story. The pair also declines to be photographed unless they are both dressed as movie characters, which leads people to suspect that the outfits have some sort of symbolic relationship to the music; as it turns out, this is just something they like to do. Perhaps the strangest thing about their friendship is that CeeLo actually refers to Burton as "Danger Mouse" in casual conversation. As far as I can tell, he is the only person who does this.

"I very rarely call him Brian," says CeeLo. "I love the name Danger Mouse. It's an oxymoron, you know. But he *is* dangerous. He is."

When I spoke to Burton at Power Plant, he was in the process of leading band rehearsals for a Gnarls Barkley tour, although—at the time—no tour schedule had been set. The future of the band is still being invented, as there is still some uncertainty about how popular *St. Elsewhere* will be in America (although it did open on the domestic Billboard charts at #2). Nonetheless, Burton says there will definitely be another Gnarls album in the future, and he already has plans to work with Black Thought from the Roots, Mark Linkous of Sparklehorse, and Blur frontman Damon Albarn (Burton recently produced the album *Demon Days* for Albarn's side project, Gorillaz).

When he describes those projects anecdotally, they sound like ordinary, conformist collaborations; what will be more compelling is when (and if) Burton can ultimately employ his so-called auteur philosophy in rock production. It will also be interesting to see if anything akin to a "Danger Mouse Sound" eventually emerges as his calling card. Traditionally, rock producers are defined by their ability to inject specific, recognizable qualities into the records they engineer. For the aforementioned Spector, it was the dense, layered "wall of sound." Steve Albini (best known for his work with the Pixies and Nirvana) consistently captures raw, jagged guitar riffs with vocals that are low in the mix; Robert "Mutt" Lange (Def Leppard, Shania Twain) specializes in polished, sculpted anthems that sound the way the 1980s felt. At this point in time, it would be impossible to categorize what a record by Danger Mouse could be expected to sound like. He doesn't have a clear signature. That might be because it's still too early in his career (Burton is only twenty-eight). However, it also might be because his aspirations don't necessitate a signature. His prototype is still being manufactured.

"Let's use Spike Lee as an example," says Burton, falling back to film analogies. "Let's say Spike Lee makes a movie with Jamie Foxx and Robert De Niro. Because of their three different reputations, you will have totally different demographics coming together for totally different reasons. But the film will still be taken seriously. In music, you don't have that. If you put Jay-Z on a record with Radiohead, it's a gimmick, because there's no central person you can depend upon to contextualize the ultimate product. But you can easily put two different actors in the same movie and have it still make sense—if the right director does it."

It must have been the autumn of 2015. My editor at *GQ* asked me to interview Tom Brady. "Sure," I say. "But there's only one subject I want to ask him about, so he better understand the nature of what I'll be asking." My editor contacts one of Brady's agents (at the time, he had several). The agent assures us that Brady *wants* to talk about the very topic I intend to inquire about. "This interview will resonate around the world," the agent insists.

We schedule a meeting in Boston. It's canceled. We schedule a second meeting. That one is canceled, too. "Tom would prefer to do this over the phone," the agent supposedly tells the magazine. "He doesn't want to look [you] in the eye when this stuff is discussed." Now I'm intrigued. What in the hell is this guy going to tell me? A photo shoot is conducted at Brady's home. The *GQ* photographer takes dozens of bizarre, memorable pictures. Tom Brady will now be on the cover of the magazine, no matter what happens during our interview. He will be on the cover of the magazine even if there's no interview at all, in all likelihood.

I'm supposed to interview Brady for about sixty minutes on a Tuesday. He calls from his car, fifteen minutes late. We make a little small talk, and then I get to the questions I need to ask. And it's immediately obvious that Brady is not going to tell me anything, and that he never had any intention of saying anything to anyone, and that it's quite possible he honestly assumed this interview was going to focus on how complicated it is to have a hot wife and an awesome apartment. What I thought was going to happen was never going to happen. It was all misdirection.

I consider this profile a failure. But I tried to make the best of it.

The Man Who Knew Too Much

Tom Brady is the greatest quarterback in NFL history.

That's just my opinion, and that opinion is fungible. If someone else had made the same claim five years ago, I would have disagreed. Five years ago, I didn't even think he was the best quarterback of his generation. But the erosion of time has validated his ascension. Classifying Brady as the all-time best QB is not a universally held view, but it's become the default response. His statistical legacy won't match Peyton Manning's, and Manning has changed the sport more. But Brady's six Super Bowl appearances (and his dominance in their head-to-head matchups) tilt the hagiographic scales in his direction. He has been football's most successful player at the game's most demanding position, during an era when the importance of that position has been incessantly amplified. His greatness can be quantified through a wide range of objective metrics.

Yet it's the subjective details that matter more.

America's fanatical, perverse obsession with football is rooted in a multitude of smaller fixations, most notably the concept of who a quarterback is and what that person represents. There is no cultural corollary in any other sport. It's the only position on the field a CEO would compare himself to, or a surgeon, or a literal general. It's the only position in sports racists still worry about.[1] People who don't care about football nevertheless understand that every clichéd story about high school involves the prom queen dating the quarterback. It serves as a signifier for a certain kind of elevated human, and Brady is that human in a non-metaphoric sense. He looks the way he's supposed to look. He has the kind of wife he's supposed to have. He has the right kind of inspirational backstory: a sixth-round draft pick who runs the 40-yard dash in a glacial 5.28 seconds, only to prove such things don't matter, because this job requires skills that can't be reliably measured. Brady's vocation demands an inexact combination of mental and physical faculties, and it all hinges on his teammates' willingness to follow him unconditionally. This is part of the reason Brady does things like make cash payments to lowly practice-squad players who pick off his passes during scrimmages—he must embody the definition of leadership, almost like a president. In fact, it sometimes seems like Brady could eventually *be* president, or at least governor of Massachusetts.

But this will never happen. When I ask if it's something he's ever considered, he responds as if I am crazy.

"There is a 0.000 chance of me ever wanting to do that," says Brady. "I just think that no matter what you'd say or what you'd do, you'd be in a position where—you know, you're politicking. You know? Like, I think the great part about what I do is that there's a scoreboard. At the end of every week, you know how you did. You know how well you prepared. You know whether you executed your game plan. There's a tangible score. I think in politics, half the

---

1. As it turns out, this was too much of a generalization on my end. After the Patriots defeated the Falcons in the Super Bowl, alt-right white supremacist Richard B. Spencer tweeted that part of the reason he liked New England was that they had three white wide receivers. It would seem racists are interested in the entire field.

people are gonna like you and half the people are not gonna like you, no matter what you do or what you say . . . It's like there are no right answers. If there were, everyone would choose the right answers. They're all just opinions."

Had Brady given this quote as a rookie, it would have meant nothing. It would have scanned as a football player with relativist views on politics. But the events of the past year imbue these words with a stranger, deeper significance. In last year's AFC championship game, the Patriots were accused of deflating the footballs below the legal level. What initially seemed like a bizarre allegation against a pair of anonymous equipment managers spiraled into a massive scandal that seemed to go on forever, consistently painting Brady as the only possible source of the malfeasance, even by his own coach, Bill Belichick, during an uncomfortable January 22 press conference. "Tom's personal preferences on his footballs are something that he can talk about in much better detail and information than I could possibly provide," Belichick said. "I can tell you that in my entire coaching career, I have never talked to any player about football air pressure."

In May, Brady was suspended by the NFL for four games. He appealed the suspension and was reinstated in time for the opening of the 2015 season. The same week, an intensely reported *ESPN The Magazine* story illustrated how NFL commissioner Roger Goodell bungled the Deflategate investigation and actively misinformed reporters. But the article was more damaging to the Patriots as an organization. It suggested Goodell purposefully over-penalized Brady and the Patriots on behalf of the other league owners, essentially as retribution for a decade of unproven institutional cheating (potentially including the first three New England Super Bowl victories, three games that were decided by a total of nine points).

Brady has never admitted to any wrongdoing. He beat the

suspension[2] without conceding anything (and in the four games he was supposed to miss, he completed 72 percent of his passes for nine touchdowns and zero interceptions). But things are different now, in a way that's easy to recognize but hard to explain. Even though he's said absolutely nothing of consequence in public, there is a sense that we now have a better understanding of who Tom Brady really is. And it's the same person we thought he was before, except now we have to admit what that actually means.

I'M INTERVIEWING BRADY at a complicated point in his life. There are several things I want to ask him, almost all of which involve the same issue. I'm told his press agent has promised an "explosive" interview, where nothing will be off the table. The initial plan is for the interview to happen in Boston, and it will be a lengthy conversation. Two days before I leave, the agent says that the interview can't happen face-to-face (and his explanation as to why is too weird to explain). It will now be a one-hour interview on the phone.

Brady calls me on a Tuesday. He's driving somewhere and tells me he has only forty-five minutes to talk. I ask a few questions about the unconventional trajectory of his career, particularly how it's possible that a man who was never the best quarterback in the Big 10 could end up as a two-time league MVP as a pro. He doesn't have a cogent answer, beyond classifying himself as a "late bloomer." We talk about the 2007 Patriots squad that went 16-0, and I ask if wide receiver Randy Moss was the finest pure athlete he ever played with. He begrudging concedes that Moss was "the greatest vertical threat," although he goes out of his way to compliment Wes Welker and Julian Edelman, too. He never

---

2. Actually, he didn't. The suspension was temporarily lifted in 2015, but that was pending appeal. He ultimately lost the appeal and had to sit out of the first four games of 2016. But the Patriots still opened at 3-1.

brags and he's never self-deprecating. He never offers any information that isn't directly tied to the question that was posed. Everything receives a concise, noncontroversial answer (including the aforementioned passage about his lack of political ambition). Realizing time is evaporating, I awkwardly move into the Deflategate material, citing the findings of the legal report published by NFL investigating attorney Ted Wells. The remainder of the interview lasts seven minutes.

There's one element of the Wells Report that I find fascinating: The report concludes that you had a "general awareness" of the footballs being deflated. The report doesn't say you were aware. *It says you were* generally *aware. So I'm curious—would you say that categorization is accurate? I guess it depends on how you define the word "generally." But was that categorization true or false?*

(*pause*) I don't really wanna talk about stuff like this. There are several reasons why. One is that it's still ongoing. So I really don't have much to say, because it's—there's still an appeal going on.

Oh, I realize that. But here's the thing: If you don't address this at all, the fact that you refused to talk about it will end up as the center of the story. I mean, how can you not respond to this? It's a pretty straightforward question.

I've had those questions for eight months and I've answered them, you know, multiple times for many different people, so—

I don't think you have, really. When I ask, "Were you generally aware that this was happening," what is the answer?

I'm not talking about that because there's still ongoing litigation. It has nothing to do with the personal question that you're trying to ask, or the answer you're trying to get. I'm not talking about anything as it relates to what's happened over the last eight months. I've dealt with those questions for eight months. It's something that—obviously, I wish that we were talking about something different. But like I said, it's still going on right now. And there's nothing more that I really want to add to the subject. It's been debated and talked about, especially in Boston, for a long time.

Do you feel that what has happened over these eight months has changed the way the Patriots are perceived?

I don't really care how the Patriots are perceived, truthfully. I really don't. I really don't. Look, if you're a fan of our team, you root for us, you believe in our team, and you believe in what we're trying to accomplish. If you're not a fan of us, you have a different opinion.

But what you're suggesting is that the reality of this is subjective. It's not. Either you were "generally aware" of this or you weren't.

I understand what you're trying to get at. I think that my point is: I'm not adding any more to this debate. I've already said a lot about this—

You haven't. I wouldn't be asking these questions if you had. There's still a lack of clarity on this.

Chuck, go read the transcript from a five-hour appeal hearing. It's still ongoing.

I realize it's still ongoing. But what is your concern? That by answering this question it will somehow—

I've already answered all those questions. I don't want to keep revisiting what's happened over the last eight months. Whether it's you, whether it's my parents, whether it's anybody else. If that's what you want to talk about, then it's going to be a very short interview.

So you're just not going to comment on any of this? About the idea of the balls being underinflated or any of the other accusations made against the Patriots regarding those first three Super Bowl victories? You have no comments on any of that?

Right now, in my current state in mid-October, dealing with the 2015 football season—I don't have any interest in talking about those events as they relate to any type of distraction that they may bring to my team in 2015. I do not want to be a distraction to my football team. We're in the middle of our season. I'm trying to do this as an interview that was asked of me, so . . . if you want to revisit everything and be another big distraction for our team, that's not what I'm intending to do.

But if I ask you whether or not you were generally aware of something and you refuse to respond, any rational person is going to think you're hiding something.

Chuck, I've answered those questions for many months. There is no—

Were you not informed by any of the people around you that these questions were going to be asked?

(*sort of incredulously*) No. I was—

No?

This is ongoing litigation.

Okay, well, I appreciate you taking—

I appreciate it.

—the time to talk to me. Sorry, man.

Okay.

So what did Brady say during his June 23 appeal testimony, in response to a question about whether he authorized the deflation of the footballs? "Absolutely not." When asked if he knew the footballs were being deflated (even if he never specifically requested that this happen), he said, "No." Which was (obviously) the answer I assumed he would give when I posed the same question to him in this interview. I did not think he would contradict any statement he gave under oath. But I still needed to establish that (seemingly predictable) denial as a baseline, in order to ask the questions I was much more interested in. Specifically . . .

- At what point did you become aware that people were accusing you of cheating?
- Do you (or did you) have any nonprofessional relationship with Jim McNally and John Jastremski, the Patriot equipment managers at the crux of this controversy?

- Do you now concede the balls probably were deflated, or is that a total fiction?
- Do you believe negligibly deflated footballs would provide a meaningful competitive advantage, to you or to anyone else on the offense?
- How do you reconcile the Patriots' statistically minuscule fumble rate, a rate that inexplicably plummeted around 2007? Is that simply a bizarre coincidence?
- If you had no general awareness of any of this, do you feel like Bill Belichick pushed you under the bus during his January press conference? Were you hurt by this? Did it impact your relationship?

These questions shall remain unasked, simply because Brady refused to repeat a one-word response he claims to have given many times before. Now, I'm not a cop or a lawyer or a judge. I don't have any classified information that can't be found on the Internet. My opinion on this event has as much concrete value as my opinion on Brady's quarterbacking, which is exactly zero. But I strongly suspect the real reason Brady did not want to answer a question about his "general awareness" of Deflategate is pretty uncomplicated: He doesn't want to keep saying something that isn't true, nor does he want to admit he committed perjury. And I realize that seems like a negative thing to conclude about someone I don't know. It seems like I'm accusing him of both cheating and lying, and technically I am.

But I'm on his side here.

Yes, what Brady (allegedly) did was unethical. It's also what the world wants him to do. And that may seem paradoxical, because—in the heat of the moment, when faced with the specifics of the crime— consumers are programmed to express outrage and disbelief and self-righteous indignation. But Brady is doing the very thing that prompts athletes to be lionized; the only problem is the immediacy of the context. And that context will evolve, in the same direction it always does. Someday, this media disaster will seem quaint.

THE OAKLAND RAIDERS of the 1970s broke every rule they could, on and off the field, sometimes for no reason. They were successful and corrupt, and fans living outside the Bay Area hated who they were. But nobody hates the '70s Raiders now. In fact, we long for those teams, nostalgic for the era when their sublime villainy could thrive. It's widely assumed Red Auerbach bugged the opponent's locker room when he coached the Celtics in the sixties, an illicit subterfuge retrospectively reimagined as clever and industrious. When former Tar Heel basketball player Buzz Peterson talks about the greatness of his college roommate Michael Jordan, he sometimes recounts a story of the evening Jordan tried to cheat Peterson's grandmother in a card game, an anecdote employed to reiterate how MJ was so supernaturally competitive that even elderly women got sliced. The defining memory of Kansas City Royal legend George Brett involves the illegal use of pine tar on his bat, an unambiguous infraction[3] that was ultimately reversed on appeal, just like Brady's suspension.

---

3. It must be noted, however, that the old MLB rule involving limitations on pine tar was not based on any fear of a player gaining an unfair advantage. It was introduced by miserly Minnesota Twins owner Calvin Griffith, who noticed that too many baseballs were being discontinued during games because of random tar marks. Griffith simply didn't want to keep buying new baseballs, so he moved to restrict the amount of pine tar a player could apply to his bat. But pine tar never really helped anyone hit the ball harder. In fact, many people in and around baseball knew that Brett's bat was not regulation, but no one cared. It seemed like a meaningless infraction. The sneaky individuals in this scenario were Yankee manager Billy Martin and third baseman Graig Nettles, who both knew Brett's bat was illegal but waited until a crucial moment in a 1983 game to call it out.

"I'm the pine tar guy," Brett would say years later. "And it's not a bad thing to be remembered as."

In the present, we overvalue the rules of sport and insist anyone caught breaking those parameters must be stopped, sanctioned, and banned. But as the decades slip away, such responses tend to invert. Who won and who lost matters less than the visage of the experience; as long as nobody got hurt and nobody took drugs and nothing was fixed by gamblers, a little deception almost becomes charming. A deficiency of character *adds* character, somehow. It proves that the cheater cared.

The Patriots are the Raiders of now, despite the fact that the Raiders still exist. They push the limits of everything, and that's how they dominate. Sometimes that limit-pushing is lawful and brilliant: When Belichick placed six eligible receivers on the field against the Ravens in last year's divisional playoff, it was a stroke of strategic genius. Sometimes that limit-pushing is (perhaps) significantly less than totally legal. But it's all philosophically essential to what makes them who they are. They don't need to cheat in order to win, but it certainly doesn't hurt. I mean, how do rich people stay rich? By avoiding all the taxes specifically designed for rich people. How does a football franchise sustain a dynasty within an NFL system designed to instill parity? By attacking the boundaries of every rule in that system, at every level of the organization. And in both cases, the *perception* of those actions does not matter to the individuals involved. Perception is other people's problem. Brady does not hide from this: "I don't really care how the Patriots are perceived . . . I really don't."

There is nothing more attractive than a person who does not care if other people find him attractive.

These are all just games. Within the grand scheme of existence, they have no intrinsic value. A game can only matter as much as the involved players believe it to matter. This is why no one watches the Pro Bowl. It's also what makes Brady different from normal people, and from other quarterbacks: He will do whatever it takes to win, regardless of what that win represents. He is, by definition, a winner. Which is what everyone has *always* said about him. We always knew this. He is precisely the man society demands him to be. It's just that society doesn't like to think about what that means in practice.

Before I asked Brady about Deflategate, I asked him about playing golf with Donald Trump. He explained how this is an amazing experience, and how you never really know what the actual score is, and that there's always some sort of side bet, and that Trump always goes home with the money. I ask him if this means Trump cheats, as it's hard to imagine how someone could *always* win, particularly since *Golf Digest* estimates Brady's handicap as an 8.

"Nah," says Brady. "He just—he doesn't lose. He just doesn't lose."

The scoreboard is the scoreboard is the scoreboard. Everything else is just, like, *your opinion*, man.[4]

---

4. In the wake of Trump's (seemingly unimaginable) presidential victory and the Pats' (maddeningly improbable) comeback win in Super Bowl 51, a few people asked if I thought the final passages of this story were some kind of eerie, disturbing prophecy about what was going to happen in the future. I don't think it was, in any way. But so many people wanted to connect those events that almost any published relationship seemed worthy of reconsideration. The day after the game, the analytics website FiveThirtyEight.com actually published a story with the headline "The Super Bowl Wasn't Really Like the Election." Oh, really? A pro football game wasn't like a national presidential election? How shocking. All this really illustrated was the central pop culture problem of 2017: Suddenly, there was only one way to think about *anything*. Every public discussion needed to be a political discussion, and any discussion that wasn't was not worth having.

Institutional Rockism

Just a few thoughts on the next seventy-eight pages, since most of this stuff is self-explanatory:

- One of the things I love about covering uncool artists is the inevitable recognition that groups widely described as "hated" are almost always more popular than groups widely described as "beloved."
- I wrote a satirical overview of the Beatles catalog for *The Onion*'s *A.V. Club*. I remain amazed by how many of their readers had no idea this was a joke. This was further amplified by some idiot (or collection of idiots) who used my fake article as source material for Wikipedia entries on the various Beatles albums.
- I wrote about the video for Beck's "Loser" for the twenty-fifth anniversary of *SPIN* magazine, which is kind of like writing about Gayle King's favorite sweater for the twenty-fifth anniversary of *Oprah Magazine*.
- Everything in my *Chinese Democracy* review remains true.
- Everything in my *Lulu* review remains true, except the part about it being supernaturally appalling. It's merely terrible.
- The conceit behind the VORM experiment was concocted by other people, and the whole thing felt like a fadeaway twenty-three-foot jumper with the shot clock running down. But the fabricated math equation holds up surprisingly well, except that you need to know a lot about the Strokes in order to get it.
- I don't expect most people who buy this book will read a ten-thousand-word essay on KISS. It is, however, twice as good as a five-thousand-word essay on KISS.

The Opposite of Beyoncé

You tell people you're seeing Creed and Nickelback in concert—on the same night, at roughly the same time, in two different venues—and it suddenly becomes a stunt. Just describing the premise seems schlocky—it's like Def Leppard playing on three different continents in twenty-four hours, or maybe something David Blaine would attempt if he worked for the FUSE network. The assumption is that this is some type of ironic endurance test, and that no person could possibly enjoy the experience of seeing the most hated (yet popular) rock band of 2001 followed by the most popular (yet hated) rock band of 2012. But this is what I wanted to do: I wanted to see Creed at New York's intimate Beacon Theatre (performing their 1997 album *My Own Prison* in its entirety), followed by Nickelback in front of eighteen thousand people at Madison Square Garden.

I did not do this because I particularly like or dislike either band. I did it because other people like and dislike them so goddamn much.

THURSDAY EVENING, seven o'clock. A thin man stands outside the Beacon Theatre, smoking a cigarette and compulsively checking his phone (from across the street, he looks a little like Martin Starr). The man's name is Adam Semanchick, a twenty-six-year-old cabdriver from Bayonne, N.J. We stand on the sidewalk and chat about Creed; he's envious that I'm seeing both Creed and Nickelback on the same night, and he asks if I know how to get tickets to tomorrow night's sold-out Shinedown show at Best Buy. This is a person who really, really likes rock music.

"Creed was always more pop-ish," he tells me. Semanchick would have been eleven when *Human Clay* was released in 1997. "I usually preferred stuff like Slipknot and Disturbed. Heavier music. And the fact that Creed seemed Christian made them uncool. But they always wrote good songs, and they were a *safe* band. That's the key word. *Safe*. They didn't oversell their theatrics. Plus, they sing about things that any normal person is going to relate with. One of their songs talks about being 'six feet from the edge.' Depression is universal."

It's disarming to hear someone discuss Creed with such even-handed lucidity; normally, people who talk about Creed want to position themselves as distanced from what Creed is alleged to represent (and perhaps that's what Semanchick is doing here, but it doesn't feel like it). "I like all rock music," he continues. "Why would I make an exception for Creed? To be honest, I think rock is dying in the culture. They don't even play it on the radio anymore. At this point, there's really just underground metal and classic rock. That's all 'rock' is now. So I wanted to see this show."

Closer to the venue's entrance, two women from Brooklyn are waiting for someone. These women are sisters, both forty-one years old. "You're twins," I stupidly note. It turns out they're actually triplets and the woman they're waiting for is sister #3. We have a brief discussion about Creed's iconography. The first sister (her name is Nia) rejects the idea that Creed's lack of respect is remotely meaningful to the experience of loving them. "I don't listen to what anyone says about music," she tells me. "If I like a band, I like a band. I've seen Creed six times. They're never boring. Never. And I've seen *a lot* of boring shows from other people." I ask her what bands have been boring. Her instantaneous response is Incubus. But she was also disappointed by Bon Jovi, Chevelle, and Duran Duran. "I was so disappointed by Duran Duran," she says. "I really wanted that night to be great."[1]

I slink into the Beacon at 7:20 p.m. The first thing I see is a huge poster promoting a memoir from Creed vocalist Scott Stapp. The book is titled *Sinner's Creed: The True Story of Fame, Grace, and Redemption as Only Scott Stapp Can Tell It*. The interior theater doors don't open until 7:30, so people are milling around the lobby, drinking beers and frozen margaritas. Obviously, this is an older, balding crowd; one guy has brought his own homemade popcorn in a cylindrical Tupperware container, which is something you probably wouldn't see at a Japandroids show. I'm shocked by the distance some of these people have traveled to see this concert. One couple (George and Stacey Wilson-Howell) flew in from Dubai, a fifteen-hour flight. "Just a flick of his sweat," Stacey tells me. "That's all I want. Just a flick of Scott Stapp's sweat." This sentiment symbolizes his fame, her grace, and my redemption (as only Scott Stapp can tell it).

THE MUSIC STARTS one minute before eight p.m. Creed's opening act is called Eve to Adam. They are directly (and profoundly) influenced by Creed, all the way down to giving themselves a name that would prompt most average ticketholders to wrongly assume they're a Christian rock band. The singer brings a bottle of Jameson onto the stage, but he doesn't take a swig until after the last song. He sings

---

1. Nia's sister Annie had a more straightforward explanation for why she was at the show: "Creed is my Bible. I listen to them every day, and I don't like a lot of other bands. If you love someone's music, you find truth in it. I have a two-and-a-half-hour bus ride every day, which I hate. But Creed changes the way I feel."

exactly like Stapp and facially resembles *Around the Horn* host Tony Reali (this is mostly a compliment). The music is competent but unnervingly, relentlessly, idiotically straight ahead; they're like a fictional rock band invented by Daniel Clowes, deliberately designed to represent the polar opposite of alt-cool. At one point they cover Alice Cooper's "School's Out," but the rhythm section appears to be playing Metallica's "For Whom the Bell Tolls." It's the high point of the set. The lead guitarist wears a super-long scarf and reminds me of a grunge Warren DeMartini (again, this is mostly a compliment).

The singer is gracious, thanking the audience after almost every song (he will dedicate their final number, "Reach," to the U.S. armed services). He likes people, but only if they are physically in front of him. "This next song is dedicated to all the Internet tough guys who talk a lot of shit on the computer but would never say shit to your face," he declares before they play a tune called "Run Your Mouth." With only 1,305 followers on Twitter, I would not have guessed there were a lot of clowns trolling Eve to Adam, but I suppose there must be. The band does exist.

THE MUSIC OF CREED is powerful. That's not necessarily the same as "good," but it's something. They perform a simple trick on (seemingly) every track: A song will open with an uncomfortably subdued constriction that abruptly drops into a pulverizing wave of melodic distortion, instantly generating a hyperreal level of drama that can only be discounted if you consciously pre-decide to view the technique as preposterous. This is the central potency of the band's songwriting, but also its downfall. The key to being appreciated by pop critics is the act of taking your own music less seriously than the people who adore it (Stephen Malkmus is probably the best contemporary example). Creed seems to exemplify the opposite. Creed takes itself more seriously than its own fan base, which makes logical (but not practical) sense. Now, the reason I keep including the word "seems" is that I don't know if this is actually true; the band might consider the entire trajectory of their career totally hilarious. But their *posture* is serious. As I watch them onstage, they don't seem to be having fun in any context. The various musicians are dressed in a style best described as "business casual," assuming their business is happening in East Texas.

In a histrionic world where *American Idol* and *The Voice* somehow represent the apotheosis of vocal culture, you'd think Stapp would deserve the Congressional Medal of Honor. His bearlike delivery defines the great/terrible conceit (when Stapp truly goes for the jugular, his howl is like an F-14 flying forty feet off the ground). He paces around and seems randomly unhinged, periodically slapping his own chest like Kevin Garnett in the playoffs. Everyone in the front row wants to touch him, but respectfully so; sometimes they only need to touch his fingertips.

Creed's highest artistic achievement is the (excellent) song "My Own Prison," the first single they ever released. It's Creed at their utmost Creediest. Lyrical themes include despair, self-loathing, Golgotha, drugs, the shackles of self-awareness, metaphorical lions, actual lions, hypocrisy, *Crime and Punishment*, and the desperate notion of surrendering one's agency to a Higher Power. The payoff explodes at the end, where Stapp insists, "I created, I created, I created, I created, I created, I created my own prison." Free will: intact.

I've long wondered if this song is popular inside actual prisons.

"MY OWN PRISON" is the third number in Creed's set. By the song's conclusion, it's almost 9:30. I leave the Beacon and get in a cab to MSG, a stop-and-go ride that will take almost twenty minutes.

Sitting in the back of the taxi, there's not much for me to do except think about the group I just saw and the group I'm about to see. And what I think about is this: Over the past twenty years, there have been five bands totally acceptable to hate reflexively (and by "totally acceptable," I mean that the casual hater wouldn't even have to provide a justification—he or she could just openly hate them and no one would question why). The first of these five acts was Bush (who, bizarrely and predictably, was opening for Nickelback that very night). The second was Hootie and the Blowfish, perhaps the only group ever marginalized by an episode of *Friends*. The third was Limp Bizkit, who kind of got off on it. Obviously, the last two were Creed and Nickelback. The collective animosity toward these five artists far outweighs their multiplatinum success; if you anthologized the three best songs from each of these respective groups, you'd have an outstanding fifteen-track album that people would bury in their backyard.[2]

Or maybe only I think like this. Maybe the only kind of person who thinks like this is the kind of person who doesn't really care, which is probably the person I am. Maybe I'm looking at this in the least meaningful way possible. Several years ago, I met a history professor from the University of Oklahoma who worked on the doomed 1988 presidential campaign for Michael Dukakis. One of the things I asked him was when he (and all his coworkers) realized that

---

2. I realize arguments could be made for more than five bands. For example, I almost included Stone Temple Pilots, but that opinion seems to be changing. I also considered the Bravery, although they weren't loved enough to be hated in a meaningful way. Some might lobby for the Dave Matthews Band, but that group slightly contradicts the premise—if you criticize DMB within earshot of even one of their fans, you will be forced to justify every negative feeling you possess to the fullest extent of the law. You will end up having a twenty-minute conversation about Boyd Tinsley's mandolin playing. The only people crazier than fans of Dave Matthews are fans of Tori Amos (who, by the way, I *love* and will not accept criticism of).

Dukakis was not going to win. His answer surprised me: He said they *always* believed Dukakis was going to win, even as the results were rolling in on election night. "Presidential campaigns exist inside their own reality," he told me. "They have to. It's the only way they can work."

The same could be said about loving a band that everyone else prefers to ridicule. Your worldview must align with your construct. At the Beacon, I sat in front of a thirty-one-year-old man named Anthony Cona.[3] He told me he'd once met the drummer and bassist from Creed in a Charlotte, N.C., hotel bar, and that both were extraordinarily nice, normal people. "Those guys didn't have to talk to me," he said, "I wouldn't have felt any differently about Creed if they hadn't. But they *did* talk to me, and actually went out of their way to do so." This being the case, I asked Cona if he had any idea why so many people despise the very idea of Creed, particularly since they don't seem musically controversial or aesthetically polarizing. Here again, I found myself surprised by the response.

"The media deemed them as Christian Rock, so some people assumed they were preachy," he said. "But the bigger problem was that they were equated with Pearl Jam. That doesn't matter so much now, but it really mattered when they were new. Pearl Jam has already achieved mainstream success, so everyone thought Creed was piggybacking on the mainstream success of Pearl Jam. That's what turned everyone against them. That's why they got punished."

It's important to remember that every reality is always happening at the same time.

---

3. Cona first saw Creed in 1997, when they were opening for the Gary Cherone–era Van Halen at Madison Square Garden: "When Creed played, the house lights were still on. The audience wasn't paying attention at all. But they still acted like there were twenty thousand people watching them. They worked so hard. That's when I was hooked."

I ARRIVE at Madison Square Garden just before ten p.m. While I jog up three flights of non-operational escalators, I can hear the closing riffs of the Nickelback single "Photograph" reverberating throughout the arena's catacombs. When I finally surface amidst the altitude of section 103, Nickelback frontman Chad Kroeger is tenderly coaching the audience on how to properly respond to the next song. "Come on, ladies," he says, "let's pretend you're thirteen fucking years old at a Justin fucking Bieber concert." His argument makes a soft landing.

It's hard to get inside the existential paradox of Kroeger's life on tour: Every day, he gives interviews to journalists and radio DJs who directly ask him why no one likes his band. Every night, he plays music to thousands of enraptured superfans, many of whom love him with a ferocity that's arguably unhealthy. Every concert ends with a standing ovation; if he feels motivated, he spends the remainder of the night partying with forgettable strangers who will remember him for the rest of their lives. Eventually, Kroeger falls asleep. And then he wakes up in a beautiful hotel room, only to read new articles about how everyone in North America hates his band.

There is not one part of his life that's real.

The day before the New York show, Kroeger appeared on a Philadelphia radio station[4] and was asked (of course) why people hate Nickelback so vehemently. "Because we're not hipsters," he replied. It's a reasonable answer, but not really accurate—the only thing hipsters unilaterally loathe is other hipsters, so Nickelback's short-haired unhipness should theoretically play to their advantage. A better answer as to why people dislike Nickelback is tautological: They hate

4. Mix 106.1 FM.

them because they hate them. Sometimes it's fun to hate things arbitrarily, and Nickelback has become an acceptable thing to hate. They're technically rich and technically famous, so they just have to absorb the denigration and insist they don't care. They have good songs and they have bad songs, and the bad songs are bad enough to build an anti-Nickelback argument, assuming you feel like that's important. But it's never required. It's not like anyone is going to contradict your thesis. There's no risk in hating Nickelback, and hating something always feels better than feeling nothing at all.

Kroeger is a borderline genius at his craft. (And I don't mean a genius like Einstein. I mean a genius like Nikki Sixx.) He listens to the radio, studies every hit, deconstructs how those songs succeed, and then creates a composite simulacrum that cannot be deconstructed. "Bottoms Up" is about drinking your face off. "Animal" is about getting a hand job in a car. "How You Remind Me" is about being reminded of something you once forgot. I have no idea what "Something in Your Mouth" is about (I'm guessing dentistry school). His lyrics are sexist, though I'm sure they'd be considered empowering if performed by anyone who wasn't male and isn't in a band called Nickelback. The machinations of the live show are full-on hair metal: At one point, the band boards a spacecraft and is hydraulically suspended thirty feet in the air, although nobody in the crowd seemed to find this especially unusual. The gender split of the audience looked to be about fifty-fifty.[5] That ratio mildly surprised me, although I don't know why (probably my own prejudice). More surprising was the degree to which the security staff at MSG clearly loves this music; you don't often see ushers singing along with the band onstage, but that's what was happening here. They knew every

---

5. Forty percent female in the pit, sixty percent female in the grandstand.

word[6] to every chorus. Nickelback's core demographic is vaster than Alberta.

The group's strength is that they understand the tropes of classic rock (both musically and philosophically). The group's weakness is their obsession with transposable power ballads, most of which sound like what would happen if Bob Rock helped Coldplay write a really loud song for Garth Brooks (which would undoubtedly be the most popular song in the history of mankind, were it to literally exist). The one transcendent Nickelback song is the semi-acoustic "Rockstar," a dilemma for all those who want to erroneously pretend that Kroeger has no sense of irony. "Rockstar" has a faultless construction—it's simple, true, sarcastic, and aspirant. I suppose those four qualities also describe Nickelback, which is another reason why humorless people will always hate them.

But hey: That's their role. That's their job. They've created, they've created, they've created, they've created, they've created, they've created their own prison. And it's probably awesome, or at least close enough.

—April 2012

---

6. Inasmuch as anyone "knows all the words" to anything.

Like Regular Music, Except Good

Like most people, I was initially confused by EMI's decision to release remastered versions of all thirteen albums by the Liverpool pop group "Beatles," a 1960s band so obscure that their music is not even available on Bandcamp. The entire proposition seems like a boondoggle. Who is possibly interested in old music? And who would want to listen to *anything* inconveniently delivered on massive four-inch metal discs with sharp, dangerous edges? The answer: no one. When the box arrived in the mail, I briefly considered smashing the entire unopened collection with a ball-peen hammer and throwing it into the mouth of a lion. But then, against my better judgment (and because I was being paid to do so), I decided to give this hippie shit an informal listen. And I gotta admit—I'm impressed. These hipsters were mad prolific.

It is not easy to categorize the Beatles' music. More than any other group, their sound is best described as "Beatlesque." Its uplifting pastiche offers myriad tentacles: It's akin to a combination of Badfinger, Oasis, Cornershop, and every other rock band that has ever existed. The clandestine power derived from the compelling autonomy of their personnel—each Beatle had his own kitschy persona, even when they dressed identically. There was John Lennon (the mean one), Paul McCartney (the hummus consumer), George Harrison (the best dancer), and drummer Ringo Starr (the Cat). Even the most casual of consumers will be overwhelmed by the level of invention and the degree of change displayed over this scant eight-year recording career, a span complicated by both the tragic death of McCartney in 1966 and the addition of Lennon's wife, Yoko Ono, in 1968, a woman so beloved by the band that they requested her physical presence in the studio during the making of *Let It Be*.

There are 217 songs on this anthology, many of which seem like snippets of conversation between teenagers who spend an inordinate amount of time at the post office. The Beatles' "long play" debut, *Please Please Me*, arrived in 1963, opening with a few rudimentary remarks from Mr. McCartney: *"Well, she was just seventeen / If you know what I mean."* If this is supposed to indicate that the female in question was born in 1946, then—yes, I know exactly what you mean, sir. If it means something else, I don't get it. These sensitive, genteel-yet-stalkerish Beatles sure did spend a lot of time thinking about girls. Virtually every song they wrote during this period focuses on the establishment and recognition of consensual romance, often through paper and quill ("P.S. I Love You"), sometimes through monosyllabic nonsense ("Love Me Do"), and occasionally about oral sex ("Please Please Me"). The intensely private Mr. Harrison asks a few questions two-thirds through the opus ("Do You Want to Know a Secret") before Mr. Lennon obliterates the back door with the greatest rock voice of all time, accidentally inventing Matthew Broderick. There are a few bricks hither and yon (thanks for wasting 123 seconds of my precious life, Bobby Scott and Ric Marlow) but—on balance—I have to give *Please Please Me* an **A**, despite the fact that it doesn't really have a single.

Things get more interesting on *With the Beatles*, particularly for audiences who feel the hi-hat should be the dominant musical instrument on all musical recordings. Only one track lasts longer than three minutes, but—structurally—it would appear that the Beatles were more musical than any songwriters who had ever come before them, even when performing material written for *The Music Man*. It's hard to understand why the rock press wasn't covering the Beatles during this stretch of their career; one can only assume that the band members' lack of charisma and uneasy rapport made them unappealing to the mainstream media. Still, the music has verve—*With the Beatles* earns another **A**.

A Hard Day's Night provided the soundtrack for a 1964 British movie of the same name, a film mostly remembered for its subtle advocacy of euthanasia. The album initiates like the Pixies' "Here Comes Your Man" and never gets any worse. These poor Beatles would end up living quiet, desperate lives filled with sheep and heroin, but at least they aspired to wisdom: Though they'd covered "Money (That's What I Want)" in '63, they had now advanced to the cognitive realization that money cannot purchase love. It was a period of inner growth and introspection—they wanted to know why people cry and why people lie, and they embraced the impermanent pleasure of dance. They also experimented with the harmonica, but that turned out okay. I was originally going to give *Hard Day's Night* an A−, but then I heard the middle eighth from "You Can't Do That" (*"Ev'rybody's greeeeeen / 'Cause I'm the one who won your love"*), so I'm changing my grade to **A**. I assume the accompanying movie is on Hulu or something, but I don't feel like searching for it.

The Beatles get darker and (I guess) cheaper on *Beatles for Sale*, now suddenly fixating on their insecurities ("I'm a Loser") and how difficult it is to waltz a girl into bed when her ex is a corpse ("Baby's in Black"). There are a bunch of unexpected covers on this album, so it's kind of like Van Halen's *Diver Down*. It only earns a **B**, despite the tear-generating pleasure of "I'll Follow the Sun." More importantly, *Beatles for Sale* sets the supper table for *Help!*, a mesmerizing combination of who the Beatles used to be and who they were about to become. The signature track is "Yesterday" (the last song Mr. McCartney recorded before his death in an early morning car accident), but the best cut is "You're Going to Lose That Girl," a song still oozing with moral ambiguity. Is "You're Going to Lose That Girl" an example of Mr. McCartney's fresh-faced enlightenment (in that he threatens to punish some random dude for being an unresponsive boyfriend), or an illustration of Mr. Lennon's quiet misogyny (in that he views women as empty, non-specific possessions that can be pillaged from male rivals)? What makes Beatles lyrics so wonderful is not that they can be interpreted to mean whatever the listener wants; what makes them wonderful is the way they seamlessly adopt contradictory interpretations as the listener matures. It's unfathomable how a couple of going-nowhere guys in their early twenties could be this emotively sophisticated, but that's why *Help!* gets an **A**, despite the title's insertion of a totally extraneous exclamation point (which kind of makes the band seem like bloggers from 2004).

After Mr. McCartney was buried near Beaconsfield Road in Liverpool, Beatles bass-playing duties were secretly assigned to William Campbell, a McCartney soundalike and an NBA-caliber pothead. This lineup change resulted in the companion albums *Rubber Soul* and *Revolver*, both of which are okay. Despite its commercial failure, *Rubber Soul* allegedly caused half-deaf Brian Wilson to make *Pet Sounds* (this is also why EMI has released a mono version of the entire Beatles catalog—it allows consumers to experience this album the way Wilson did). If you like harmonies or guitar overdubs or the sun or Norwegian lesbians or taking drugs during funerals or the invention of sound, you will probably enjoy these records. *Rubber Soul* gets an **A–** because I don't speak French. *Revolver* gets an **A+**, mostly because of "She Said She Said" and "For No One" but partially because I hate paying taxes.

The year 1967 proved to be a turning point for the Beatles—an overwhelming lack of public interest made touring a fiscal impossibility, thereby forcing them to focus exclusively on studio recordings. Spearheaded by the increasingly mustachioed Fake Paul, the so-called Rad Four donned comedic Technicolor dream coats, consumed seven hundred sheets of mediocre acid on the roof of the studio, and proceeded to make *Sgt. Pepper's Lonely Hearts Club Band*, a groundbreaking record no one actually likes. A concept album about finding a halfway decent song for Ringo, *Sgt. Pepper* has a few satisfactory moments ("Lovely Rita" totally nails the experience of almost having sex with a city employee), but this is only **B+** work. It mostly seems like a slightly superior incarnation of the Rolling Stones' *Their Satanic Majesties Request*, a record that (ironically) came out seven months after this one. Pop archivists might be intrigued by this strange parallel between the Beatles catalog and the Stones catalog— it often seems as if every interesting thing the Rolling Stones ever did was directly preceded by something the Beatles had already accomplished, and it almost feels like the Stones completely stopped evolving once the Beatles broke up in 1970. But this, of course, is simply a coincidence. I mean, what kind of bozo would compare the Beatles to the Rolling Stones?

After the humiliating public failure of *Pepper*, the Beatles returned to form with *Magical Mystery Tour*, an unsubtle compilation of the trippiest ("Blue Jay Way") and kid-friendliest ("Your Mother Should Know") material they ever made. "I Am the Walrus" seems like sarcasm, but "Penny Lane" makes me want to purchase a digital camera and apply to barber college. Will history ultimately validate *Magical Mystery Tour* as the band's signature work? Only time will tell. **A.** Now hitting on all sixteen cylinders, the Beatles bolted back to the woodshed for *The Beatles*, a blandly designed masterwork that could inspire any reasonable California citizen to launch a race war. To this day, we don't know much about the four men who comprised the Beatles, but listening to this exceedingly non-black album makes one detail wholly clear—these guys truly loved each other. How else could they make such wonderful music? In fact, they adored and trusted each other so much that they didn't even feel the need to perform some of these songs together. It must have been a great era to be in this band. Amazingly, they even wangled a cameo from noted blues musician Eric Clapton (best known for his contributions to a John Mayall album I once found used for four dollars). *The Beatles* is almost beyond an **A+**; in retrospect, they probably should have made this a triple album. They could have just included the five *Pepper*-y songs from *Yellow Submarine* (**C–**), which I think might have been a Halloween record.

Let It Be comes next (or last, depending on how you view the time-space continuum), and it's a confusing project—it's often difficult to tell who is playing lead guitar, and many of the songs could be about either having sex or not wanting to be involved with society (which is sometimes the same thing). Fake Paul's beard looks tremendous and his increasingly less lilting songs are beautiful, but his focus is askew; he seems like a guy who wants to make a record with his wife (which is what John was already doing, although for less reasonable motives). "I've Got a Feeling" is my preferred track, but it's also the first time I really don't believe what these fellows are trying to sell me. I give *Let It Be* a **B–**, although the Replacements get an A and the cast of *Sesame Street* gets a B+.

The artwork for *Abbey Road* seems eerily familiar (that's actually my car in the photo's background), but the music it symbolizes is almost alien—I don't know why they wrote a song about the least compelling *Clue* character, but that's par for the course for these chain-smoking longhairs. The opener sucks (seems as crappy as mid-period Aerosmith), but Mr. Harrison follows with a wedding song that effortlessly proves why people who try to quantify visceral emotion should just stop trying. The entire band seems unserious on this endeavor, but in the best possible way—for the first time in a long time, they sound as free as they look. That said, the audio quality is unusually heavy and detailed; one suspects most of the arduous lifting on *Abbey Road* fell on the shoulders of Jeff Beck producer George Martin. The album ends perfectly, except that Fake Paul decided to add a superfluous twenty-four-second mini-song that wipes away any historical closure *Abbey Road* might have otherwise achieved. The real Mr. McCartney (R.I.P.) would have never considered such a move. I give *Abbey Road* an **A**, but begrudgingly.

I've noticed this EMI box set also included a gratuitously titled singles collection, *Past Masters*, but I'm not even going to play it. How could a song called "Rain" not be boring? Have you ever listened to regular rain, pelting a bedroom window as you drift off to sleep? Annoying! I feel like I've heard enough. These are nice little albums, but I can't imagine anyone actually shelling out Bitcoins to buy these unwieldy physical monstrosities. There's just too much excellent music on the Internet, and you don't even have to pay a penny. Sure, you might find the instructional, third-person perspective of "Sie Liebt Dich" charming and snappy (particularly if you're trying to learn German in the most complicated way possible), but first check out "myspace.org," a new Internet-based website with forward-thinking musical spiciness. That is the future. The Beatles had some talent, but it's a little like listening to an old man talk about gramophones and sarsaparilla and the war in Korea. Get in yer coffin, Grandpa. Give it up. I'm looking through you, and I don't see shit.

—September 2009

Non-Suppressive Slacker

Here's what happened when MTV played Beck's "Loser" for the first time in 1994: People watched it and said things like "I guess this is an okay song."

Here's what else happened when MTV played Beck's "Loser" for the first time in 1994: The culture inverted itself, weirdness was mainstreamed, everyone stopped combing their hair, people slept more, dirtbags began using the word "art" in casual conversation, people purchased broken turntables at stoop sales, and the boy who would become Michael Cera entered kindergarten.

Here's what nobody said when MTV played "Loser" for the first time: "Well, I guess this is what we're doing now."

Here's what everybody realized when MTV played "Loser" for the first time: *Well, I guess this is what we're doing now.*

WHEN A COLLECTIVE HISTORY of the 1990s is written (and then re-written, and then retweeted) in some distant future, all the pop historians will mention the impact of "Smells Like Teen Spirit." That song will serve as lynchpin for whatever supposedly happened in the cultural chasm between Gordon Gekko and Mohamed Atta. Someday, "Smells Like Teen Spirit" will be part of the public domain, and filmmakers will use its opening riff to specify the '90s in the same way we use "The Charleston" as shorthand for the '20s. In a hundred years, it might be the only song from the '90s the average American can recognize—the title and the artist will be lost, but its abstract sound will be emblematic of an era. Its caricature *grungeness* will survive, and all those future humans who think about the not-so-distant past will care about that. "Smells Like Teen Spirit" was over-produced and impenetrable, but its impact was organic and interpretative—it was an unanticipated watershed whose meaning changed over time. And that makes it completely unlike "Loser," a song that galvanized how 1994 felt in a most unnatural way.

When you listen to "Loser" in the present (or—even better—if you watch the video), it seems like an engaging, strange song. Not a *truly* strange song, but a *conventionally* strange song. The lyrics are faux-Dylan surreal, the music is primitive, and the hook is immediate. The images from the video are like a 16-millimeter university art film: stock cars from the '60s, a musician dragging a casket to nowhere, unsexy cheerleaders, a Rasta Man getting high. The experience of watching this in 2010 is like watching Richard Linklater's *Slacker* on VHS—the aesthetic has now been duplicated so often that it's impossible to remember how different it once seemed. It arrived in the pre-Internet era, so deducing what Beck was saying in the chorus was borderline impossible (many thought the Spanish phrase *"Soy un perdedor"* was actually "Slide open the door," which made even less sense than the ultimate actuality). People wanted to figure out what "Smells Like Teen Spirit" was supposed to signify, but nobody tried that with "Loser." You immediately knew it was about nothing. Beck paradoxically achieved his nonexistent goal—he sounded like an artist who was lazy *on purpose*. And this would not have been important if "Loser" had merely been a novelty hit. But that's not what it was.

THE FIRST TIME I heard "Loser" was also the first time I ever heard of Beck, which isn't unusual. What was unusual is that both of those things were promoted to me in my living room, as a commodity, apropos of nothing. Before it debuted on MTV's *Alternative Nation*, the network's flannel-clad VJs were promoting the shit out of "Loser," no differently than if it had been the newest release from a band that was already mega-famous. This is partially because "Loser" was already (technically) old—it had been released as an indie single on Bong Load Records in March 1993 (Bong Load pressed only five hundred vinyl copies, but college radio stations played it compulsively). Cool kids were already aware of who Beck was. But most of the world is not cool, so we found out on MTV. That alone seemed meaningful. People had been accusing MTV of dictating public taste for years, but now it was really happening: A mildly avant-garde single by a person we'd never heard of was already famous enough to open an episode of *Alternative Nation*, the less edgy offspring of *120 Minutes*. It was like waking up the morning after a coup and discovering the new president was a hobo in a scarf.

People like to compare "Loser" to Radiohead's "Creep," but that relationship is bogus. There's a narrative to "Creep," and the protagonist's self-loathing is supposed to be a real feeling—when Beck asked people to kill him, only a fool would think he was serious. Smashing Pumpkins followed "Loser" with the metalesque "Zero," but that was self-loathing as bandwagon chic—by the fall of '95, it was simply the sentiment alt-gods were supposed to express. And it was "Loser" that made that happen. "Loser" was lifestyle branding: It took a vision of unspecific, apolitical apathy and made it charming and desirable. Overnight, it became much easier for white people to be hip. All you had to do was look weird and act weirder.

Remember those John Hughes movies from the 1980s, where Andrew McCarthy and his overachieving rich friends inevitably ran the high school? Nobody buys that shit anymore. It's a distant reality that seems completely unreal. Ever since MTV pre-decided "Loser" was the future of middle-of-the-road coolness, the underclass has become the overclass. The counterculture has become a product that's available to everybody. And this didn't happen naturally; it happened because somebody made that choice (and the rest of us didn't know any better). Which, on balance, is probably the greatest thing MTV ever did for anyone.

—August 2010

Democracy Now!

Reviewing *Chinese Democracy* is not like reviewing music. It's more like reviewing a unicorn. Should I primarily be blown away that it exists at all? Am I supposed to compare it to conventional horses? To a rhinoceros? Does its preexisting mythology impact its actual value, or must it be examined inside a cultural vacuum, as if this creature is no more (or less) special than the remainder of the animal kingdom? I've been thinking about this record for fifteen years; during that span, I've thought about this record more than I've thought about China, and maybe as much as I've thought about the principles of democracy. This is a little like when that grizzly bear finally ate Timothy Treadwell: Intellectually, he always knew it was coming. He had to. His very existence was built around that conclusion. But you still can't psychologically prepare for the bear who eats you alive, particularly if the bear wears cornrows.

Here are the simple things about *Chinese Democracy*: Three of the songs are astonishing. Four or five others are "very good." The vocals are brilliantly recorded and the guitar playing is (generally) more interesting than the guitar playing on the *Use Your Illusion* albums. Axl Rose made some curious (and absolutely unnecessary) decisions throughout the assembly of this project, but that works to his advantage as often as it detracts from the larger experience. So: *Chinese*

Democracy is good. Under any halfway normal circumstance, I would give it an A.

But nothing about this circumstance is normal.

For one thing, *Chinese Democracy* is (pretty much) the last Old Media album we'll ever contemplate in this context. Artists will continue to make "albums," but only as a gimmick or a packaging device. This is the last record that will be marketed as a collection of autonomous-but-connected songs, the last album that will be absorbed as a static manifestation of who the band supposedly is, and the last album that will matter more as a physical object than as an Internet sound file. This is the end of all that, partially because the recording process started five years before those specific qualities even had theoretical alternatives. But the more meaningful reason *Chinese Democracy* is abnormal involves (a) the motives of its maker and (b) how those motives embargoed what the definitive product eventually became. The explanation as to why *Chinese Democracy* took so long to complete is not simply because Axl Rose is an insecure perfectionist; it's because Axl Rose self-identifies as a serious, unnatural artist. He can't stop himself from anticipating every possible reaction and interpretation of his work. I suspect he cares less about the degree to which people *like* his music and more about *how it is taken*, regardless of the listener's ultimate judgment. This is why he was so paralyzed by the construction of *Chinese Democracy*—he can't write or record anything without obsessing over how it will be received, both by (a) the people who think he's an unadulterated genius, and (b) the people who think he's little more than a richer, red-haired Stephen Pearcy. To him, all of those disparate opinions have identical value. So I will take *Chinese Democracy* as seriously as Axl Rose would hope, and that makes it significantly less simple. At this juncture in history, rocking is not enough.

The weirdest (yet stupidly predictable) aspect of *Chinese*

Democracy is the way 60 percent of the lyrics seem to directly comment on the process of making the album itself. The rest of the vocal material tends to suggest some kind of abstract regret over an undefined romantic relationship punctuated by betrayal, but that might just be the way all hard rock songs seem when the singer plays a lot of piano and only uses pronouns. The craziest track is called "Sorry," which resembles spooky Pink Floyd and is (possibly?) directed toward former GNR drummer Steven Adler, although I suppose it might be about Slash or Stephanie Seymour or David Geffen. It could even be about Jon Pareles, for all I fucking know—Axl's enemy list is pretty Nixonian at this point. The most uplifting songs are "Street of Dreams" (a leaked song previously titled "The Blues") and the exceptionally satisfying "Catcher in the Rye" (a softer, more sophisticated reworking of "Yesterdays" that occupies a conceptual self-awareness in the vein of Elton John or mid-period Queen). The fragile ballad "This I Love" is sad, melodramatic, and pleasurably traditional. There are many moments where it's impossible to tell who Axl is talking to, so it feels like he's talking to himself (and inevitably *about* himself). There's not much cogent storytelling, but it's linear and compelling. The best overall description of the literary quality of the lyrics would probably be "effectively narcissistic."

As for the music—well, that's actually much better than anticipated. It doesn't sound dated or faux-industrial, and the guitar shredding that made the final version (which I'm assuming is still predominantly Buckethead) is alien and perverse. A song like "Shackler's Revenge" is initially average, until you get to the solo—then it becomes the sonic equivalent of a Russian robot wrestling a reticulating python. The second solo on the obtuse "Riad N' the Bedouins" is something like R2D2 having either an orgasm or a panic attack. Whenever people lament the dissolution of the original Guns N' Roses, the person they always focus on is Slash, and that makes sense (his unrushed blues metal was the group's musical vortex). But it's actually better that Slash is not on this album. What's cool about *Chinese Democracy* is that it truly does sound like a new enterprise, and I can't imagine that being the case if Slash were dictating the sonic feel of every riff. The GNR members Rose misses more are Izzy Stradlin (who wrote or cowrote many of the band's most memorable tunes) and Duff McKagan, the underappreciated bassist who made *Appetite for Destruction* so devastating. Because McKagan had worked in numerous Seattle-based bands before joining Guns N' Roses, he became the de facto arranger for many *Appetite*-era tracks, and his philosophy was always to take the path of least resistance. He pushed the songs in whatever direction felt most organic. But Rose is the opposite. He takes the path of *most* resistance. Sometimes it seems like Axl believes every single Guns N' Roses song needs to employ every single thing that Guns N' Roses has the capacity to do—there needs to be a soft part, a hard part, a falsetto stretch, some piano plinking, some R&B bullshit, a little Judas Priest, subhuman sound effects, a few Robert Plant yowls, dolphin squeaks, wind, overt senti-mentality, and a caustic modernization of the blues. When he's able to temporarily balance those qualities (which happens on the title track and "I.R.S.," the album's two strongest rock cuts), it's sprawling and entertaining and profoundly impressive. The soaring vocals crush everything. But *Chinese Democracy* sporadically suffers from the same problem that paralyzed proto-epics like "Estranged" and "November Rain": It's as if Axl is desperately trying to get some un-makable dream song from inside his skull onto the CD, resulting in an overstuffed maelstrom that makes all the punk dolts scoff. His ambition is both noble and wildly unrealistic. It's like if Jeff Lynne tried to make *Out of the Blue* sound more like *Funhouse*, except with jazz drumming and a girl singer from Motown.

The most compelling question throughout *Chinese Democracy* is never "What was Axl doing here?" but rather "What did Axl *think* he was doing here?" The tune "If the World" sounds like it should be the theme to a Roger Moore–era James Bond movie, all the way down to the title. On "Scraped," there's a vocal bridge that sounds strikingly similar to a vocal bridge from the 1990 Extreme song "Get the Funk Out." On the aforementioned "Sorry," Rose suddenly sings an otherwise innocuous line (*"But I don't want to do it"*) in some bizarre, quasi-Transylvanian accent, and I cannot begin to speculate as to why. I mean, one has to assume Axl thought about all of these individual choices a minimum of a thousand times over the past fifteen years. Somewhere in Los Angeles, there's gotta be four hundred hours of DAT tape with nothing on it *except* multiple versions of the "Sorry" vocal. So why is this the one we finally hear? What finally made him decide, "You know, I've weighed all my options and all their potential consequences, and I'm going with the Mexican vampire accent. This is the vision I will embrace. But only on that one line! The rest of it will just be sung like a regular non-dead American." Often, I don't even care if his choices work or if they fail. I just want to know what Rose *hoped* they were supposed to do.

On "Madagascar," he samples MLK (possible retribution for "One and a Million"?) and (for the second time in his career) the movie *Cool Hand Luke*. Considering that the only people who will care about Rose's preoccupation with *Cool Hand Luke* are those already obsessed with his iconography, the doomed messianic message of that film must resonate with his very being. But how does that contribute to "Madagascar," a meteorological metaphor about all those unnamed people who wanted to stop him from making *Chinese Democracy* in the insane manner he saw fit? Sometimes listening to this album feels like watching the final five minutes of the *Sopranos* finale. There's no acceptable answer to these types of hypotheticals.

Still, I find myself impressed by how close *Chinese Democracy* comes to fulfilling the absurdly impossible expectation it self-generated, and I not-so-secretly wish this had actually been a triple album. I've maintained a decent living by making easy jokes about Axl Rose for the past ten years, but what's the final truth? The final truth is this: He makes the best songs. They sound the way I want songs to sound. A few of them seem idiotic at the beginning, but I love the way they end. Axl Rose put so much time and effort into proving that he was super-talented that the rest of humanity forgot he always had been. And that will hurt him. This record may tank commercially. Some people will slaughter *Chinese Democracy*, and for all the reasons you expect. But he did a good thing here.

—November 2008

Metal Machine "Music"

The universe is predisposed to hate this new Lou Reed–Metallica album *Lulu*, and I totally get that. This album is not really designed for people who like music. It sounds like what it is: an old, weird misanthrope reciting paradoxical nonsense over a wall of arbitrarily selected guitar sludge. Anyone who tries to suggest it's surprising in any way needs to reexamine his or her propensity for being surprised. I'm sure there will be a sector of Metallica's core audience who will feel "betrayed" by this project, mostly because Metallica fans enjoy the sensation of betrayal.[1] I suppose a handful of Lou Reed obsessives will consider this record hilarious as long as they don't have to listen to it, and I'm certain some contrarian rock critic will become Internet Famous for insisting it's more subversive than *Transformer* and a musical reaction to both Occupy Wall Street and the subpar drum production on *St. Anger*. It will be legally

---

1. An abridged list of things Metallica has done to cause its fan base to feel betrayed: getting haircuts, making a video for "One," headlining a Lollapalooza tour no one really liked, responsibly dealing with their alcoholism, writing a song that required James Hetfield to sing on key, hiring a replacement for bassist Cliff Burton, replacing the bassist who replaced Cliff Burton, not having enough bass on . . . *And Justice for All*, not writing songs that were eleven minutes long, suing the same people who purchased their T-shirts, writing the song "4x4," wearing trousers that cost more than $33, and transitioning away from a lyrical preoccupation with killing other people (toward a lyrical preoccupation with killing themselves).

purchased by the 13,404 Metallica completists who saw *Some Kind of Monster* on opening weekend, unless the album is exclusively sold at Wal-Mart, in which case it will enter the Billboard charts at #2. *Rolling Stone* will give it three and a half stars and then pretend it never happened; meanwhile, people who thought *The "Priest" They Called Him* was a brilliant idea will hold a vague, misplaced grudge against Dave Mustaine while sleepwalking to the methadone clinic.

It is not a successful record.

It might be a successful simulation of how it feels to develop schizophrenia while suffering from a seven-month migraine, although slightly less melodic.

Yet there's still something vital about *Lulu* that needs to be remembered, even as you rip it off MediaFire and immediately forget the name of every single track: *This was the dream.* If considered in a vacuum, this absurd collaboration that no one wants to take seriously (or even play more than once) is the ultimate manifestation of what was once viewed as the idealized, unattainable goal of mainstream art. Just by existing, *Lulu* represents at least four things:

1. Two historically significant artists merging unrelated genres for no defined reason.
2. Adult, self-aware musicians following their own creative vision, devoid of commercial pressure or responsibility.
3. An attempt to produce something authentically different from anything we've ever heard before, motivated only by a desire to see what will happen.
4. A confident, unvarnished attempt at taking arcane high art (*Lulu* is based on theatrical German Expressionism from the early twentieth century) and repackaging it for denim-clad teenagers huffing gas in Arizona parking lots.

If you think about *Lulu* within those specific parameters, it seems admirable. It almost feels important. But those thoughts are annihilated by the inevitable experience of actually hearing it. If these geniuses had consciously tried to make a record so simultaneously dull and comedic, they'd never have succeeded; the closest artistic equivalent would be what might have happened if Vincent Gallo had been a script consultant for *The Room*. To be fair, the end of the album does have one song that's mildly okay—a dreamy, unaggressive twenty-minute exploration titled "Junior Dad" that will probably resonate with Damien Echols. There's also a track called "The View" that's pretty mind-expanding if you pretend the lyrics are literally about watching *The View*. But the rest of *Lulu* is as appalling as logic demands. If the Red Hot Chili Peppers acoustically covered the twelve worst Primus songs for Starbucks, it would still be (slightly) better than this. "Loutallica" makes Super Heavy seem like Big Star. But this is what happens in a free society. Enjoy your freedom, slaves.

As a rule, we're always supposed to applaud the collapse of the record industry. We are supposed to feel good about the democratization of music and the limitless palette upon which artists can now operate. But that collapse is why *Lulu* exists. If we still lived in the radio prison of 1992, do you think Metallica would purposefully release an album that no one wants? No way. Cliff Burnstein from Q Prime Management would listen to their various ideas, stroke his white beard, and deliver the following forty-five-second pep talk: "Okay, great. Love these concepts. Your allusion to Basquiat's middle period was very apt, Lars. Incisive! But here's our situation. If you guys spend two months writing superfast Diamond Head songs about nuclear winter and shape-shifting, we can earn $752 million in eighteen months, plus merchandizing. That's option A. The alternative is that you can make a ponderous, quasi-ironic art record about 'the lexicon of hate' that will outrage *The Village Voice* and mildly impress Laurie Anderson. Your call." Ten minutes later, Bob Rock would be parking his Lexus at the studio. Which is not to say that musicians should reflexively adhere to the static desires of their fan base, because that's bad, too; on a personal level, I'm glad Metallica and Reed[2] tried this, if only because I'm always a fan of bad ideas. They've earned the right to overreach. But if the fundamental goal of Metallica is to make good music, it seems like trying to get rich while doing so dramatically improves their creative process. The constraints of late capitalism really work for them; they're extraordinarily adept at making electrifying heavy rock that's designed to generate revenue. The reason *Lulu* is so terrible is that the people making this music clearly don't care if anyone else enjoys it. Now, here again—viewed in a vacuum—that sentiment is admirable. But we don't live in a vacuum. We live on earth. And that means we have to accept the real-life consequences of a culture where recorded music no longer has monetary value, and that consequence is *Lulu*.

When I awoke yesterday morning, I immediately read a few online stories attempting to debunk the "myth" of Tim Tebow's win over the Miami Dolphins. The alleged "myth" is that everyone erroneously believes Tebow is a great pro quarterback. In truth, this notion is neither myth nor reality—no one closely following pro football thinks Tebow is anything other than who he is. There are people who love his ability to succeed despite his mechanical problems, and there are those who adore him as a symbol, and there are those who think it's exciting that someone can win NFL games in nontraditional ways, and there are others who dislike him because he's the

---

2. It should be noted that I'm mostly looking at this situation from Metallica's perspective, mostly because Reed's motives are impossible to comprehend. It's possible that—from his position—this is actually the most commercial thing he's ever attempted. I also think it's possible he convinced Lars Ulrich that alienating the people who love you is an important part of being important. Which, of course, is true.

highest-profile Christian in a Christ-o-centric landscape, and there are many who are sick of hearing his name two hundred times a day, and there are a few who believe criticizing Tebow somehow makes them more sophisticated. But you simply don't find intelligent people who are confused about his actual ability, if only because those qualities are discussed and analyzed endlessly. The only myth about Tim Tebow is that the public is somehow ill-informed about his strengths and weaknesses. It's a myth that exists only so that critics can point out how it isn't valid. This type of straw-man construction happens all the time. For much of my life, I lived under the fable that record labels were inherently evil. I was ceaselessly reminded that corporate forces stopped artists from doing what they truly desired—they pushed musicians toward predictable four-minute radio singles that frowned upon innovation, and they avariciously turned art into a soulless commodity that MTV could sell to the lowest common denominator. And that did happen, sometimes. But some artists need that, or they end up making albums like this.

—Autumn 2011

2 + 2 = 5

If all art aspires to the condition of music, all the sciences
aspire to the condition of mathematics.

—*George Santayana*

We are the robots.

—*Kraftwerk*

t's easy to be cynical, but I'm not like that. Nope. No way. I prefer to
focus on the ultra-super-positive, which is less depressing and more
financially rewarding. I give props to my ninjas and kudos to my serfs.
I attack reality with well-placed, non-ironic, nonrefundable LOLs. I'm
not afraid to tell people how great they are, even if they're average or
less-than-average or openly evil. So let's all put aside our petty com-
plaints and be real, if only for a moment: As a society, we're pretty
awesome.

Now, I'm not referring to *American* society, per se; I'm referring to
human society, starting with the Mesopotamians and ending with
the first wave of solo projects from Odd Future. As a species, we're
totally killing it. We've already accomplished way more than we deserve: the Great Wall of China (not to mention the numerous Chinese restaurants that share its name), the Renaissance (I wasn't

directly involved with this, but whatever), the moon landing ("maybe"), and countless other triumphs that can't be counted (as they are unaccountable). We've almost totally conquered polio, racial intolerance, and werewolves. Assuming we exclude most of Europe during the twelfth century, it's been a quasi-terrific, can't-miss, semi-delicious nine thousand years—and we humanoids have been the catalyst for everything. Dark-hearted humanity critics always want to rave about how "brilliant" dolphins are, but do dolphins have Twitter? No. They don't even have Tumblrs.

WE ARE THE PEOPLE, AND WE ARE OUTSTANDING.

And yet . . . not perfect.

Not quite. There's still a lot of greatness to be achieved. We're still struggling with cold fusion and time travel. It seems like our ACLs are constantly tearing. Cats remain undomesticated. Many of the existential paradoxes originally raised by post-Renaissance philosopher Gallagher continue to haunt us (parking on driveways, driving on parkways, etc.). To truly live, man must forever joust against himself. He must wage war against his own sexy demons. And I think we'd all agree that one of these demons looms larger than all others combined—we still haven't figured out a way to arbitrarily turn art into math.

Well, that is about to change.

That is about to VORM.

Several weeks ago, members of the Bill Simmons Institute for Randomly Idealized Utopian Statistics (B-SIRIUS) asked me to create a formula that mirrored the popular baseball statistic VORP, an acronym for "Value Over Replacement Player." The VORP metric (popularized by MIT-schooled *Baseball Prospectus* writer Keith Woolner) attempts to isolate the merits of a particular hitter or pitcher in comparison to a fictional "replacement player"—a hypothetical straw man who's an average fielder and a mediocre hitter. "Would it be possible," pondered the ever-pondering Simmons, "to create an identical statistic for music in the popular genre of rock 'n' roll? Is there a mathematical way to calculate how essential a given musician is to his or her band, and would it then be possible to extrapolate that artist's value in comparison to other artists in competing groups?"

My response to this query was, "Of course not, that's stupid, it will never work, it's antithetical to the very concept of creative endeavor, art is by nature ephemeral and impossible to quantify, and there isn't even anyone who wants this statistic to exist." But then we did it anyway.

ROCK VORM! (Part I): Inside the Numbers

So how could this be done? How can one quantify how valuable someone like Mick Taylor was (or wasn't) to the Rolling Stones, relative to the drug addict who came before him (Brian Jones) or the alcoholic who came after (Ron Wood)? And is there any mathematical means for comparing Taylor's specific worth to a similar guitarist from a different era (say, Izzy Stradlin of Guns N' Roses), or to someone who plays a totally different instrument in a totally different scenario (such as Human League keyboard player Ian Burden)?

The short answer is, "Probably not." But the long answer is the only one we care about, so let's keep going . . .

Start with the premise that every band[1] is comprised of 100 points.

These 100 points encompass the totality of every group in every

---

1. It's important to note that this formula only works with full bands, not solo artists. It also doesn't work if the band is fundamentally one person who gets credit for everything, like the Steve Miller Band, Ben Folds Five, LCD Soundsystem, NIN, or Aldo Nova.

context, regardless of the band's popularity or the quality of their work—the Kinks, Los Lobos, Geggy Tah, Broken Social Scene, and your high school ska band are all built on the same 100-point scale. If you were to start a band today with the first four people you encounter in the company bathroom, that band would have an immediate composite value of 100 points. These 100 points are broken into five weighted categories, and the points are distributed among every individual who's ever been an official, full-time member of the collective. The five categories are as follows:

1. **Songwriting (40 points):** Since the most important aspect of any band is the music they create and perform, this is the heaviest category. Points are awarded for both the amount of songs a specific individual wrote and the quality of those songs over time (hit singles count more than album tracks, but timeless, iconic anthems count more than ephemeral hits). If we use the Beatles as an easy example, Lennon and McCartney would get 17 points apiece, George Harrison would get 6, and Ringo would get 0. In a band like Creedence Clearwater Revival, John Fogerty would get 37 points and the other three members would each get one. If a band doesn't write any of its own material, no points are awarded to anyone.

2. **Sonic Contribution (20 points):** This relates to how much an individual contributes to the "sound" of a band—essentially, how much they are personally responsible for what the group sounds like as a unit. Since the main thing most people notice about pop music is the vocal track, lead singers have a clear advantage (in the case of Blondie, Debbie Harry would get 18 of the possible 20 points). Lead guitarists also tend to score higher, especially in metal bands. Both of these

disparities stand to reason, since singers and guitarists are traditionally the hardest aspects of any lineup to replace. However, highly distinctive backing vocals can also play a role—someone like Van Halen bassist Michael Anthony would be awarded as many points (3) as former lead singer Sammy Hagar (and only one point less than David Lee Roth), since his soaring background vocals were essential to all VH studio recordings for almost thirty years.[2] Musicians who produce their own records themselves (Jimmy Page, Jeff Lynne, Tom Scholz) also score higher in this category.

3. **Visual Impact (10 points):** Mostly an aesthetic taxonomy, "visual impact" pertains to how much someone contributes to the look and memory of the band. When you envision a group like Culture Club within your own mind, whom are you imagining? In all likelihood, you're almost exclusively imagining Boy George, so he scores a 9 (Mikey Craig, better known as "the black guy in Culture Club," gets the remaining 1 point). In Cheap Trick, Robin Zander, Rick Nielsen, and Bun E. Carlos all get 3 points apiece, but Tom Petersson only gets 1. In Interpol, ex-bassist Carlos D would get 5 points, Paul Banks would get 2, and everyone else gets 1. This is a hard category to describe, but it's easy to calculate once you grasp the concept.

4. **Live Performance (10 points):** This is a two-pronged qualifier. The first part of the equation is self-explanatory—it

---

2. And just in case you're curious—Eddie Van Halen would get 8 points within this rubric. Alex Van Halen would get 2. Wolfgang Van Halen and Gary Cherone both receive 0. I would love to squeeze one more point onto AVH's ledger (his snare drum sound on *OU812* is so tight it sounds synthetic, and side two of *1984* remains percussively unassailable), but 20 is the max number for this category. There were just no extra points to go around, and I always feel a moral obligation to stick to my own fake rules.

measures how captivating the musician comes across during a live concert or in a recorded video. (Is the person watchable onstage? Do they try? If they don't try, how cool do they look while not trying?) The second part of the equation involves how they conduct themselves "in reality"—basically, the degree to which they treat their entire life as a performance. What do they say during interviews? How do they behave in public? Do they ever appear on TMZ? This is an exceptionally strong metric for Courtney Love.

5. **"Attitude" (5 points):** This connotes how much value someone offers as a human idea (regardless of how that idea manifests itself musically). It rewards people who represent who or what a band supposedly "is." In Duran Duran, Nick Rhodes get 3 of the potential 5 points; in the Sex Pistols, Sid Vicious would have gotten 4; in Motörhead, Lemmy gets all 5. These points specify how accurately a person embodies the perceived spirit of the entire group, and it typically contradicts the scoring pattern from the first two categories (for example, Jack White only gets 1 point here, but Meg White gets 4). People who smoke a lot of cigarettes or are often photographed while drinking in airports tend to do well within this classification.

6. **Intangibles (15 points):** This is everything else about the candidate—a swirling jambalaya of all that makes a musician essential: smarts, chemistry, sexuality, drug use, infidelity, insanity, a bizarre origin story, a propensity for crime, memorable dance moves, inappropriate joking about fatal diseases, their personal taste in guitar strings, a strident unwillingness to sell out, a charming willingness to sell out immediately, high-profile ownership of dragon pants, involvement with the H.O.R.D.E. Festival, involvement with

Farm Aid, involvement with Hear 'n Aid, boating accidents, cult membership, non-membership in the Cult, emaciation, obesity, a willingness to wear neckties for promotional photographs, a willingness to compose the theme song to *That Thing You Do!*, a willingness to collaborate with Bob Ezrin, a checkered history of collaborating with Lenny Kravitz, anachronistic facial hair, and/or the inability to be the person in the band who is not Joe Walsh.

The calculation of these five categories is how the so-called Gross VORM is generated—you take one member of any random band and figure out how many points he or she warrants. So let's do that right now; as our stylish guinea pig, we'll use Strokes guitarist Albert Hammond Jr.

Gross Rock VORM & Adjusted Rock VORM (Part II): [Subject— Albert Hammond Jr.]

Here's how Hammond scores within the five categories we just outlined:

1. **Songwriting (6 out of 40):** On the early Strokes albums, vocalist Julian Casablancas wrote almost everything (J.C. would probably get a career score of 25 in this category). But the most recent Strokes album (*Angles*) gives songwriting credits to all five members equally, and Casablancas wasn't even in the studio (he mailed in his vocal tracks electronically). Albert is now a registered factor. Hammond also made two solo records that sound like decent Strokes facsimiles,

so one assumes he must play a role in the creation of actual Strokes songs. As such, he gets 6 of the remaining 15 points that didn't go to Julian.

2. **Sonic Contribution (3 out of 20):** The two most distinctive aspects of most Strokes tracks are Casablancas's woozy-sloth vocals and Fab Moretti's precision drumming. Moreover, one could argue that Hammond is the second most important guitar player in a band with only two guitars. He only gets 3 points here, which hurts.

3. **Visual Impact (4 out of 10):** In the past, I would have given Hammond 6 points here, as he's traditionally been "the most Stroke-like" Stroke. That will remain true over time, since the image of the Strokes we'll all inevitably remember is how they looked in 2001. However, Hammond recently went to rehab, lost a bunch of weight, and cut his hair; this costs him two points of visual impact. He gets a 4.

4. **Live Performance (6 out of 10):** When you watch the Strokes perform live, Hammond is usually the only person who seems excited to be there. He supposedly selects clothing that makes dancing easier, and he sometimes makes jokes during interviews that are authentically funny. He gets the lion's share of these points.

5. **Attitude (1 out of 5):** All the Strokes get 1 point apiece. In this regard, they are equal.

6. **Intangibles (7 out of 15):** Hammond's father recorded at least one song ("It Never Rains in Southern California") that's probably better than any song the Strokes have ever made. Al Jr. wears three-piece suits on warm days, holds his guitar like Buddy Holly, is pictured smoking (!) in the liner notes for *Is This It*, and has not dated Drew Barrymore. In a

broad sense, Hammond's role in the Strokes is inherently intangible; as a result, he dominates this category.

We now have Albert Hammond Jr.'s Gross Rock VORM: 27 (this is slightly higher than two of the other three Strokes, but lower than the irreplaceable Julian, who pulls down a 41). Yet this is only his *gross* score; since there are five members of the band, we need to divide by five. This is how we establish the Adjusted Rock VORM (ARV).[3] Hammond's ARV is 5.8, which denotes how much more valuable he is to the Strokes than any random rhythm guitarist they could pull off the streets of lower Manhattan. We work from the premise that our hypothetical replacement musician would earn an ARV of 1.0, which means Hammond's is 5.8 times better.

This statistic, however, only tells us how Hammond performs in comparison with his own group. How does he compare to the world at large? That's more complicated, which brings us to Part III . . .

Calculating the "Real" Rock VORM (Part III)

Since every band starts on the same 100-point scale, the GRM and the ARV only allow us to measure a group against itself, which generates a logic gap (certainly, the 19 points Morrissey gets for being the principal lyricist in the Smiths doesn't accurately compare with the 19 points Pete Wentz gets for being the principal lyricist in Fall

---

3. Since we're trying to figure out how *irreplaceable* a musician is, the size of the group matters quite a bit. If a band is a duo (or even a trio), losing one member constitutes breaking up entirely. Conversely, this is also why every member of the Wu-Tang Clan and the Polyphonic Spree has an astoundingly low ARV.

Out Boy). In order to calculate someone's "Real" Rock VORM (RRV), we need to multiply their personal ARV by the "established value" of the group itself. A group's established value encompasses all aspects of its existence (musical and otherwise). All bands are ranked on a scale of .01 to 1.0, with the Beatles representing the 1.0 designation. Due to space limitations, I can't list the established value of every single band who has ever existed—but here's a partial list:[4]

> 1.0: The Beatles
>
> .989: The Rolling Stones
>
> .98: Led Zeppelin
>
> .97: The Jimi Hendrix Experience, the Beach Boys, the Velvet Underground, Pizzicato Five
>
> .929: Black Sabbath, CCR
>
> .914: Steely Dan, Bad Brains
>
> .91: The Replacements, the Smiths
>
> .909: The Stooges, the Carpenters
>
> .86: Thin Lizzy
>
> .825: Pavement, Radiohead, the Grateful Dead, the Police
>
> .81: R.E.M., godheadSilo
>
> .78: Nirvana, Parliament-Funkadelic
>
> .71: ZZ Top
>
> .7099: The Pixies
>
> .685: Queen, NRBQ
>
> .642: The Faces, Fleetwood Mac, Cheap Trick
>
> .635: Oasis, Sleater-Kinney, Rush
>
> .6: The Drive-By Truckers, Sleep
>
> .59: Sonic Youth, Mötley Crüe, the Go-Go's

---

4. The research for this portion of the abstract was modeled after the work of mid-'90s musicologist Ronald Thomas Clontle and surveys the same core demographics (Lawrence, Kansas; Gainesville, Florida).

.55: My Morning Jacket, Rancid, Thomas Jefferson Slave Apartments

.543: The Fall, Journey

.53: The Chills, the Eagles, the Stone Roses, Cinderella

.47: Metallica, U2, Soundgarden, Japandroids

.469: REO Speedwagon, Hüsker Dü, Wings, Best Coast, Slade

.444: Sweet, Poison, Crosby Stills & Nash, Depeche Mode, Supergrass

.39: Ra Ra Riot, Cornershop, Dokken, Roxy Music

.345: Aerosmith, Styx, Paramour, Black Oak Arkansas

.32: Uriah Heep, Grizzly Bear

.3: Spacehog[5]

.28: Rage Against the Machine, Rilo Kiley, the Doors

.24: Primus, Black Flag, Yngwie J. Malmsteen's Rising Force

.2: The Dave Matthews Band, Wavves, Foo Fighters

.18: April Wine, the Black Eyed Peas, Joy Division

.15: Incubus, Spoon, Gaslight Anthem, Iron and Wine

.1: Porno for Pyros, Kaiser Chiefs, Bat for Lashes, Asia

.05: Crash Test Dummies

.025: Green Day, Alabama

.01: The Fabulous Thunderbirds

I will concede that some of these rankings are debatable. The scores themselves are also fungible and constantly evolving: In 1995, Elastica would have received a .61 (on par with the likes of My Bloody Valentine); today, Elastica would get a .35 (somewhere just below the Moody Blues). Regardless, these scores are what we use to establish

---

5. Just in case you're keeping score at home: ".3" is also the score typically applied to semi-successful (but still unsigned) bar bands who are known on a local level. If you're currently in an unsigned bar band and you suck, use ".22" instead. Use ".11" if you're in an unsigned band that plays noise rock.

any specific individual's "Real" Rock VORM—we multiply his or her ARV with the preexisting established value of his or her band.

So let's conclude our look at Albert Hammond Jr.: His "Adjusted Rock VORM" was 5.8. As a band, the Strokes' overall value is .51 (roughly in the same neighborhood as Fugazi and Britny Fox). When these two factors are multiplied, the final product is 2.958. And that, my mathematical friends, is the worth of Albert Hammond Jr.: His "Real" Rock VORM is 2.958, which means he is better than any rock musician with a lower RRV (and worse than anyone whose RRV score is higher).

Problem solved. Next problem.

—some random afternoon in 2011

Advertising Worked on Me

1.

I love writing about KISS. I love it too much, probably. I've written about this band semi-constantly for the past twenty years, sometimes for reasons that weren't justified and sporadically with motives that weren't justified and intermittently with logic that wasn't justified. But KISS goes into the Rock & Roll Hall of Fame this week, so today I'm Timothy Olyphant.

2.

The New York–based rock and roll group KISS formed in 1972, when two workaholic Jews (guitarist Stanley Eisen and bassist Chaim Wits) aligned forces with two irresponsible boozehounds (drummer Peter George John Criscuola[1] and guitarist Paul Frehley). Their adopted stage names are household, unless you are very young, crazy old, or not interested in loud music: Paul Stanley, Gene Simmons, Peter Criss, and

---

1. Oddly, many sources suggest that the sequence for this name should actually be George Peter John Criscuola (which transposes "George" with "Peter"). But Peter Criss's autobiography (*Makeup to Breakup*) says differently.

Ace Frehley (the latter adopting "Ace" because "the band didn't need another Paul"). The group was spawned upon the dissolution of Simmons and Stanley's previous band Wicked Lester, a folk-rock five-piece Simmons likes to compare to the United Nations (due to their mixture of ethnicities and non-uniform physical appearance). Wicked Lester scored a record deal with Epic, but most of the music was never officially released. Some of the tracks would fit on the soundtrack to *Hair*.

From the standpoint of how instantly recognizable they are to people who barely care, KISS is among the most famous rock bands in the history of the idiom. This is a function of their initial nine-year decision to appear in public only as theatrical characters allegedly representing their inner natures, once categorized by critic Chuck Eddy as "a cat, a bat lizard, something with one black star on one eye and something with one silver star on each eye." Soon after inception, the band knocked out three albums in the span of twenty-four months, all on the ill-fated, drug-enriched label Casablanca. None sold particularly well; combined sales were fewer than 300,000 units. KISS responded to this failure by counterintuitively rerecording many of these unsuccessful songs in concert and releasing a double live album, titled *Alive!* It charted for 110 weeks. KISS fans classify KISS as the best live arena act of all time, almost to the point of utter obviousness; those who hate KISS will usually concede they were (once) a competitive live act, but only if you were in middle school.

Throughout the last half of the '70s, KISS operated as the biggest band in the world—although not because of record sales (groups like Fleetwood Mac and the Eagles sold way, way more). KISS just sort of declared that their enormity was reality and reality elected to agree. They were popular enough for every member of the band to release a solo album on the same day and to have their actual blood mixed into the ink of Marvel comic books; they were popular enough to star in one of the most structurally irrational movies ever made and to sleep with the likes of Diana Ross. They were popular the way Pepsi is popular. But somewhere around 1979, a lot of odd and foreseeable things started happening in persistent succession: They made a disco album, Peter was fired, they made a concept album, Ace quit, they took off the makeup, they fired the guy hired to replace Ace, the guy who replaced the guy who replaced Ace got a bone disease, they sued a record label, they temporarily rediscovered popularity, the drummer who replaced Peter died from heart cancer, the original quartet reunited for $144 million, they created a 3-D concert experience (despite the fact that life itself is already three-dimensional), Peter quit twice, Ace quit again (replaced by a guy who once painted Paul Stanley's house), Gene blamed the Internet for ruining music, Paul played the lead in *Phantom of the Opera*, and every original member wrote an autobiography. And now it's today, and KISS is still my favorite band, for reasons I incessantly attempt to articulate to varying degrees of imaginary success.

3.

In his essay collection *The Disappointment Artist*, Jonathan Lethem writes about his insecurity over analyzing the legacy of Philip K. Dick, an author whose best work had already been chronicled and whose worst work is relatively awful. Early in the piece, Lethem sums up his feelings with a lyric from Bob Dylan: "I'm in love with the ugliest girl in the world." I strongly relate to this sentiment, particularly since that's literally what Gene Simmons resembled in 1986.

KISS doesn't make it easy for fans of KISS. There's never been a rock group so effortless to appreciate in the abstract and so hard to love in the specific. They inoculate themselves from every avenue of revisionism, forever undercutting anything that could be reimagined as charming. They economically punish the people who care about them most: In the course of my lifetime, I've purchased commercial recordings of the song "Rock and Roll All Nite" at least fifteen times (eighteen if you count the 13-second excerpt used in the introduction to "Detroit Rock City" on *Destroyer*).[2] Considered alone, this is not unusual; there are lots of bands who capitalize on the myopic allegiance of their craziest disciples. In 2009, Pavement announced a reunion tour and asked their most dogged fans (myself included) to purchase tickets a whopping fifty-three weeks in advance. Every decision was premeditated for maximum fiscal impact. "Instead of one announcement mapping out the entire tour itinerary," noted *The Washington Post*, "concerts have been announced one by one, in a fine-tuned sequence seemingly designed to maximize profits in every possible way." It was savvy business, and almost no one complained. Yet Pavement would never *brag* about this level of calculation. They would rationalize their actions, or they'd remind the media that they never explicitly said they wouldn't add extra shows, or they'd chuckle about the swindle only when no one else was around. Pavement would still take the money, but they'd simply (a) say nothing, (b) feel bad about it, or (c) *pretend* to feel bad about it.

But not KISS.

When KISS cajoles people into paying more money than the market demands, they tell everyone they know. They give instructional

---

2. This is mostly because "Rock and Roll All Nite" tends to show up on pretty much every record KISS has been involved with since 1992. I originally purchased the song on the studio album *Dressed to Kill* on cassette when I was in high school, and then again on CD in college, and then a third time when they remastered their existing catalog in 1997. I performed the same triple-buy for *Alive!* and for *KISS: Double Platinum*. I only purchased the import *KISS Killers* once (on CD), and I only had *Smashes, Thrashes & Hits* on tape. I think I might have found *Alive III* used, but I know I got both *You Wanted the Best, You Got the Best!!* and *Greatest KISS* at Best Buy. "Rock and Roll All Nite" is on all of those purchases. It's also on the symphonic album they recorded in Melbourne, Australia, and the soundtrack to *Dazed and Confused*, and it appears twice on the KISS box set. The fact that it's not included on the *Detroit Rock City* movie soundtrack still shocks me.

interviews about how future bait-and-switch endeavors can be designed and they adopt the new model for all future undertakings. Moreover, they insist the exchange was mutual. They say the experience they offer is singular and nontransferable, and that anyone who isn't willing to pay for the KISS experience isn't a KISS fan (and therefore does not matter, or perhaps even deserve to exist). It's the guiding principle behind everything KISS does: In order to "qualify" as a KISS supporter, you have to be a KISS *consumer*. And this is non-negotiable—it doesn't work any other way. If you try to enjoy KISS in the same way you enjoy Foghat or Culture Club or Spoon, you'll fail. You might like a handful of songs or appreciate the high-volume nostalgia, but it will inevitably seem more ridiculous than interesting. To make this work, you need to go all the way. And this is because the difficult part of liking KISS—the manipulative, unlikable part—is how you end up loving them.

4.

This Thursday, Nirvana will also be inducted into the Rock Hall, in their first year of eligibility (it was the fifteenth try for KISS). No one disputes the validity of this inauguration. Coincidentally, a pre-famous Nirvana covered a KISS song in 1990, performing "Do You Love Me" on a compilation titled *Hard to Believe*. Nirvana historians care about this because it's one of the only Nirvana recordings where forgotten ex-guitarist Jason Everman plays in the studio; KISS historians care about this because it gives credence to the theory that KISS directly influenced Nirvana (and should therefore be credited as rightful progenitors of grunge, not unlike Black Sabbath and Neil Young). I'm not sure how sincerely one can take the latter claim, since (a) Nirvana seems to be making fun of the song as they play it, and (b) it's often impossible to differentiate between what Kurt Cobain liked, what Kurt Cobain mocked, and if his mockery had any relationship to his actual feelings. (KISS is also Pearl Jam's Mike McCready's favorite band, which might have been enough to make Cobain hate them at the time.) My gut feeling is that Nirvana covered "Do You Love Me" because they thought it was comically masculine. But there's one moment in their cover version that I always think about: It's the moment where the singer is directly addressing the song's female antagonist, an opportunistic groupie obsessed with the trappings of fame and success. Among the various things she likes is "all the money, honey, that I make." But Nirvana was singing this song in 1990, when they were broke and unknown. This being the case, they changed the words: Instead, they sing, "All the Mudhoney that I make." Which, I suppose, was intended as a funny little in-joke for Mark Arm not to laugh at. But twenty-four years later, that joke feels different. When I hear it today, it seems like Nirvana was both fascinated and amused by KISS. It seems like they liked the structure of the song, viewed the lyrical details as ironic, and enjoyed the process of recording it. But the idea of directly talking about how rich they were—even before they actually were rich—was just too unnerving for them to accept and replicate, even sardonically. It was so counter to what they valued (or—more accurately—what they *aspired* to value) that they felt more comfortable making a joke about the word "honey."

They couldn't even force themselves to pretend to talk like the band they were pretending to honor.

5.

Here's a statement only a fool would contradict: There's never been a band inducted into the Rock & Roll Hall of Fame whose music output has been critically contemplated *less* than the music of KISS, at least among the people who voted them in. I can't prove this, but I'd guess 50 percent of the voters who put KISS on their Rock Hall ballot have not listened to any five KISS records more than five times; part of what makes the band so culturally durable is the assumption that you can know everything about their aesthetic without enjoying any of it. That perception doesn't bother me, and I certainly don't think it bothers the band. In many ways, it works to their advantage. Still, I definitely disagree with anyone who thinks these albums are somehow immaterial. It's traditionally hard to get an accurate appraisal on their value, because most people who write about KISS either don't care at all or care way too much. The fact that I'm publishing this essay arguably puts me in the latter camp (and that argument is not terrible). But it doesn't feel that way. I know what I know: A few of these records are great, most are okay, several are bad, and some should be buried in sulfur. An objective person could assess the Kinks' catalog with identical language. I, however, have not listened to all thirty-five Kinks albums enough times to properly do so. But I've listened to all these KISS records enough to do this . . .

Kiss (1974): The first song on the first album is "Strutter," which (coincidentally or unfortunately) might be the clearest, classiest rock song KISS ever produced. I suppose a cynic might claim it was all downhill from there. But that's stupid: All five tracks on side 1 are unambiguously excellent—simple, chewy, and stylized (employing the best possible connotations of all those modifiers). "Cold Gin" makes poverty seem as exhilarating as alcoholism[3] and "Let Me Know" remains the

---

3. "Cold Gin" (written by Frehley) is supposedly what you drink when your heating system breaks down and the landlord isn't around to fix it, and "the cheapest stuff" is all that's required for these

most underrated song in their entire forty-year history. The stuff on side 2 is slightly weaker . . . but if Paul Westerberg considers it halfway canonical, the plaintiff has no further questions. The straightforward reality is that if KISS had died in a boating mishap the week this record hit stores, the same people who currently hate them would insist this 35-minute document is a forgotten progenitor of punk, on par with the Stooges. KISS would be remembered as a catchier, savvier version of the New York Dolls, and only Morrissey would disagree. **GRADE: A**

***Hotter Than Hell* (1974):** This is one of the most poorly mixed albums ever released. Not surprisingly, that type of technical failure—when awarded the luxury of time—slowly becomes romantic. *Hotter Than Hell* now seems ultra-honest: In the '90s, a handful of indie weirdos tried to make their records sound this cheap on purpose. The songwriting is exceedingly minimal and uncommonly naturalistic ("Comin' Home" and "All the Way" in particular). "Parasite" is one of the rare early KISS riffs that qualify as traditionally metallic; rarer still, it's also inventive and influential (you'll recognize its chord progression on Gang of Four's "What We All Want" and "Ghetto Life" by Rick James). Of course, the main artifact people tend to recall about this album is "Goin' Blind," a dirgelike Gene Simmons power ballad about a ninety-three-year-old man having an affair with a sixteen-year-old girl. (The detail about the age difference was actually concocted by Paul.) It's hard to understand why this kind of May–December

---

purposes. However, I'm still not sure why you would specifically want *cold* gin if you were trying to stay warm. Not room-temperature gin? Too many syllables?

romance would be a fantasy for any normal twenty-five-year-old, but I suppose it has a certain Dark Crystal appeal. The consensus is that the narco-woozy solo on "Strange Ways" is the most arresting guitar work Ace Frehley ever got on tape, but the universality of that sentiment is heavily based on Dimebag Darrell's expressed opinion before he got murdered. Audiophiles may note that *Hotter Than Hell* was remastered in 1997, thereby making its appalling production extra loud. **GRADE: A–**

***Dressed to Kill* (1975):** Superchunk drummer Jon Wurster once claimed that the opening track ("Room Service") is the worst song ever made by anyone, but his logic is flawed. Wurster seems skeptical that a stewardess on a commuter airline would decide to have sex with Paul Stanley simply because his body language implied he was annoyed by an impending flight delay. Anyone who truly understands KISS knows that this sort of thing happens to Paul constantly (he even wrote a song about it in 1989—"Read My Body"—where he compares his penis to a font). More importantly, the guitar riff on "Room Service" is borderline life-affirming (sort of glam-pop Chuck Berry). "Getaway" is a snappy Ace track (sung by Peter), "C'mon and Love Me" is an introduction to the black magic of Susan Miller, and the blandly titled "She" has got to be the only rock song in history to rip off the Doors, reference John Wayne's *Hondo*, promote prostitution, and launch the future commerciality of grunge.[4] It should also be noted that "Rock and Roll All Nite" closes *Dressed to*

---

4. It directly influenced Pearl Jam's "Alive," although I don't think anyone would have figured this out if the always affable Mike McCready hadn't directly said as much in a *Guitar School* interview.

Kill, although this fledgling version sounds like it was recorded on a microcassette inside an aluminum grain bin. "Rock and Roll All Nite," by sheer public response, is the greatest song KISS ever made. So how good is that, really? In his book *Revolution in the Head*, British critic Ian MacDonald analyzes every composition the Beatles recorded in the studio, of which he cites 188. By my half-drunk estimate, "Rock and Roll All Nite" is better than 93 of these tracks, along with 12 ties. So the best song by KISS would be (at worst) the 95th best song by the Beatles. Which is outstanding.   **GRADE: B+**

Alive! **(1975):** Side 1 is 80 percent perfect, eradicating whatever sonic problems the first three studio albums may (or may not) have had. Side 2 is 75 percent perfect, albeit less bombastic (which matters, since that's the whole idea here). Side 3 lasts for-fucking-ever. Side 4 is loose and cliché and joyous and indefatigable, and Paul's stage banter proves he truly had zero interest in drinking culture (since he somehow doesn't know there's a proper name for vodka mixed with orange juice). I don't enjoy live albums, but I enjoy this one.   **GRADE: A+**

Destroyer **(1976):** Produced by conceptual taskmaster Bob Ezrin and considered the closest KISS ever came to making a conventionally classic album, *Destroyer* is actually more uneven than most of the band's output from this period. "Detroit Rock City" is overrated and monotonous, an opinion validated by the fact that people who hate KISS tend to begrudgingly concede it's okay. Conversely, the sleazy flash of "King of the Nighttime World" sounds better every year it ages. "God of Thunder" would have been cooler had Ezrin retained the proto-disco tempo of its original demo. "Shout It Out Loud" is supposed to remind people of "Rock and Roll All Nite," which would feel more functional if the public somehow failed to remember that "Rock and Roll All Nite" is the only song KISS always, always, always plays. The guys in the group can't seem to agree on whether they initially thought "Beth" was brilliant or terrible, but they all concede it paid for itself a hundred times over. "Do You Love Me" springs off the speakers like a mongoose and allows the listener to imagine the members of KISS reading about themselves in magazines and worrying that all the glossy photographs will prompt women to expect them to pay for dinner. Ace doesn't play on "Sweet Pain" (allegedly due to a local card game), so Ezrin brought in some guy from Alice Cooper to pretend he was a castrated Ted Nugent. The cover art makes for an excellent T-shirt and a decent golf visor; the spoken-word intro displays questionable news judgment; if this record was weather, it would be partly cloudy with a 40 percent chance of mastodons. **GRADE: B**

Rock and Roll Over **(1976):** There's a nice 2007 documentary about a teenager with Asperger's syndrome titled *Billy the Kid*, and the kid in question (Billy) loves KISS. Another person with Asperger's, John Elder Robison (the brother of memoirist Augusten Burroughs), was actually employed by KISS and designed a lot of Frehley's exploding guitar equipment. I don't have Asperger's, but my behavior at certain dinner parties sometimes prompts my wife to suspect otherwise. Now, I'm not arguing there's a provable medical connection here. If your child likes KISS, don't call your family practitioner. But there's something about *Rock and Roll Over* that makes me wonder about the empathetic disconnect inherent to this type of music. *Rock and Roll Over* is a collection of ten songs, eight of which are explicitly about human physicality but only one of which intersects with human emotion. Many of these tracks exhibit an awkward distance between personal actions and interpersonal feelings, including the ones with straightforward narrative threads ("Baby Driver" is about an obsession with transportation). "Hard Luck Woman" was originally written for mid-period Rod Stewart and sounds exactly like a song originally written for mid-period Rod Stewart; this is, of course, exceedingly positive. "Makin' Love" is the closest Ace ever comes to Jimmy Page, which is as positive as positive gets. Mostly unrelated, but not totally: 1976 also marks the historical period when Gene Simmons was briefly obsessed with behaving like an animatronic robot. **GRADE: A–**

***Love Gun* (1977):** This is KISS at its utmost KISS (so if you don't like this, you don't like KISS): Excellent Eddie Kramer production, the third-best Peter song, the second-best Ace song, and no dead weight (unless you hate the Crystals cover at the end, which I don't). Personally, I've never been a big fan of the title track, as the faux-Bonham drumming reminds me of hearing a jackhammer at six a.m. But I guess it's not bad for a song written completely inside Paul's head while he stared out the window during a cross-country flight (although this also means Paul was sitting on an airplane and thinking about metaphors for his cock, a preoccupation that skews uncouth). **GRADE: A**

Alive II (1977): "The idea of not having to be in the studio with each other for all those hours certainly made sense to everyone," was the retrospective analysis of ex–KISS manager Bill Aucoin. That's a curious reason for recording a second live album, but—with KISS—the ends justify the means. "I Stole Your Love" is the musical equivalent of giving five Heinekens and an El Camino to a fourteen-year-old who thinks *2 Fast 2 Furious* was based on real events. A lot of this material isn't actually live (I believe Paul once said, "It was as live as it needed to be"), but these oversexed diplomats never claimed to be Bon Iver. The extra studio tracks on side 4 allegedly exist to fulfill an arcane contractual obligation, but a few cuts are quite likable ("Rocket Ride" and the Dave Clark Five cover especially).   **GRADE: A–**

Double Platinum (1978): The first of about 547 greatest hits packages, all of which will contain "Rock and Roll All Nite." The song selection is appropriate, but everything was remixed and compressed (and somebody took the guitar solo off "Strutter" for no defensible reason).   **GRADE: C–**

KISS: Ace Frehley (1978): This record includes "Rip It Out" and a cover of Hello's "New York Groove," which is just about as vintage as any of these jokers are gonna get from here on out.   **GRADE: A**

KISS: Gene Simmons (1978): This record features Joe Perry, Cher, one Doobie Brother, Janis Ian, Donna Summer, an homage to silent film star Lon Chaney, and a faithful cover of a song off the *Pinocchio* soundtrack. It's also about having sex in a Holiday Inn, with a drum intro that vaguely mirrors

"Escape (The Piña Colada Song)" and a passable Big Bopper impersonation. **GRADE: B**

***KISS: Paul Stanley* (1978):** This record has a track where Paul Stanley insists it's "alright" if a woman wants to have noncommittal sex with him, because he's just that kind of open-minded dude. The Cheap Trick–ish, Raspberry-flavored "Wouldn't You Like to Know Me" should have been a minor hit. "Hold Me, Touch Me (Think of Me When We're Apart)" managed to crawl up to #46 on the Hot 100 and might have gone higher if the song title didn't seem like Jewel's unpublished poetry airbrushed onto the side of a unicorn. **GRADE: B+**

***KISS: Peter Criss* (1978):** This record was released by Peter Criss in 1978. **GRADE: D**

***Dynasty* (1979):** This is a sellout, frozen-face, Studio 54–obsessed Plexiglas superdisc, which makes me want to like it. Perversely, I do not. "I Was Made for Loving You" is a wide-angle caricature with a paint-by-number guitar solo—it sounds like what would happen if you hauled a $79 Casio keyboard into a cave and hit the "DISCO" function. Paul has claimed he was simply trying to prove that absolutely anyone could write a disco song and have it chart in the top 10. It got to #11. Space Ace covers the Stones for coincidental symbolism and Gene rhetorically asks if the illusion of celebrity defines his improbable charisma. These are the high points. The worst songs ("X-Ray Eyes" and "Save Your Love") are only classified as "songs" because that seems to be the accepted nomenclature. **GRADE: D+**

Unmasked (1980): Here we have the group's unabashed pop album with a dreadful cartoon cover, confused by its own irony. Much of this material is underrated (except for "Torpedo Girl," which is worse than advertised). "Shandi" sounds silly the first time you play it, but it's an authentically beautiful song with sincere sentimentality—and it was so popular in Australia that KISS was able to leverage a stadium tour across the entire continent. "Tomorrow" and "Is That You?" showcase Paul's considerable aptitude as a working-class creator of formalist radio fare. The Simmons number "She's So European" is one of his most oblique attempts at romantic exposition, though the phrase "She's So European" might just be code for "She's So Annoying." All told, *Unmasked* remains an absorbing period piece and an essential text for anyone trying to figure out what these maniacs consider mainstream pop. Peter Criss was still officially the drummer for this release, but he doesn't play on any of these songs (it's all Anton Fig, who eventually got a job with David Letterman). That doesn't hurt. Of course, *Unmasked* is also Ace at his absolute septic tank worst, which does. **GRADE: B+**

(Music from) The Elder (1981): Undeniably the most fascinating KISS album by a factor of ten, this is the soundtrack to a movie that does not exist,[5] fueled by

---

5. Due to its nonexistence (there is not even a script), deducing the plot for *The Elder* solely from its corresponding music is more or less impossible. It appears to be set in a version of the past that is actually the future, focusing on a boy recruited by a medieval organization called the Order of the Rose. A British metal writer named Seb Hunter is currently trying to make this film happen, but there's absolutely no chance that KISS will give him the rights to this music. Which means we will eventually have the soundtrack to a film that does not exist and a film inspired by a soundtrack it can't actually use.

mountains of cocaine the band members did not ingest.[6] Only two songs have any relationship to the rest of the group's catalog: the exceptional Ace cut "Dark Light" (cowritten by Lou Reed) and the confrontational closer, "I" (perhaps the first translucent glimpse into Simmons's Randian objectivism). There's now an urban legend that suggests this is the only KISS album that ever got a positive review in *Rolling Stone* magazine, but the writer merely compared it to Jethro Tull (and it's not really a compliment). This is the Rubicon that changed KISS forever: They actively made a record solely for the critics, earnestly believed the work was exceptional, and found themselves humiliated in front of an audience who had pre-decided to hate them. In response, Paul and Gene reversed their original feelings (they now claim to hate all the songs), rejected the entire notion of taste, and decided to view any art created for non-commercial purposes as inherently false. This album will never be appreciated objectively, unless we can find a way to play it for someone who (a) likes theatrical classical rock but (b) has no idea that KISS ever existed. **GRADE: A–**

Killers (1982 import): KISS was so embarrassed by *The Elder* that Paul grew a beard. To mitigate the damage, his record label sheepishly sent yet another greatest hits collection around the world (with the most popular edition landing in Japan). The track listings vary from country to country, but all versions include four new songs—"I'm a Legend Tonight"

---

6. The ingestion was primarily performed by Ezrin, an amazing producer who probably got caught up in his own genius. Which he now admits: "There are great moments (on *The Elder*) for sure, and some classics buried in the mix. But on the whole, it's way too self-indulgent and way too overproduced. It's also not fully realized."

(dumb and boring), "Down on Your Knees" (dumber still, but less boring), "Partners in Crime" (meh), and "Nowhere to Run" (blah). *Killers* was hard to find, overpriced, and repetitive, so if you own this album you obviously love the band already (regardless of what they were trying to accomplish). **GRADE: B–**

Creatures of the Night (1982): This is the album "real" KISS fans are supposed to adore, and it tends to be the project most lauded by the band itself ("I like *Destroyer, Creatures,* and *Revenge,*" Simmons once remarked, although I'm pretty sure he was promoting *Revenge* at the time of this remarking). To this day, Paul continues to unsuccessfully deny he wrote "I Still Love You" about the actress who played Tom Hanks's girlfriend on *Bosom Buddies* (Donna Dixon, something of a sassier Suzanne Somers). *Creatures of the Night* is the most metal KISS record (in response to *The Elder*) and also the worst-selling (because of *The Elder*). At times, it traffics in heaviness for the sake of heaviness, which would be okay if KISS was an organically heavy band (which they aren't). Still, Eric Carr is like the '85 Bears on drums and the best material is pulverizing ("War Machine," cowritten with Bryan Adams, is the last monolith Simmons ever made and an indispensable snapshot of his militaristic persona). The songs are all worth spinning if you're lifting weights or moving furniture or oxy-acetylene welding. Ace had exited the band at this point, so a then unknown Vinnie (Cusano) Vincent provides most of the recognizable guitar playing (although I get the impression the number of uncredited session players employed here falls somewhere in the vicinity of Steely Dan's *Gaucho*). This was also the period where Eddie Van Halen allegedly asked Gene

Simmons if he could join KISS, an anecdote Gene has told approximately four thousand times and Eddie has told approximately never. **GRADE: B+**

It was at this juncture in the KISS chronology that they stopped wearing makeup and became a straightforward hair band, albeit with more credibility and less youthful indiscretion (no drugs, basically). Readers of early-'80s rock magazines may recall many bizarre interviews with Paul and Gene where they were asked if it would be difficult for them to record music without the greasepaint, thus suggesting that many reporters somehow assumed KISS wore makeup in the studio. What the visual alteration ultimately meant was that the records now had to stand on their own, so many (most?) people stopped caring. Some of the group's creative limitations were pushed to the surface: "You'd be hard pressed to name another band that wrote all its own songs over such a long period of time without ever learning how," noted Rob Sheffield for *Rolling Stone*. Here again, I am forced to disagree, even if I can't think of another band that fits that description better. And at least I know Rob put in the work (he classified *Hot in the Shade* as "polished and diverse" when he was still writing for *SPIN* in 1990). For those keeping book in the outfield, KISS re-donned the kabuki gear in '96, impacting their songwriting exactly as much as logic would dictate.

Lick It Up (1983): A successful comeback project (with Vincent updating the guitar sound and writing material competitive with the rest of popular culture, or at least competitive with Dokken). With the face paint vanquished, Paul holds the singular spotlight while Gene becomes the tall guy on bass. "All Hell's Breaking Loose" deserves some credit for inventing rap-rock, although that's a little like complimenting Vlade Divac for inventing flopping. The title cut remains a live standard and sounds better when played faster than intended (which usually happens), but—at least in the studio—Gene wanted everyone to stay in the so-called monster plod. **GRADE: B**

Animalize **(1984):** Vinnie was fired by KISS and replaced by Mark St. John (who would make only one album before contracting Reiter's syndrome, a rare strand of arthritis). Simmons contributes almost nothing except a lyrical passage that compares someone's vagina to a fireplace (I still dig the primordial riff, though). Stanley handles everything else (including the production and the album art), almost like McCartney after the other three Beatles lost interest. "Heaven's on Fire" is a great effort, and all the nihilistic grandstanding on side 2 is uninspired but understandable. I realize this isn't exactly a ringing endorsement, but the group was in shambles and still managed to yield a competent double-platinum rock record. Time has proven that Paul is the only member of the band who never stopped caring. **GRADE: B**

Asylum **(1985):** Writing about how the visceral physicality of unencumbered intercourse offers fleeting escape from the constructed tedium of day-to-day subsistence is not a bad premise for a pop song. However, naming that song "Uh! All Nite" slightly detracts from that premise. In '85, Gene was still acting like a deadbeat dad and poor Paul was running out of ideas; Bruce Kulick had taken over on lead guitar and had to make the milkshakes for everyone else. *Asylum* is, to its credit, '80s KISS returning (regressing?) to their '70s sound, and I guess it's admirable these guys were still trying to put out a fresh album every goddamn year, even if the main motive was avoiding bankruptcy.   **GRADE: B**

***Crazy Nights* (1987):** The album title is *Crazy Nights*. The single is titled "Crazy Crazy Nights." The chorus of the single states that these are "Crazy, Crazy, Crazy, Crazy Nights." (Well, that escalated quickly.) The penultimate track is "Turn On the Night." The ultimate track is "Thief in the Night." A lot seems to be happening nocturnally. Your appreciation of this music will be proportional to your appreciation of Desmond Child and/or your ability to know who Desmond Child is.   **GRADE: C–**

Smashes, Thrashes & Hits* (1988)*: Another greatest hits money grab, except this time it sounds like Paul remixed or rerecorded almost everything on the record. This required Eric Carr to sing his own studio version of "Beth," which seems like a lot of work for the sole purpose of making Peter Criss feel bad. The anthology includes two new songs that are humiliating for all involved, although enough time has passed to make "Let's Put the X in Sex" moronically delightful.   **GRADE: C**

***Hot in the Shade* (1989):** Due to the year it was released and the year I was born, I probably listened to this album 300 times, roughly 296 more than necessary. It's most noteworthy for Simmons's Trumpian decision to start singing about the wonders of capitalism without any fear over how that might look, hence "Cadillac Dreams" and "The Street Giveth and the Street Taketh Away." The rest is pretty much sleepwalking, though. **GRADE: D–**

Revenge **(1992):** Created in the wake of Carr's death and released within the vortex of grunge, *Revenge* was well-received by KISS fans, opening at #6 on the Billboard album chart before dropping like a donkey down a mine shaft. Ezrin is back as producer, as is Vinnie Vincent as a cowriter. Gene grew a goatee and Paul bought a leather duster, so you know a lot of deep consideration went into this. This record might seem okay if it wasn't alleged to be outstanding; not unlike Zima and the city of Las Vegas, every single exposure is slightly worse than the one before. It includes a cover of an Argent song they made for the *Bill & Ted's Bogus Journey* soundtrack, but I would not travel through time to hear this again. **GRADE: B–**

Alive III **(1993):** There's a decent version of "I Love It Loud" on here, which I think was even on the radio for two or three weeks. They stick "Rock and Roll All Nite" in the middle of the set, which is absurd. Francis Scott Key gets a writing credit. A reasonable comparison is *The Godfather, Part III*. **GRADE: D**

KISS Unplugged **(1996):** Contrived by MTV in order to reunite the original band (and complicit with Paul and Gene, who suddenly had an "outside" reason for the reunion everyone always suspected was inevitable), this is of high interest to completists (an earnest "See You Tonight"!) and fundamentally irrelevant to everyone else (an earnest "See You Tonight"?). **GRADE: B+**

Carnival of Souls: The Final Sessions **(1997):** Recorded before the reunion agreement was signed and released in order to kill time, *Carnival of Souls* illustrates the direction late-period KISS was going before people remembered they used to be awesome. That direction, it seems, was the New Sincerity—songs about child abuse, songs about hate, songs with titles like "I Walk Alone" (sung by the recently exiled Bruce Kulick), and no anthems or memorable melodies. This is the anti-KISS. I might add that it's also anti-good, but that would be cheap. I'm bumping it up one half letter grade for the peculiarity of its ambition. **GRADE: C**

Psycho Circus **(1998):** The long-awaited reunion of the original KISS lineup and the worst album the band ever made. Frehley's "Into the Void" is the strongest cut on the album, and also terrible. **GRADE: F**

KISS Symphony: Alive IV **(2003):** This was recorded with the Melbourne Symphony Orchestra in Australia. If you own this album, it means (a) you own every album on this list, (b) "Shandi" was your wedding song, or (c) you are a member of the Melbourne Symphony Orchestra. **GRADE: D**

Sonic Boom **(2009):** Those who believe Head East's "Never Been Any Reason" is the best song of the '70s might vaguely enjoy the track "When Lightning Strikes," and it sometimes seems like C. C. DeVille is playing guitar on "Never Enough."

The lead single ("Modern Day Delilah") is akin to something off *Revenge* that was supposed to sound like *Creatures of the Night*. I know a few people who like this album, but they always start their positive proclamations with the sentence, "You know, I actually thought this wasn't so terrible." That's almost supportive, kind of. **GRADE: C–**

Monster (2012): The twentieth KISS studio album, recorded so that KISS could say they've made twenty studio albums. The twentieth Rolling Stones album was *Dirty Work*, which sounds like *Sticky Fingers* by comparison. When R.E.M. made an album titled *Monster*, it felt like the least heavy record ever made by a band trying to be heavy on purpose. Yet it's still heavier than this. **GRADE: F**

I don't think there's much risk of any member of KISS entering the Rock Hall as a solo artist, particularly since the Hall isn't even willing to induct any member who wasn't in the original lineup (not even Eric Carr, who was in the band for eleven years). But just in case . . .

Let Me Rock You (Peter Criss, 1980): No, seriously, I insist . . . allow *me* to rock *you*. **GRADE: D–**

Out of Control (Peter Criss, 1982): This is probably cheating, but *Out of Control* becomes fascinating if you pretend Peter Criss is actually Harry Nilsson. You just have to listen to the lyrics of a song like "In Trouble Again" and imagine how they'd come across if they reflected problems and scenarios that actually happened in Nilsson's life, as opposed to things that may have happened to Peter Criss. You might also want to get super-high for this, but I would never advocate drugs.   **GRADE: D**

Vinnie Vincent Invasion (Vinnie Vincent Invasion, 1986): A Joycean masterwork. The Reagan administration's *Blow by Blow*. Nine and a half perfect songs (because even I get a little bored during "Back on the Streets"). This was either the second- or third-best rock album released in '86, depending on your relative feelings toward *Master of Puppets* and *The Queen Is Dead*.   **GRADE: A+**

Frehley's Comet (Frehley's Comet, 1987): It took almost ten years to make this album, which feels about right: The opener ("Rock Soldiers") is the rare example of a man writing a song about the defining moment of his own life while somehow managing to misremember almost all of the factual details.[7] "Love Me Right" is direct and "Dolls" is obtuse, yet both are closer to Old KISS than whatever New KISS was doing in 1987. The best cut is "Calling to You," which was (not exactly surprisingly) written by the bass player in 1982. Is this the KISS corollary to *All Things Must Pass*? Yes, if we are somehow legally obligated to pretend such a thing exists.   **GRADE: B+**

---

7. A first-person story describing a near fatal car wreck, "Rock Soldiers" states in its first lines, *"It was back in the summer of '83 / There's a reason I remember it well."* However, the accident actually occurred in the spring of 1982. Later in that same verse, Ace claims, *"The Devil sat in the passenger's side / Of DeLorean's automobile."* However, Ace wasn't driving the car (Anton Fig was), and the vehicle was a Porsche. It should be noted that Frehley did have an unrelated incident with a De-Lorean in 1983 on the Bronx River Parkway, but there was no accident (just a DUI).

Second Sighting (Frehley's Comet, 1988): Ten songs, written in about ten minutes. One is pretty good. Two or three are okay. Difficult to remember which are which.   **GRADE: D+**

All Systems Go (Vinnie Vincent Invasion, 1988): Featuring vocalist Mark Slaughter[8] and his 287-octave range, this was a step backward for the self-absorbed Vinnie. The shredding on "Dirty Rhythm" is a respectable rewrite of "Fits Like a Glove," and "That Time of Year" might work at a really dismal prom—but there's something disenchanting about a record where the music is fast and the atmosphere is ponderous. Vincent performs a few bars of "The Star Spangled Banner" at the front of side 2, which I'm sure was very inspiring to all the Soviet émigrés who defected to America in order to work at Tower Records.   **GRADE: B–**

Trouble Walkin' (Ace Frehley, 1989): There's a leathery cover of ELO's "Do Ya" on this post-Comet project, and a few members of Skid Row make cameos. But the main thing this record did was give people an excuse to purposefully mishear the phrase "I am trouble walking" as "I have trouble walking," which was a far more accurate categorization of the person singing the lyrics.   **GRADE: C+**

---

8. Following this album, the other three members of Vinnie Vincent Invasion managed to kick Vinnie Vincent out of his own band. They proceeded to form Slaughter and opened for KISS in the summer of 1990. In 2011, Vincent was charged with domestic abuse in Nashville, but the charges have been "retired," whatever that means. Simmons regularly refers to Vincent as the most self-destructive person he's ever met and insists he was never an official member of KISS (as Vincent refused to sign the paperwork necessary for liability insurance).

Euphoria **(Vinnie Vincent Invasion, 1996):** The only thing you need to know about this four-track EP is that it includes a song called "Get the Led Out" which does not resemble Led Zeppelin in any significant way, to the point where I suspect Vinnie honestly misspelled the word "lead" and just had to pretend like this was artistically intentional. **GRADE: D**

Union **(Union, 1998):** Bruce Kulick seems like a decent person with a reasonable sense of humor. The singer on this album is the vocalist from Mötley Crüe who is not Vince Neil. Kulick is now a member of Grand Funk Railroad (who still play forty shows a year). This is not actually a record review. **GRADE: I**

Asshole **(Gene Simmons, 2004):** Too on-the-nose. Although it does include a track cowritten with Bob Dylan, so maybe it deserves a Nobel. **GRADE: F**

Live to Win **(Paul Stanley, 2006):** I sometimes suspect this record is a heavily veiled description of Paul's fractious relationship with Gene. Stanley's memoir halfheartedly insists their relationship has slowly improved over time, and they evidently like each other enough to co-own a minor league football franchise. But Paul also writes, "[Gene] chose to ignore his underlying issues and instead committed himself to creating an external façade and persona that, unfortunately, he felt required to knock down anyone who threatened his singularity in the spotlight." He also deflates the notion that Simmons is some kind of financial genius: "Gene's most successful venture in business was promoting the perception that he was a savvy businessman." When Paul got married in 2005, he did not invite Simmons to the wedding. **GRADE: C–**

***Anomaly* (Ace Frehley, 2009):** For eight stellar minutes (the wobbly "Pain in the Neck" and a cover of "Fox on the Run"), this is a B+ effort. But then there are forty-six additional minutes. **GRADE: C–**

So where does this leave KISS "academically"? My grading system[9] saddles the group with a cumulative G.P.A. of approximately 2.56, although it jumps to 3.16 if you only count the albums released during the first makeup era (which seems to be how the Rock Hall is viewing the band). If you include all the later solo projects, the grade point dips to 2.34, arguably below the Mendoza Line for inclusion into an institute that supposedly rewards eminence. But one must also realize (a) my grading reflects no larger consensus, (b) great works amplify an artist's musical legacy more than subpar works erode it, and (c) we all know that this is beside the point, anyway (because this, as always, is about KISS—the rules are different).

6.

I support the Rock & Roll Hall of Fame, as a physical building. It's a pleasant structure to meander around when you're loaded. There's a futuristic room where you can lie on the floor and watch videos on a massive TV, and it's right next to the Great Lakes Science Center (so you can visit both venues without reparking your car). Of course, as an *institution*, the Rock Hall is totally devoid of meaning. But this is no one's fault. There's no way the Rock & Roll Hall of

---

9. I counted each album as a three-credit class; solo albums were worth two credits apiece and double albums were worth four. I have to assume the mathematical accuracy of my grading would matter to KISS, or at least to Gene Simmons (since he started his professional life as a sixth-grade teacher at P.S. 75 in Spanish Harlem).

Fame could ever be definitive or authoritative, simply because there's no shared agreement over what rock music is supposed to do. Say what you will about the Baseball Hall of Fame, but at least we all agree on the point of the game it celebrates. We know that individual success at baseball reflects (a) the ability to generate runs or (b) the ability to stop an opponent from generating runs. But what is the point of pop music? What constitutes success? Everyone has an opinion, but no one knows for sure. There are players in the Baseball Hall of Fame who might not deserve induction, but I can't think of a single inductee considered *terrible* by a subset of baseball fans. There are, however, many people—including members of the Rock Hall committee, most notably Dave Marsh—who'd classify KISS as terrible. So how does one rationalize the canonization of a group that some people don't even view as satisfactory?

Well, maybe like this:

If you want the Rock Hall to be exclusively comprised of serious artists who've been granted elite status through critical consensus, that's fine. That's an acceptable thing to want. But the facility won't have much utility as a tourist attraction (because only critics will care) and it won't eliminate the central problem of inclusion (since art is still subjective). If you make mass popularity the main criterion, things get even worse—the Rock Hall becomes Twitter. If you think voters should consider both of those qualities equally and simultaneously, you end up with what we have now—a club that places Laura Nyro alongside Metallica, regardless of how unconnected they seem to anyone with a relationship to both. But there is at least one metric that makes sense to me: the number of people who *really* care about an artist, demonstrated over time. This does not privilege the taste of an exclusive class of people who get to decide for everyone else, nor does it mechanically reflect a raw numeric census of anyone who once purchased an album or attended a concert. I'm referring to the long-term accumulation of people who are exceptionally invested in a particular artist's existence; essentially, I'm referring to the kind of people crazy enough to care whether a few musicians they've never met are inducted into a mythical society that serves no non-symbolic purpose. Certainly, every major artist has a handful of fans that fit into this category. But some have way, way more. And if an artist's output fosters that kind of following on a mass scale for multiple generations, they've obviously done something right. They've created art that validates itself, and which doesn't need to be validated by anyone else.

One thing I've learned in my life is that—creatively—it's better to have one person love you than to have ten people like you. It's very easy to *like* someone's work, and it doesn't mean that much; you can like something for a year and just as easily forget it was ever there to begin with. But people remember the things they love. They psychologically invest in those things, and they use them to define their life (and even if the love fades, its memory imprints on the mind). It creates an immersive kind of relationship that bleeds into the outside world, regardless of the motivating detail. In pop music, the most self-evident example is the Grateful Dead, although Rush and the Smiths fall into the same class. Another example is Fugazi. Two others are Bikini Kill and the Insane Clown Posse. These are artists who diametrically impact how substantial factions of people choose to think about the universe. The social footprint they leave is deeper than their catalog.

This is why KISS must be accepted as meaningful.

As a counterexample, take a band like Boston: The first Boston record has more good songs than any KISS record, and Tom Scholz is more talented than all the members of KISS combined. The eponymous 1976 Boston LP sold 17 million copies, roughly equating with the aggregate sales for all KISS studio records involving the original members. I'm a massive fan of Boston, as is much of middle-aged

America. There are more reasonable people who *like* the music of Boston than there are reasonable people who *like* the music of KISS. But Boston is not in the Rock & Roll Hall of Fame, and very few listeners care. Nobody feels betrayed or outraged. And this is because there aren't enough humans who *love* Boston for nonmusical reasons. Such creatures exist, but they are few and far between. Those of us who dig Boston only tend to think about them when "More Than a Feeling" or "Something About You" comes on the radio; conversely, those of us who dig KISS think about them all the time. They (we?) buy new KISS records they (we?) know we won't like, and the purchase still feels essential. It almost wouldn't matter if the CDs were blank, because KISS has transcended music and become something else entirely. And if you are not going to lionize the transposition of creation and emotion—if you're not going to lionize the ability of a musical band to matter more as a concept than as a mere producer of sound—I'm not sure what we're pretending to do here.

7.

When asked the question "Why KISS?" there's always a temptation to respond with, "Why anything?" It's a low-impact existential response that spikes the whole argument; the implication is that all obsessions are fundamentally identical and that the chosen subject is just an arbitrary placeholder for the desire to care about anything at all. It's definitely the easiest way to make a non-ridiculous case. It does not, however, seem accurate. I don't think loving KISS is the same as loving *The X-Men* or Christopher Priest or *Veronica Mars* or Liverpool F.C., or even the same as loving Alice Cooper or Marilyn Manson. There's something unique about how the process of fixation metabolizes with KISS, and—as I consider what the quality is—I find myself a little disturbed by the possible answers. But it still gets us closer to the truth. The question is not, "Why KISS?" or "Why anything?" The question is, "Why would someone love the obstinate, outlandish version of something when there are so many alternative options that would be easier to appreciate and more credible to espouse?" In other words, what is so extra-good about something the intellectual world tells me is ultra-bad?

It comes down to three things.

The first part involves self-imposed Stockholm syndrome. The second part involves a fallacious sense of ownership, which is related to the first part. And the third part involves most of the world being wrong.

Part I: I know KISS is fucking me over, and I don't remember a time when I didn't know this. I know they view me as a robot. As far as KISS is concerned, I exist only to buy the same old material they keep repurposing while unconditionally investing my thoughts into the same self-mythologizing anecdotes they keep telling, over and over again.[10] But here's the thing: *I like it.* I enjoy giving KISS my money—it's one of the only extensions of consumerism that provides me with genuine gratification. At this point, the process of acquiring KISS minutiae is not that different from experiencing it. If someone sends me a KISS book, I read it the same day it arrives, even if I've read every fact and detail before. That's almost preferable, somehow (it reminds me of who I am). I might start casually following Arena League football now that Gene and Paul own a team, the LA KISS. In fact, I might buy an LA KISS T-shirt (I once purchased an Ace

---

10. These anecdotes include: Ace showing up to his band audition wearing sneakers that did not match, Gene asking Peter if he would be willing to wear a dress in order to join the band, how the photo session for the *Hotter Than Hell* album cover was insane and debauched, how "Rock and Roll All Nite" was written as an attempt to consciously create an anthem in the style of Sly and the Family Stone's "Dance to the Music," how the original title of "Beth" was "Bec" (short for "Rebecca") but Gene thought it would make people assume it was about Jeff Beck, et al.

Frehley baseball jersey, although I can't recall ever wearing it). Has KISS trained me to think like this, or did I train myself? Doesn't matter, because I don't feel this way about anything else. By interweaving capitalism so intimately with the very idea behind why they exist, wasting money on KISS is actually *pleasurable*. I like being a prisoner. I wouldn't if the stakes were higher, or if it wasn't my choice. But the stakes are low and the choice is my own. And within this slavery comes an interesting kind of freedom, elucidated in Part II.

Part II: I own KISS. I don't own the trademark to their logo and I don't dictate their tour itinerary and I can't request that they clean the leaves out of my storm gutters.[11] But I have complete intellectual autonomy over my interaction with KISS, as does every other person immersed in the KISS Lifestyle. This is what happens when a band surrenders themselves to total commoditization: Because KISS does not pretend that what they do is motivated by some idealistic truth, you are able to eliminate the blind hero worship that so often comes with pop idolatry. KISS is adored by their base, but only when they're literally onstage, exercising the overt signifiers of arena rock; the moment they exit the arena, that same fan base views them skeptically and objectively. Ask a crazed KISS fan if he or she thinks Gene Simmons and Paul Stanley are "good people"—you may be surprised by the response. KISS fans are obsessed with the band's greatest missteps (*KISS Meets the Phantom*, the failure of *The Elder*, the exact year

---

11. Although this is partially how Tommy Thayer became the band's current guitarist. Thayer started his career in the '80s pop metal band Black n' Blue. Two of the group's records were produced by Gene Simmons. Thayer left Black n' Blue in 1988 and went on to portray Ace Frehley in Cold Gin, one of the better KISS tribute bands. He eventually started working for KISS in a business capacity, sometimes as a tour manager (whenever I interviewed KISS in the '90s, he would set up the phone calls) and sometimes as a gopher (he helped paint Paul Stanley's bedroom and cleaned Gene Simmons's storm gutters). When Frehley quit in 2003, he adopted the same role in KISS that he had played in Cold Gin. He became Fake Ace. The only flaw is that his technical prowess prompts him to play the old KISS songs a little too accurately, which sometimes makes the concerts oddly clinical.

Gene and Paul started wearing wigs, etc.). We love the petty darkness. The single best book about the group is titled *KISS and Sell*, written by their former business manager and built on gossipy details about their byzantine (and sometimes mortifying) financial framework. It's just freely accepted that KISS fans can love KISS and still think they're jerks. As such, it's a balanced relationship. It's a real relationship. Which brings us to . . .

Part III: There are multiple levels of *realness*, none of which are absolute. A movie is comprised of actors pretending to be other people on a set that represents a place that isn't there, so it's not real; the ideas and themes of a movie, if created and performed by talented artists, can be acutely, profoundly real. This fake/real dichotomy is understood by everyone. Yet that contradiction confuses people when applied to KISS. When the critical world looks at KISS, they see adults pretending to be characters they are not, projecting unsophisticated music about fantasy emotions, presented as a means of earning revenue. What they do not see is that this is how almost all rock music would appear to an alien. It is inside the genre's very DNA, all the way back to Elvis. So KISS is not a cheaper, exploitive translation of rock. KISS is the living definition of rock's electrifying unreality, presented with absolute transparency. And the many rational, intelligent people who disagree with that are simply wrong (not about everything, but certainly about this).

8.

Full disclosure as we touch rock bottom: I did not want KISS to make the Rock & Roll Hall of Fame. I thought it would be cooler if they didn't. I liked the idea of KISS coming to represent the opposite of whatever the Rock Hall purports to be. I find it strange that the people who hated KISS at the height of their powers will now be allowed to amend their position in retrospect (I felt the same about Black Sabbath and Rush, but I guess those floodgates are now open forever). Still, I know they deserve it, and I know the band is happy about it,[12] and I want the band to be happy. You know, it's so goddamn crazy: I always refer to the guys in KISS by their first names, as if we're somehow friends or acquaintances. It feels stupid to do this, and sort of childish. But that's what happens when something enters your life and (impossibly, inexplicably, irrevocably) never leaves. I've thought about KISS way too much over the past three decades, but still not as much as I'd prefer. There is just no group that's more fun to think about. There are some that are more fun *to listen to*, but that's a different question. Whatever KISS did, they did it right, including the things they did wrong. They have no rival and they have no peers. Advertising worked on me.

—April 2014

---

12. Actually, this might not be completely true. Gene Simmons has slammed the Hall for failing to include any non-original KISS members and Paul Stanley gave an interview to *Classic Rock* where he said he didn't feel honored to be inducted or nominated. I was glad Paul said that. This, of course, isn't quite the same as saying he wasn't happy about the award, but it did make me wonder if he's lost interest in the part of his job that requires pretending. That's certainly the impression one gets from his autobiography, *Face the Music*. Unlike the other KISS memoirs, Stanley's is legitimately revealing: He writes about his bizarre family life as a child, the fact that he was born deaf in one ear, and the crippling insecurity that plagued him throughout his entire career. He's also unflinchingly up-front about his feelings toward the other members of the band, most of whom will not enjoy reading his categorizations. He's even a little harsh toward the guys who are dead.

Who Wants to
Live Forever?

Hero in Black

October 28, 2013

When a famous man dies, his critics tend to vaporize (at least temporarily). The type of pundit who disparages the newly dead always comes across like an opportunistic coward, and almost every postmortem potshot has the opposite effect of its intention. When a problematic man dies, you don't dwell on the qualities that made him a problem. There's simply no point in attacking a man who is no longer there.

Unless that man is Lou Reed.

Then there *is* a point, and it explains everything else.

Reed died yesterday at the age of seventy-one. You probably won't find an obituary that fails to mention the cantankerous complexities of his character. In the punk oral history *Please Kill Me*, Reed's nastiness is literally described as "famous," which is absolutely accurate. He was uncommonly famous for acting like a prick. It was essential to who he was as a public figure. He was the single most famous jerk in an idiom supersaturated with jerks hoping to be famous. But that's not why his death is such a loss. That's not what's important. What's important is that this universally shared opinion about Lou Reed's persona never made *anyone* question the merits of his work. You were allowed to think whatever you wanted about who he was as a person (mostly because he didn't seem to care), but there was never any argument over the veracity of his genius. Few rational listeners injected their discomfort with Reed's personality into the experience of hearing his records; even fewer concluded that the way he sometimes acted in public eroded the insight of his output. You might say, "I hate Lou Reed," but you couldn't say, "I hate Lou Reed and I hate all his music." If you did, it only meant you had terrible taste in everything. And this is why Reed's life was such a philosophical, unparalleled success: He proved that the only thing that truly mattered about an artist was *the art*. Everything else was just something amusing to talk about.

Start at the beginning. Start with *The Velvet Underground and Nico*. You play the record once. You play it again. Maybe you've heard it many times before, but it always sounds less reassuring than you expect. The first track is fragile. The second track is gravel. All eleven songs make you think about stuff you normally ignore. Maybe your first thought is, "This music seems like it could have been recorded last week." The album is forty-six years old, so the realization is amazing. But then you think something else: "You know, these songs are still *weird*. The voices are bizarre. The structures are so simple they almost seem amateur. Some of these ideas are crazy." So then you start to wonder how this contradiction could exist. You wonder how something this old could feel so in step with everything that's happened in popular culture over the past forty-six years, yet still manages to strike the audience as perverse and unorthodox and consumed with otherness. It makes no sense: Something that sounds this modern should also feel familiar; something that feels this strange should also sound like it belongs to a different age. But it doesn't sound rote and it doesn't sound anachronistic. It is, in all likelihood, the most irrefutably timeless rock music anyone has ever made—not necessarily the *best*, but the most aesthetically durable. The smartest rock music ever made, all things considered. "Heroin" wasn't the first song written about heroin, but it was the first song about heroin that was *titled* "Heroin." It was not a metaphor to unpack. It arrived unpacked. You just had to deal with it. And since Lou Reed was the man who wrote it, you just had to deal with him, too.

The four Velvet Underground studio albums are enough to validate and excuse every other transgression Reed ever committed. In a span of five years, he changed rock entirely (and he didn't even need to sell many records in order to do so). And he knew this. And he used this. He used it to become the kind of figure that—outside of Bob Dylan—didn't really exist in popular music: His work became significant simply because he was the specific person who made it. That was its value. Had he been a fraud, such a transference would have spelled disaster; fortunately, he was the opposite. Did he release some bad solo records? Absolutely. Some of the worst. But they only *sounded* bad. They were still worth thinking about. They had to be judged on a different scale, with different criteria, for different reasons. In the forty-six years since *The Velvet Underground and Nico*, there have been other musicians who've occupied this cultural vocation. But never to this degree, and never without trying a little too hard.

In 1975, Reed released *Metal Machine Music*, a four-sided sixty-four-minute collection of itchy guitar feedback with no words or melody. In the original liner notes, Reed claimed no one he knew had ever listened to the entire thing, including himself. If you purchased it on vinyl, you eventually realized the fourth side concluded with a "locked groove." This meant that—if you didn't manually lift the needle off the record—it would never stop playing (thereby subjecting its listener to an endless, joyless squeal). He made an album that sounded terrible on purpose and figured out a way to make it last forever. It assaulted the people who supported him and exasperated the label that paid him to create it. Now that he's dead, it's tempting to argue that the mere existence of *Metal Machine Music* is cool and subversive, almost as if the only thing that matters was the premise. But it's not just the premise. It's not just that Reed thought it would be funny to do this.[1] It's not a parody or an urban legend. *Metal Machine Music* is a real thing. You can hold it in your hands. You can drop it on the floor. It's a tangible document that illustrates the militant fringe of what can be produced with the rudimentary tools of rock 'n' roll, designed by someone who never adequately explained what his original motive was. It's not merely cool that it exists. It's amazing that it exists. It's wonderful, regardless of the notes. And while thousands of lesser mainstream artists could have easily produced an album with similarly unlistenable sounds, only Reed actually did so. Only Reed made this album, sold it to a hundred thousand people, and moved on to something else entirely.

And this is the point.

The point is not that Reed had the ability to make really great records (*Transformer*, *The Blue Mask*) interchangeably with really bad ones, or that he had the leverage to alienate the very people who liked him the most, or that he will always be the model for a certain kind of East Coast gutter-punk elitist. The point is that he was exactly what he claimed to be: an actual artist who made actual art. He was aware of what he was doing and he did it anyway. He followed no one and left us with a shitload of sublime artifacts that only he could have forced into reality. He hauled the water. And everything else about him? Every journalist he insulted?[2] Every audience member he

---

1. Although that was probably part of it.
2. I suppose it's a little self-serving to mention this, but I think it's safe to say that a small part of Lou Reed's legacy will be that he elevated rock criticism more than any other musician I can think of. This can be seen through his relationship with Lester Bangs, his spoken-word interludes on the

ridiculed? The Warholian celebrity he amplified and perverted? His hubris? It changes nothing and signifies even less. It would not matter if he had murdered a hundred innocent people—the guitar riff on "Sweet Jane" would be no less unassailable (even if we all had to pretend otherwise). The work is what matters, and he is the person who did the work.

Some art is real.

---

live album *Take No Prisoners*, and the surprisingly excellent review he wrote for Kanye West's *Yeezus* LP. It could also be argued that the Velvet Underground invented the idea of a band that only critics appreciate, even though more or less everyone appreciates them today.

417

Villain in White

August 12, 2011

Jani Lane was the first person to speak from the stage at the first concert I ever paid money to see, a 1989 show at the West Fargo Fairgrounds featuring Warrant, Great White, and Ratt. In retrospect, that was a real triple bill of tragedy: Ratt's Robbin Crosby was the first major '80s metal figure to contract HIV, Great White was the accidental catalyst for the death of one hundred people at a 2003 show in Rhode Island, and—today—the news broke that Lane was found dead at the age of forty-seven in Woodland Hills, California. As I type this sentence, the cause of death has not been reported . . . but this was a forty-seven-year-old musician who died in a hotel room. Do the math.

It's easy to compliment the dead, but that's often the only time we admit noncontextual truths: Jani Lane was an incredible frontman, particularly in 1989. He was loquacious and funny and famous-looking, and Warrant tried *so hard* to be entertaining—they probably played for only forty minutes, but they clearly did not want all the teenage girls wearing Ratt T-shirts in the mud to feel remotely ripped off. The only song most of the crowd knew was "Down Boys," which they may have played twice. I remember they played "Heaven" and everybody sort of instantly knew this would be a super-successful single that a lot of guys would pretend to hate during prom. Considering how emotionally invested Warrant seemed in playing for eight thousand people in a city they knew nothing about, it must have been a wonderful time to be the singer in a band engineered for joy and hugeness. Yet I wonder how often Jani Lane was happy during the twenty-two years that followed. He had success, but it was the kind of success that's hard to appreciate.

Lane wrote most of the music for Warrant and was particularly excited about the release of what would be their second album, a record he wanted to title *Uncle Tom's Cabin*. He thought the hypothetical title track, "Uncle Tom's Cabin," was the most sophisticated thing he'd ever composed, and it probably was. But the people at Columbia Records thought it was too understated and "political" (or something), so they told Lane to write an anthem that was consciously unserious. He supposedly wrote "Cherry Pie" in less than fifteen minutes, made several million dollars, and regretted having done so for the next fifteen years. When you interviewed Lane during the late '90s, he would talk about "Cherry Pie" like a man who'd thoughtlessly married a gorgeous woman and immediately realized he'd irrevocably altered the very meaning of his life, but I guess Lane did that, too (he married the woman from the "Cherry Pie" video, Bobbie Brown, in 1991—but they divorced in '93). He sighed a lot. He still made jokes, but they were dark as fuck.

Warrant had bad timing. They were blamed for killing heavy metal, even though they never exhibited any interest in being heavy or metallic. The band was forced into a genre of music after that genre had already peaked, which meant they were both artificially pushed by industry insiders (who refused to accept that glam was fading) and unfairly maligned by trendy fans (their '91 tour with Trixter and Firehouse was mocked by everyone, including the kids who went to the show and sheepishly conceded it was awesome). Lane often told a story of walking into the Columbia offices in 1993 and expecting to see a framed poster of Warrant in the reception hallway, because that's where it had always been. When he saw that this picture had been replaced by a likeness of Alice in Chains, he knew it meant something bad. But he kept trying. He really did. He still loved music. Critics will forever argue that the pop he made was fundamentally fake, and I understand what that argument entails. But Lane was not a fake person. When he did (what amounted to) a solo tour in '96, he would make this weird pact with the audience: He would openly tell the crowd that he'd play all the old songs he kind of hated if they would just be willing to listen to the new songs he liked. That might sound desperate, but that's not how it felt at the time. It made him seem reasonable. He understood how expectation functioned and he realized that the experience of entertainment had no relationship to how non-fans viewed the quality of his work. Lane was significantly less pretentious than most of the credible musicians who usurped his role in the popular culture.

Lane's life got weird post-1996: A native of Northeast Ohio (and born with the paradoxical name of John Kennedy Oswald), he moved back to Cleveland and briefly became a chef. He gained weight and started wearing eyeglasses. People thought this was hilarious, because guys who used to sing in rock bands are evidently supposed to live off blueberries and have 20/20 vision. He appeared on one of those terrible VH1 shows about losing weight and temporarily replaced the lead singer of Great White; he made a power pop album that would have appealed to old Warrant fans if they'd only known it existed. He got a DUI and spent four months in jail. He leaves behind a nineteen-year-old daughter who probably looks a lot like the beautiful girls who used to be in Warrant videos. He died in a Comfort Inn, which just seems depressing as hell. I can't tell if he had an obviously great life or a quietly tragic life. Probably both, which is how it goes for most people.

All art is real.

(1928–2013)

'd spent the day with my father at the hospital. He was not responsive and did not seem to recognize that I was there. I was actually hoping this was the case, since any sign of consciousness would mean he was equally aware of everything else that was happening, all of which was terrible.

That night I was back at my brother's farm, watching Notre Dame play Michigan. My dad loved Notre Dame football, so the game adopted a heavy symbolic significance inside my mind. I knew he wasn't watching it; I knew there was no way a television was on in the ICU. Throughout the first half, I wondered how many casual discussions I'd had with my father about what high school players Notre Dame was in the process of recruiting. It sometimes seemed like the main thing we talked about.

Tommy Rees threw a bad pick late in the second quarter and Michigan took a 27–13 lead. At halftime, I went into the basement to get more beer. When I returned, what I saw on the TV made me simultaneously happy, bewildered, and despondent: It was the rapper Eminem, standing in the press box with Brent Musburger and Kirk Herbstreit, having the least natural conversation I've ever witnessed.

Mass media makes a lot of things about life confusing, one of which is the recognition of age and maturity. Whenever I watch sports on TV, I always feel like I'm watching athletes who are somehow older than I am, even though this is almost never true (even when I watch golf). It infantilizes me. Meanwhile, seeing Eminem generates the opposite sensation: We're the same age, but it often feels like he's fifteen years younger. When *The Slim Shady LP* was released in 1997, I was already a full-on taxpayer. His work was brilliant, but also juvenile. It was like Zappa. His worldview seemed like an inaccurate reflection of the generation we both occupied. I knew he was the most technically proficient rapper I'd ever heard (at least in terms of wordplay and verbal dexterity), but I did not relate to him in any context that wasn't a self-construction. This falls in stark contrast to my relationship with Brent Musburger, a stranger whose intertwinement with my existence is unnaturally cavernous. The number of raw minutes I've listened to Musburger speak aloud undoubtedly dwarfs the amount of time I've spent listening to almost anyone I know personally (I mean, there just aren't that many non-cult scenarios where it's normal to listen to the same person talk for three and a half straight hours on a weekly basis for thirty years). I have an ongoing fantasy where I randomly meet Musburger in a T.G.I. Fridays and we end up watching a MAC game together on the bar television; I imagine Brent expressing enthusiastic opinions about the complimentary pot stickers. So now I'm watching this unnatural cultural collision (contrived by ABC for purposes of marketing), and I instantaneously find myself annoyed by the online reactions that have not yet been written. I know everyone is going to insist this interview is awkward and idiotic and hilarious. But I'm in the mindset to be moved, so it moves me. I pretend like it doesn't, but it does.

Here is Eminem, placed in a situation where he knows he will be mocked if he doesn't make his discomfort obvious. He's promoting the use of "Berzerk" as weekly bumper music for college football, a song that (not coincidentally, I'm sure) samples a Billy Squier riff so familiar that it seems wholly reasonable to hear it on prime-time network television. He knows he's actively rebranding himself as the classic rock version of hip-hop, which is his best commercial option and (almost certainly) an evolution he never imagined or desired. But he's being cool about it. When Herbstreit asks what about his new album makes him most excited, he gives two answers that are different versions of the same truth: His first response is, "Nothing." His second is, "To just be done with it." This does not seem like sarcasm. I believe it's how he really feels about this record, and maybe about his whole career. Still, he's trying to make this work. He's trying to build a weird bridge to somewhere reasonable. He forces his way through the publicity he knows is his responsibility. He sincerely compliments Brent on his broadcasting career and goes out of his way to note the passing of Pat Summerall. Musburger tries even harder: He drops Rick Rubin's name into the conversation and asks a needlessly specific gambling question that derives (for reasons unknown) from the state of Montana. Who are these anonymous Montana-based degenerates who want to know Eminem's take on an NFL point spread? And why is Eminem so reluctant to respond to this innocuous query?

I suspect it's because he actually cares about the answer.

People don't worry about the idea of a Generation Gap anymore. That notion has been replaced by a Technology Gap. The possibility of parents and children sharing the same cultural interests has increased dramatically over the past twenty-five years; today, the central bifurcation is how that communal culture is accessed and interpreted and experienced. Yet there are still certain chasms forged by the rudimentary passage of time. Musburger is, by all accounts, a deeply conservative guy (I love whenever he announces Cal home games, because he inevitably says something amusing and reactionary about the student body). It's hard for me to imagine him listening

423

to a song like "Berzerk" without wondering what the hell happened to the world he helped create. But you know what? He's still engaged with that world. He still wants to know what Eminem thinks about the Detroit Lions. Sure, you could argue he's just doing his job. But there is no condescension in his voice. There is no distaste with the assignment. What we have is an old man saying, "Look—I don't really understand what you do or why people care. But I don't need to understand it in order to know it has value." And what we have in response is a younger man saying, "I realize you have to treat me like a celebrity, because that's the reason I was pushed into this press box. But I am not your equal. That's not possible. I will never respect myself as much as I respect you."

The promotional segment ends and the game returns. Notre Dame mounts a comeback but fails in the fourth. I finish the rest of the beer, take an Ambien, and go to bed around midnight. Ten minutes later, my brother knocks on the door and says the whole family has to go back to the hospital immediately. So that's what we do.

Something Else

As a youth, I enjoyed heavy metal music. I may have mentioned this once or twice before. But like any quasi-discerning lunatic, there were still a handful of metal bands I did not appreciate, most notably AC/DC. I certainly owned cassette copies of *Back in Black* and *Who Made Who*, and I listened to both of those tapes hundreds of times before I was old enough to vote. But I didn't *love* AC/DC, at least when compared to glam bands like Mötley Crüe and W.A.S.P. and Faster Pussycat. At the time, my three-pronged reasoning was that I disliked the singing style of replacement Brian Johnson, I found songs like "Big Balls" and "Thunderstruck" willfully puerile, and that Angus Young declined to pyrotechnically shred out on solos. What I now realize is that those opinions were just a way for me to rationalize a subterranean level of aesthetic anxiety I didn't have the mind or lexicon to explain: AC/DC was too real for me. I preferred artifice, and AC/DC offered nothing in that regard. They ignored trends. They calculated nothing. They mechanically recorded buzz-saw rock with a level of aggression, vulgarity, and indifference many of the groups I preferred pretended to embody whenever they were interviewed. As I've aged, my affinity for the visceral straightness of AC/DC has increased; I like them more today than I did when I was fourteen. This is strange for an obvious reason (AC/DC is straight-up *designed* for fourteen-year-olds), but also for a convoluted one: My aesthetic evolution runs counter to the modern direction of pop music appreciation. It's now considered antiquated for any critic to be compelled by "authenticity" or "auteurism" or "creative integrity." Those qualities are viewed as absurd and pejorative; naked artifice (and a hyperawareness of one's own self-generated perception) is what we're *supposed* to want. Criticism, like all forms of public discourse, is mostly fashion. And my sense of fashion is always inverted. I liked fake things when I was supposed to like real things, and I never cared about authenticity until everyone else decided it was an irrelevant thing to value. I realize my peers must assume this contrarianism is a conscious decision, and (for financial reasons) I wish that were the case. But the honest explanation is that my perception of reality is so inflexibly personal that it has almost no correlation to what's happening in the world outside of my own skull. And I fear this applies not just to music, but to pretty much everything I experience.

In 2005, I published a book titled *Killing Yourself to Live*, mostly written in 2003. It was a travelogue fixated on the relationship between love and death, with particular emphasis on the latter. I used to think about dying all the time. It obsessed me. In a previous essay collection, I'd already noted that I thought about death more than I thought about sex—a perspective that was true, but also affected. I actively wanted to be that type of mischievously morbid person. I liked that I was the kind of weirdo who thought about death so much that I'd write an entire book about it at the age of thirty-three. But now I'm forty-five. I'm twelve years older than the person who wrote *Killing Yourself to Live*, with an additional twelve years of uncut garbage miles on the corporeal pedometer. I am, almost literally, half dead (I think it's possible I could live past ninety, but all the sharps in Vegas would take the under). I'm fifteen pounds heavier, arguably from food. My body is in decline. I'll eventually need to surgically replace my left knee, and maybe the right one, too. For a couple of sobering weeks one warm December, my liver stopped working—although it did heal itself, pretty much on its own.[1] You could say I've treated my body like a temple, assuming you're referring to the way Jesus treated temples. I can count all my bones. But my body is only half the equation. What was once a distant obsession is now an ongoing concern. My life simply has more death in it. My father is dead. I've had friends die, and an actuary would assert a few others are queuing up for the transition.[2] I now have two small children, which means I live in a perpetual state of fear that something terrible will happen to them, to the point where I won't watch a documentary if I know it involves the death of a child (despite my embarrassment over how cliché and preposterous that must sound to any childless person, including myself at the age of thirty-three). The practical consequences of mortality have never been more lucid. Yet here's the idiotic rub: I no longer think about death *as a concept*. Ever. It stopped fascinating me, even though it's still more fascinating than almost anything else I can think of. The possibility of my own death rarely crosses my mind, even as I grow mathematically closer to its inevitable actuality.

Now, the conventional explanation for this shift would be "denial." An uncreative therapist might suggest my fixation on speculative death dematerialized as I advanced toward nontheoretical death. She might even say I was only fascinated by dying because I was too immature to

---

1. When it comes to regenerative reinvention, livers are (evidently) the internal organ equivalent of Madonna. I just stopped drinking for six weeks and everything got better. It was a strange medical problem. I'm still a tad skeptical of the entire diagnosis, if we're being frank. Maybe I was just tired. Maybe my tongue is supposed to be black.

2. This was written just before the death of Marc Spitz, a colleague from *SPIN* magazine who unexpectedly died in his apartment at the age of forty-seven. I wasn't thinking about Spitz when I wrote this sentence, but I certainly am now.

truly understand what it signifies. But this hypothetical therapist would be wrong. That's not what this is about. What this is about is slightly crazier: Social media has murdered my interest in death.

When I was writing *Killing Yourself to Live*, I believed the notion (and meaning) of mortality was a problem not considered enough. This is a strange sentiment to express, but I felt like death was underrated. It seemed like a construct only explored as an extension of religion or art. Obviously, there had always been novels and folk songs and one-act plays about the dark fragility of existence; it's the oldest topic imaginable, particularly for poets and priests and Kenneth Lonergan. But fixating on the nonnegotiable paradox of death didn't seem like a day-to-day practice for practical people. We were conditioned to pretend it was not perpetually lurking behind every casual decision. It was not seen as a component of normal subsistence; it was a concern for people without real concerns. If you weren't looking for dead people, you didn't see them, unless you were Haley Joel Osment. And this made me want to think about dead people *constantly*, for reasons that were almost political. I believed our culture was deliberately ignoring a shared, profound experience. I believed we were not engaging with the complete experience of what it meant to be alive.

But how could I possibly believe that now?

On any given day, the only news I cannot escape is the avalanche of histrionic emotion concerning whatever famous (or semi-famous) person recently stopped living. When David Bowie died in January 2016, the level of communal online mourning was so massive (and so prolonged) that I wondered if we'd reached the apex of social media as a means for memorializing the passing of celebrities. "We can't do this for everybody," I thought to myself. "We will run out of poignant hyperboles." But then Prince died in April, and the escalation advanced. Dying used to be an occupational risk to living like a rock star, but it's now the primary thing rock stars do. I have a friend who works at *Rolling Stone* magazine, and we sometimes play a party game where we speculate on whose death would (or would not) warrant the magazine's cover. Roger Daltrey? Jackson Browne? What about Joan Baez? For a long time, almost every candidate was halfway debatable. But it's starting to seem like any artist big enough to qualify for the conversation will probably get the nod, assuming no one more noteworthy dies the same week.[3] It's almost become a business decision: The only issues of *Rolling Stone* guaranteed to sell exceptionally well are the ones with dead faces on the front.

Much like our Social Security system, there's a looming demographic dilemma with this unrestricted, all-inclusive commemoration of celebrity death. Most of the famous people currently dropping were eminent in the 1960s and '70s, and it feels like these deaths are happening constantly. But (of course) there were far more people made famous by the shallow nature of the eighties, if only because of cable TV. The nineties manifest will include the first generation of reality stars and the explosion of hip-hop; the early twenty-first century will need to encompass those who were classified as "Internet Famous," which is akin to granting amnesty to the entire Florida prison system. From here on out, there's never going to be a downturn in the number of high-profile corpses arguably worth remembering, particularly in a media landscape driven not by institutions but by any private citizen who cares enough to argue. Perversely and predictably, recognizing the death of a celebrity on Facebook has become a form of lifestyle branding: Expressing sadness over the passing of an obscure calypso musician is public proof that you care about obscure calypso music. Posting the posthumous photo of a forgotten sitcom star is proof that you were one of the few who did not forget,

---

3. I was shocked when *RS* elected not to put George Michael on the cover after he passed, but that might have been because he died on Christmas weekend (and no one was in the office).

because that sitcom has now been integrated with your own formative experience. If everyone in your news feed is mourning the passing of Garry Shandling or Joe Garagiola or Leonard Cohen, you can absolutely throw your unvarnished emotions into the mix, even if you hadn't really thought about the individual for twenty-five years. I mean, who could possibly question your motives? A man is dead.

Am I complaining about this? I am not complaining about this. Does it worry me? It does not worry me. On balance, it might be marginally good for society. If we're going to invest psychological energy into a media construction, the lives of dead strangers is better than most of the alternatives. And it's not like this is some kind of commoditization of death, unless you view the attention economy as more meaningful than the real economy. Besides, people have the right to be sad in public, even if that sadness is amplified for effect. But something positive can still be crazy. This unilateral bereavement is (quite often) psychologically bewildering, and—though I'm hesitant to admit this— a little too emotionally gratuitous for someone with my phlegmatic limitations. It has distorted my conception of death. It has, somewhat remarkably, desensitized the entire process. Sometimes a celebrity will die, and it doesn't even seem like a death. It seems like an auction.

When I heard about the passing of Prince, I was walking into a movie theater. I experienced the subsequent matinee behind a hazy veil of distraction. For two hours, the tragedy seemed so tragic. Prince was the most talented pop musician of the twentieth century, with a deep connection to the Midwest and a black belt in eccentricity. I loved his music and cared about his life, or at least I thought I did. But when I exited the theater and turned on my phone, it dawned on me that—evidently—I didn't care at all, relative to the world at large. So many other people were *performing* their love of Prince, gnashing their teeth and screaming into the void, endlessly explaining how the unfairness of this man's passing was conjoined with their own high school experience of listening to "When Doves Cry." And it didn't feel like that to me. It felt sad, but not in the way *they* were sad. I could not psychologically compete. I could not compete with the collective unreal, so I decided to think about something else.

Acknowledgments

The stories in this collection were originally assigned and edited by a variety of people. But the majority of these pieces were shaped and orchestrated by two guys: Dan Fierman and Brendan Vaughan. Both were absolutely integral to the existence of this book. I cannot thank them enough.

Other editors I need to acknowledge for their direct contributions to this anthology: Lane Brown, Sia Michel, Devin Gordon, Nick Catucci, Ryan D'Agostino, Paul Tough, Josh Modell, Steve Kandell, Gary Belsky, Gary Groth, and Sean Fennessey. I'd also like to thank the various copy editors and fact-checkers involved in the process, even if we were never formally introduced.

Finally, I must express my appreciation for Brant Rumble, David Rosenthal, Daniel Greenberg, and my wife, Melissa Maerz. Thank you.

Index

"Three-Man Weave," "That's Not How It Happened," "The Light Who Has Lighted the World," "Where Were You While We Were Getting High?," "I Need to Be Alive (in Order to Watch TV)," "I Will Choose Free Will (Canadian Reader's Note: This Is Not About Rush)," "Speed Kills (Until It Doesn't)," "Use Your Illusion (but Don't Bench Ginóbili)," "But What If We're Wrong? (Drink the Acid, Swallow the Mouse)," "Brown Would Be the Color (If I Had a Heart)," "White's Shadow," "The Opposite of Beyoncé," "Metal Machine 'Music,'" "2 + 2 = 5," "Advertising Worked on Me," "Hero in Black," "Villain in White," and "(1928–2013)" originally appeared on Grantland.

"My Zombie, Myself" originally appeared in *The New York Times.*

"There's Something Peculiar About Lying in a Dark Room. You Can't See Anything." originally appeared as the introduction to *Peanuts Every Sunday 1956–1960* by Charles M. Schulz (Fantagraphics, 2014).

"Liquid Food," "I'm Assuming It's Going to Be Fun," "Owner of a Lonely Heart," "The Enemy of My Enemy Is Probably Just Another Enemy," "A Road Seldom Traveled by the Multitudes," and "The Man Who Knew Too Much" originally appeared in *GQ.*

"C'mon Dave, Gimme a Break" originally appeared in *Billboard.*

"Everybody's Happy When the Wizard Walks By (Or Maybe Not? Maybe They Hate It? Hard to Say, Really.)," "Not a Nutzo Girl, Not Yet a Nutzo Woman (Miley Cyrus, 2008)," "When Giants Walked the Earth (and Argued about China)," and "The City That Time Remembered (Tulsa, Oklahoma)" originally appeared in *Esquire.*

"The Drugs Don't Work (Actually, They Work Great)" originally appeared in *ESPN The Magazine.*

"I Hear That You and Your Band Have Sold Your Guitars" originally appeared in *The Guardian.*

"House Mouse in the Mouse House" originally appeared in *The New York Times Magazine.*

"Like Regular Music, Except Good" and "Democracy Now!" originally appeared in *The A.V. Club.*

"Non-Suppressive Slacker" originally appeared in *SPIN.*

Each piece has been edited and augmented for this collection.